The National Security League,
1914–1922

SELECTED OTHER WORKS BY KERRY SEGRAVE
AND FROM MCFARLAND

Women and Bicycles in America, 1868–1900 (2020)
Dying for Chocolate: Cordelia Botkin and the 1898 Poisoned Candy Murders (2020)
The Electric Car in America, 1890–1922: A Social History (2019)
"Masquerading in Male Attire": Women Passing as Men in America, 1844–1920 (2018)
The Women Who Got America Talking: Early Telephone Operators, 1878–1922 (2017)
The Hatpin Menace: American Women Armed and Fashionable, 1887–1920 (2016)
Police Violence in America, 1869–1920: 256 Incidents Involving Death or Injury (2016)
Chewing Gum in America, 1850–1920: The Rise of an Industry (2015)
Wiretapping and Electronic Surveillance in America, 1862–1920 (2014)
Beware the Masher: Sexual Harassment in American Public Places, 1880–1930 (2014)
Policewomen: A History, 2d ed. (2014)
Extras of Early Hollywood: A History of the Crowd, 1913–1945 (2013)
Parking Cars in America, 1910–1945: A History (2012)
Begging in America, 1850–1940: The Needy, the Frauds, the Charities and the Law (2011)
*Vision Aids in America: A Social History of Eyewear
and Sight Correction Since 1900* (2011)
Lynchings of Women in the United States: The Recorded Cases, 1851–1946 (2010)
*America Brushes Up: The Use and Marketing of Toothpaste
and Toothbrushes in the Twentieth Century* (2010)
Film Actors Organize: Union Formation Efforts in America, 1912–1937 (2009)
Parricide in the United States, 1840–1899 (2009)
Actors Organize: A History of Union Formation Efforts in America, 1880–1919 (2008)
*Women and Capital Punishment in America, 1840–1899: Death Sentences
and Executions in the United States and Canada* (2008)
Obesity in America, 1850–1939: A History of Social Attitudes and Treatment (2008)
Ticket Scalping: An American History, 1850–2005 (2007)
Women Swindlers in America, 1860–1920 (2007)
America on Foot: Walking and Pedestrianism in the 20th Century (2006)
Endorsements in Advertising: A Social History (2005)
Women and Smoking in America, 1880–1950 (2005)
Suntanning in 20th Century America (2005)
Lie Detectors: A Social History (2004)
Foreign Films in America: A History (2004)
Product Placement in Hollywood Films: A History (2004)

The National Security League, 1914–1922

Wall Street and the War Machine

KERRY SEGRAVE

McFarland & Company, Inc., Publishers
Jefferson, North Carolina

Library of Congress Cataloguing-in-Publication Data

Names: Segrave, Kerry, 1944– author.
Title: The National Security League, 1914–1922 : Wall Street and the war machine / Kerry Segrave.
Other titles: Wall Street and the war machine
Description: Jefferson, North Carolina : McFarland & Company, Inc., Publishers, 2020 | Includes bibliographical references and index.
Identifiers: LCCN 2020043615 | ISBN 9781476682860 (paperback : acid free paper) ∞
ISBN 9781476640914 (ebook)
Subjects: LCSH: National Security League—History. | Militarism—United States—History—20th century. | World War, 1914-1918—Economic aspects—United States. | United States—Defenses—Economic aspects. | United States—Defenses—Political aspects.
Classification: LCC UA23 .S41636 2020 | DDC 940.3/1—dc23
LC record available at https://lccn.loc.gov/2020043615

British Library cataloguing data are available

ISBN (print) 978-1-4766-8286-0
ISBN (ebook) 978-1-4766-4091-4

© 2020 Kerry Segrave. All rights reserved

No part of this book may be reproduced or transmitted in any form or by any means, electronic or mechanical, including photocopying or recording, or by any information storage and retrieval system, without permission in writing from the publisher.

Front cover, left to right: Charles D. Orth, President of the National Security League; Henry Litchfield West, Executive Secretary of the National Security League (Library of Congress)

Printed in the United States of America

McFarland & Company, Inc., Publishers
Box 611, Jefferson, North Carolina 28640
www.mcfarlandpub.com

Table of Contents

Preface   1

Introduction   3

Part I. Preparedness, 1914–1917 (April 5)

1. Formation, December 1914   6
2. The Organization   26
3. The Politicians   35
4. Conferences and Conventions   43
5. Fear, Weirdness and Public Relations   60
6. The General Campaign   66
7. Critics and Impugners   91

Part II. Patriotism, 1917 (April 6)–1918 (November 10)

8. The Organization   108
9. The Politicians   116
10. Loyalty and Education   130
11. The General Campaign   155
12. Critics and Impugners   170

Part III. Americanization, 1918 (November 11)–1922

13. The Organization	178
14. The Reds	183
15. The General Campaign	192
16. Critics and Impugners	204
Chapter Notes	231
Bibliography	245
Index	257

Preface

This book examines the National Security League from its formation late in 1914 until 1922, by which point the organization was in a state of rapid decline.

It was an organization run by mainly wealthy corporate lawyers operating out of New York City, but financed away from the public eye by Wall Street and corporate money. Impetus for the formation of the group was the start of World War I in Europe, in the summer of 1914. For the American capitalist class that event marked an opportunity to reap enormous profits from the conflict. It was a time for the capitalist class to launch a major effort to increase America's military and war machine, in addition to profiting from the sale of munitions to the warring parties.

However, the project had to be pitched to the public as something very different. Also, the desired increase in America's military included an increase in a home reserve force, or some type of federalized National Guard. The latter was needed because of the fear on the part of the capitalist class that the socialism/communism ideology, then very much in the public eye and mind following the Russian revolutions of 1905 (failed) and 1917 (successful), would spread to the United States and threaten the power, status, money and property of the capitalist class. That led to the formation of the National Security League, which began with the incessant refrain that America was virtually helpless militarily, in the period up to America's formal entry into World War I. That theme was "preparedness."

From the time of American entry into the war until the cessation of the conflict in November 1918 the National Security League launched a new incessant refrain—"patriotism, loyalty." Behind that was the attempt to control the working class to the extent that workers dutifully enlisted and went overseas to become cannon fodder, and that those who remained at home were physically fit enough to work in the capitalist munitions plants and that those workers refrained from taking advantage of any manpower shortage by striking for higher wages, and so on. It was okay for the capitalist class to reap extortionate benefits from war, but it was not okay for workers to reap a few tiny extra benefits.

The third and last incessant refrain from the League began immediately after the end of World War I. That theme was "Americanization." During this period the group vigorously attacked anyone and everyone who opposed the American capitalist order.

One of the paths pursued by the League was to target politicians who opposed its agenda in any way. So enraged were the politicians, and not just the ones targeted, that formal hearings were held against the League with the result that the National Security League was found guilty of violating election spending laws of the time. However, nothing was done to the group. That was because those opposing the League were annoyed and infuriated not because of election spending violations but by the fact the League had accused them of being unpatriotic and so on. Once the hearing committee had decided it had absolved all politicians from such character slights, it was content and dropped any further action against the League. From that point onward the League rapidly faded into obscurity.

Research for this book was done using online databases with the Library of Congress' "Chronicling America" being the most useful. Also used were newspaperarchive.com and various other newspaper databases.

Introduction

This book is divided into three parts covering the period 1914 to 1922. The first part comes under the general heading of "Preparedness" and covers the League from its inception until April 5, 1917, the day before the United States officially entered World War I. Preparedness involved endless examples provided by the organization about how helpless and hopeless the United States military was and how desperately a vastly bigger military was needed. Ludicrous examples were presented to the public about invasions of America by a foreign power being imminent and, thus, a gigantic military was needed, as was a home reserve force, something along the lines of a federalized National Guard. Individual chapters in this section look at the structure and operation of the League; interaction of the group with politicians; conferences and conventions staged to make the group appear more influential; the general campaign of the group; and a final chapter on those who opposed the League and criticized it and its operations.

Part II covers the period during which the United States was officially at war, from April 6, 1917, until November 10, 1918. Once America entered the war the drumbeat of preparedness was almost immediately replaced by the clarion call for "patriotism," or "loyalty." Using that theme the National Security League hoped to be able to hold the workforce in line. The underclass had to be convinced in large numbers to go abroad and possibly die or be grievously wounded in service of the capitalists' drive to profit from war. Patriotism was also used to keep the home workforce in line and not take any advantage, undue or otherwise, to improve their lot in a situation where there might be a labor shortage. Excessive profiting from war was a privilege to be enjoyed only by the upper class; it did not extend to the workers. Individual chapters in this section look at the organization; interactions with politicians; the loyalty campaign; the general campaign; and a chapter on critics.

Part III covers the period from November 11, 1918, the end of World War I, through 1922, by which time the League was a spent force and rapidly fading from view. The theme in that period was "Americanization," in which the League did battle against the "Reds." In the eyes of the National Security League everybody who voiced any concern about the capitalist system, ranging from a trivial tinkering with the system to a total overthrow, was a Red and had to be stopped. Along the way the League had increasingly antagonized politicians by questioning the loyalty of many of them and trying to remove from office any and all who disagreed with the League and its positions. An irate Congress held hearings about the League and aired much of what had been secret—the funding of the group by the wealthy class and its real agenda of increasing the military, for one reason to be used at home to keep the underclass under control should that revolution, much feared by the capitalist class, come to pass. Although the League was found guilty in Congress of election spending limit violations, nothing was ever done to the group. Politicians who damned the League in the hearings were content to stop when they had proven, at least to themselves, that they were loyal and patriotic people. That is, when the personal slights against themselves had been vanquished the slights and crimes against the system as a whole could be, and would be, ignored. Chapters in this section address the organization, the campaign against the Reds, the general campaign, and the critics.

After exposure by the Congressional hearings, the National Security League was shamed and ridiculed and was thereafter a spent force. But, of course, the desires of the League found manifestation in other ways, in other groups. The push by the capitalist class for an increased military is still with us. The ludicrous idea that America is militarily weak remains with us on occasion. The push of the League to control the working class was not successful in its effective lifetime but has since then, arguably, been very successful. Russia was being used even then as a whipping boy by the League; there was even a news article subhead that proclaimed Russia was trying to destroy American democracy. One hundred plus years later and it is still the same.

Part I
Preparedness, 1914–1917 (April 5)

Chapter 1

Formation, December 1914

It started out with a lie. Over the life of the organization the press would regularly publish material about the League; untruths, exaggerations, outrageous claims, and so on, in an uncritical way, as though such items were factually correct news accounts. And it all began with the very first reports of the formation of this new organization. On the evening of December 1, 1914, in a hotel meeting room in New York City, a group of people gathered to plan the launch of what would become the National Security League (NSL). The group announced it would work toward bringing about a United States Congressional investigation into the condition of the army, navy and coastal defenses of the United States. This was viewed as the first step in a proposed country-wide campaign to insure the enactment of national and state regulations necessary for maintaining national security. Reportedly, it was formed that night "at a meeting of 250 representative citizens of New York." And that was a lie. There were no non-white people there; there were no women in attendance; there were no labor union representatives in the room; there were no ordinary working men there, there were not 250 people in attendance, and so on.[1]

A different account presented a slightly more accurate picture of attendance at that inaugural gathering with a headline that noted "business men in defense league," while a line of text stipulated that "150 business men" at the Hotel Belmont resolved, on December 1, to form a national security league to support the campaign started by United States Representative August P. Gardner against the nation's supposed "unpreparedness" to defend itself against invasion.

Plans for the league were formulated by S. Stanwood Menken, a wealthy lawyer with the legal firm of Beekman, Menken and Griscom. Menken was named to chair the meeting and he urged that the people were entitled to know the true defensive situation of the republic. Said Menken, "We know that, however this indescribable [World] war [I] ends, the world

Chapter 1. Formation, December 1914

will not be free from human selfishness and unwisdom, and we believe that our very capacity for success brings to us the menace of aggression. To safeguard our entity and the doctrines that we stand for we must agree upon some national policy, carefully planned so as to be available in time of necessity, either by defense of arms or through peaceful means." He added that the United States "needs a strong defensive navy and the basis in men and equipment of a larger reserve army, to be under central control free from political interference and with broad executive powers."[2]

Also at that meeting was Charles E. Lydecker. He offered a resolution asking for the appointment of a committee of 50 men to form the National Security League, to have branches throughout the nation, for the purpose of informing the people of the condition of the army and navy and for "arousing public opinion to whatever action may be found requisite." While the NSL often paid lip service to the idea of conducting an investigation into the condition of the U.S. military it had no such thought in mind. From the beginning the NSL was interested only in a bigger military in all aspects and wanted it as soon as possible.

George Haven Putnam, also at the meeting, likened New York State to Belgium (invaded by Germany in August 1914), saying that a strong opposition force "would find little difficulty in entering New York Harbor, proceeding up the Hudson and burning Poughkeepsie and Albany on its way to the north." Putnam argued that New York harbor should be guarded by a new fleet of submarines. His ridiculous and nonsensical statement was just the first of many as members of the NSL would go on to attempt to generate as much fear as possible, based on impossible examples.

Adding to the hysteria was John Winthrop Loveland, who asserted that in two weeks two nations, and in four weeks still another country, could place 150,000 men on American shores, while it would require a month for the U.S. to put in action 130,000 military men, of which 100,000 would be untrained. Loveland then attacked Andrew Carnegie, declaring that his peace movement and "a great many good clergymen in their pulpits were placing the nation in jeopardy." Representative Gardner (Republican, Mass.) was not present at the meeting but he sent a telegram to Menken asking his cooperation and inviting him to send a representative to a hearing on Capitol Hill when his House resolution came up; it was a resolution providing for a commission to investigate the adequacy of the army and navy. A few years later it was revealed that the Carnegie Corporation was the biggest donor to the NSL.[3]

Another account of the formation meeting declared that "The league was formed to work toward a congressional investigation into the condition of the army, navy and coast defenses." Again, the only purpose at that time was to increase the size of the military, not conduct some sort of unbiased investigation in which the outcome was open and with unbiased investigators willing to accept whatever conclusion the facts may have warranted. One other resolution passed asked U.S. President Woodrow Wilson to act speedily upon Gardner's resolution requesting an investigation into the armament of the U.S. and authorizing the appointment, by chairman Menken, of a committee of 50 men to organize branches of the new league "throughout the nation." One of the reasons for the organization of the NSL, according to this account, was "because under the changed conditions of international conditions, it may not be wise to entrust our national defense to hurried emergency measures."[4]

A New York newspaper published an editorial in favor of the new association, on December 3. The editor wrote that "The National Security League is the expression of a growing conviction the country over" and that the idea was all "plain common sense and precaution." The editor argued that war was a possibility for any nation, near or remote. "In the case of our own country, with its fortunate isolation, its democratic and anti-militarist spirit, its will for peace, we are surely justified in rating the chance a small one," he asserted. Erroneously he added that the NSL "calls for no vast expansion of our army and navy, and we do not understand that the National Security League sets out with any preconceived demand for increased appropriations."[5]

In light of the formation of the NSL it was remarked that a special interest was attached to the session of the 63rd Congress, that began on Monday December 7, regarding action on increasing the size of the U.S. army and navy. Noting the idea that the nation was in a state of unpreparedness it was observed that a new movement, the NSL, sought to arouse public opinion in favor of putting the army, navy and coastal defenses in a state of preparation for war and would likely carry on an "active propaganda" in Washington to achieve that end.[6]

Representative Gardner, noted as some type of catalyst for Menken and the NSL, had first gotten involved back on October 15, 1914, when he introduced into the House his resolution providing for a national security commission on inquiry into the question of the preparedness of the USA for war, defensive or offensive. It was a proposal that was not well received. Representative James Hay (Dem., VA) was chairman of the Committee on Military Affairs and he, at once, declared that no action would be taken on the Gardner resolution. President Wilson looked upon it "with disfavor." Secretary of War Lindley Garrison stated that the information Gardner desired to bring to the attention of the people could be found in the War Department reports that had already been submitted to Congress at various times. Thus, the Gardner resolution was widely expected to die quickly and quietly. Reportedly, it was that gloomy outlook for Gardner

Chapter 1. Formation, December 1914

Augustus Peabody Gardner, 1916. Gardner was a voice in the U.S. House of Representatives calling for increased militarism, in late 1914. When the National Security League was formed it cited Gardner as a main catalyst for the group.

and his proposal that the NSL had come into being with the new organization believing that the public could only be aroused on the basis of public and politicized committee hearings, as opposed to old reports gathering dust on shelves.[7]

One of those at that initial meeting was George Haven Putnam and he was not happy with some of the media coverage of the group. In a letter to the editor that was published just a few days after the first meeting he noted that the series of resolutions adopted "were adopted without dissent by the citizens present, a very representative gathering." He grumbled that most, if not all, newspapers covering the meeting did not print the resolutions in full, and denied the claims of one paper, at least, that the proceedings were "hysterical." He likened the military situation to a merchant with valuable material in a warehouse who found the neighborhood was exposed to some fresh risks from fire and so he increased his insurance. (Haven failed to point out that in such cases it was the merchant who bore the additional cost, not the general taxpayer.) Haven referred to "The recent breaking down of international relations, the evidence that with some nations at least it is not safe to put trust in treaties or guarantees." That, Haven asserted, meant that "in the judgment of many of our citizens the time has come for a larger expenditure for national insurance" (meaning a bigger military).[8]

Stanwood Menken announced on December 6 the names of the general committee he had appointed to begin to formulate plans to arouse the federal government to the necessity of improving the national defense. All the names of the men were published in the account; more than 50 were named, about 86. One of them was Cornelius Vanderbilt; another was Thomas Hamlin Hubbard, described as a philanthropist, railroad executive and financier. Another was George Emlen Roosevelt, described as a banker and railroad financier involved in no fewer than 14 railroad reorganizations. He was a first cousin, once removed, of former U.S. President Theodore Roosevelt.[9]

The question of national defense and the preparedness of the army and navy for war occupied almost exclusively the first day of the last session of the 63rd Congress, on December 7. According to one article, "It was apparent that what has become a national demand, voiced by such organizations as the National Security League, the Army League and the Army and Navy League, and by prominent individuals all over the country [note that a few prominent men and a couple of organizations herein became 'a national demand'] will be the principal feature of the legislative program for the present session, overshadowing the schedule prepared by President Wilson and the Democratic leaders."[10]

On the afternoon of December 8 the NSL's General Committee,

Chapter 1. Formation, December 1914

comprised of 50 "well known" citizens, met at the Hotel Belmont in New York City to "perfect" the organization and to formulate a definite statement of the purpose and scope of the league. The objects and aims were voted to be the following: to urge Congress to conduct an exhaustive investigation into the defensive condition of the country. The NSL insisted the organization was completely nonpartisan and not committed to any bill then before Congress. As a result of any such inquiry the group would urge "a practical policy for creating a national defense and a scientific work thereon." Those men who attended that meeting were described by a reporter as "busy bankers, merchants, publicists, lawyers, physicians, engineers and brokers...." All 50 were in attendance. Committees were established to draw up the group's aims. Set up were separate committees on the navy, the army, coasts, defenses, the militia, a legislative committee, one on finances, one on extension of the NSL (establishing branches), one on membership, and a finance committee. That last committee was to be comprised of the league chairman, secretary, treasurer plus the chairmen of the various committees. One of those at the meeting, W.C. Church, remarked that an investigation was most needed to show the nation was in a "most deplorable condition" with respect to its defenses.[11]

Criticism of the National Security League only rarely surfaced. But, on those rare occasions the real aims and purposes were outlined. A brief editorial in a Richmond, Virginia, newspaper saw through the subterfuge of the group's utterances. That editorial, in its entirety, stated; "Manufacturers of arms and armor ought to be willing to open their hearts and contribute generously to the support of the National Security League. If it is successful in its ambitions, it will add security to their bank accounts at any rate."[12]

In the middle of the same month the NSL was formed and took a lead role in trying to generate an hysteria about the need for a bigger army and navy, an item appeared suggesting that the hysteria was misplaced. According to the account the "most formidable armada" ever assembled under the American flag would be seen at the naval station at Guantanamo in the following month, for maneuvers. That fleet was to be composed of 21 battleships, nine of them the most powerful type of "super dreadnought," and was to form an escort for President Wilson through the Panama Canal.[13]

In the same newspaper on the same date as the above item was an article that painted a somewhat different picture of the situation. The article featured drawings of a field artillery piece, to scale, for each of eight nations, supposedly indicating artillery strength. In order, by scale, the nations were ranked as follows; Russia, Germany, France, Austria, Italy, Japan, England, and United States. No actual numbers were given. Nor was the reader given any guidance as to whether or not each nation counted field artillery in the same fashion. By taking the area of each drawing, roughly, it appeared that Russia had an artillery 150 times as big as the United States while England had one 50 times as big. General Leonard Wood was chief of staff of the U.S. army and he prepared the drawing as part of his last report to the Secretary of War. Wood was an embodiment of United States colonialism, imperialism and militarism and was involved in all the military occupations of the time. If the U.S. was indeed short of troops at home it could be placed in the fact that America had so many troops deployed in occupying and plundering other nations. He was Governor-General of Cuba from December 1899 to May 1902; Wood was Governor of Moro Province in the Philippines from July 1903 to April 1906. Later he was Governor-General of the Philippines from October 1921 to August 1927. As well, he was Chief of Staff of the United States Army from April 1910 to April 1914. In that latter year U.S. President Wilson replaced Wood as Chief of Staff. Wood was a strong advocate of the Preparedness movement, a stance that alienated him from Wilson and led to his replacement. Nor did Wood limit his dispensing of imperialistic militarism to foreign nations. Already a member of the U.S. Army in the 1880s, Wood participated in the last battle against Apache chief Geronimo in Arizona, in 1886.[14]

A meeting took place in the middle of December that attracted a reported 1,500 men who jammed a meeting room at the Hotel Astor in New York City. It was comprised of "business men, merchants, bankers, professional men, manufacturers, importers and exporters..." who gave their approval of the call for "adequate" military preparedness for America. Held under the auspices of the Merchants Association, the meeting featured a number of speakers with several of them being from the NSL: Menken, Putnam, Frederic R. Coudert, and W.C. Churchill. It was argued at the meeting

General Leonard Wood (between 1915 and 1920) was responsible for the "missile gap" information listed herein and went on to become a prominent member of the NSL. He lobbied for increased militarism while still a member of the United States military and then lobbied from the outside through the League.

that the U.S. Army had just 25,000 regulars and only 120,000 militia men or National Guard members. Of that latter number it was claimed that only 50,000 to 60,000 were "reasonably efficient or well trained." And the needs of the U.S. Navy were considered just as pressing. As well, there was a need to provide and lay up in reserve a sufficient supply of arms and ammunition.[15]

The new association remained busy during the remainder of December. At one meeting William T. Hornaday suggested that bonds for $10 million should be floated by the U.S. Treasury to pay for the extra expense of a bloated military. George Wingate argued that lessons in marksmanship be given in the public schools. The latter was the beginning of what would increasingly occupy the time of the NSL in the future—to drive their militaristic points into children and the teachers of those children. That drive would be under the guise of patriotism and loyalty through a rigid militaristic system, which gave cover for a ruthless capitalistic class as it amassed enormous profits.[16]

The National Security League had designated special committees, composed of the "leading experts" on those subjects throughout the U.S., said the group, to investigate the condition of the army, navy and militia. It was asserted that by the time their reports were presented, the finance, membership and branch organization committees of the NSL "will be in a position to bring them forcibly to the attention of every community in the country." That was the belief of Menken who stated that the disclosures of the League would result in the appointment of a commission, by the President and Congress, that would finish the probe his League had begun.[17]

The group regularly drew in big names of the day to espouse its cause, many of them former military men and cabinet officers. One was a former secretary of the Navy, Charles J. Bonaparte, who declared a "lively discussion" was then underway in Washington and the whole nation "as to the sufficiency or remedies for the insufficiency of our forces of land and sea." Bonaparte was, of course, preaching the NSL line and argued for a bigger army and a bigger navy and for sooner rather than later.[18]

Stanwood Menken was the listed author of a lengthy piece that appeared in a New York City newspaper on December 27, 1914. It took up about two-thirds of a page. Three other articles on the remainder of the page also came out in favor of military increases. How prepared, Menken wondered, was his county to meet the attack of any enemy. All of the military increases demanded by the NSL, and others, in the period from 1914 to early 1917 were based on a need to shore up the military in order to meet an enemy country that would attack the United States; that is, the purpose of an increased military was seen by the NSL as a defensive necessity. Offensive use was never mentioned. World War I was underway (starting on July 28, 1914) but nobody then envisioned the U.S. entering that conflict. How likely was it that America would be attacked by a foreign power? Looking backward from today it was over two hundred years since such an event took place. The last time the continental United States was attacked by the forces of a foreign government was the War of 1812.[19]

In the course of an interview in May 1915 Menken elaborated on the formation of the NSL. He explained that the circumstances of the war that broke out in Europe in the summer of 1914 set a good many people thinking about the condition of the United States. "We had no desire to take part in that war and there seemed to be no reason to believe that we would become involved in it," but in case of some situation we would need an enormous amount of preparatory work. There had been a group of seven men who sat down together and decided to form the National Security League. Those seven founders were S. Stanwood Menken, Herbert Barry, George Haven Putnam, Lawrence F. Abbott, J. Mayhew Wainwright, Charles E. Lydecker, and Franklin Q. Brown. At the hotel meeting in December 1914, Menken explained, they realized they would have a "grave task to undertake to arouse public sentiment to the point at which the Government would be forced to take such steps as we believed to be vitally necessary."

Even when he gave that interview, in May 1915, Menken insisted, "it is not, and never has been, our purpose or our effort to kindle a war spirit in our people." That was, of course, exactly what the NSL set out to do. According to Menken, the new organization realized that before they could make an appeal to the country to join the group's effort, "we would have to present the case with as powerful an array of facts and arguments as could be made, and accordingly we began a systematic preparation of what we felt would be convincing data." In order to achieve that result the NSL set up a wide array of committees to prepare reports on various aspects of its plans for military expansion. They wanted a large force available to meet a possible invasion by a foreign power. To that end they advocated for a bigger army and navy and a bigger militia, or National Guard.

The reporter who wrote this piece mentioned the other aspect behind the formation of the National Security League. That was the matter of social control at home; the suppression of labor and dissidents in general, anyone who challenged the American form of capitalism. Said the reporter, "We believe it is possible for secret armed organizations to be formed in the United States which by concerted action could so embarrass this government at a critical time as to endanger the very existence of this nation. Our armed forces should be strong enough at least to overcome any disloyalty of that nature."[20]

Men who were prominent in the organization were often very wealthy. There were even wealthier individuals behind them who financed the association. However, it would be some years before that cabal of super wealthy capitalists was exposed. Some of the wealthy men involved with the League in its earliest days included August Peabody Gardner. He came from a wealthy background and was a Harvard graduate. He studied law at Harvard Law School but never practiced the profession, "instead devoting himself to the management of his estate." He married into even more money when he wed Constance Lodge, daughter of Henry Cabot Lodge. Gardner was a Representative in the United States House from November 1902 until May 1917, where he sat as a Republican. Charles E. Lydecker (1851–1930) was a law graduate from Columbia University in 1873. Like many of the men in the group, Lydecker had a long involvement in the military and was once president of the National Guard Association. As well, he was Public Administrator for New York City from 1889 to 1893. George Haven Putnam (1844–1930) was a publisher, being president of G.P. Putnam's Sons for its first 52 years of existence, from 1872 onward. He was the son of George Palmer Putnam, an important American book publisher. George was born in London, England, where his father was establishing a branch of his New York City publishing company, Wiley and Putnam. On his father's death George took over the business (with his brothers) and renamed it G.P. Putnam's Sons. In 1894 he hired the 26-year-old Theodore Roosevelt as a "special partner." After his stint as U.S. President (1901–1909), Roosevelt continued to agitate in favor of militarism and worked with the NSL.[21]

S. Stanwood Menken (1870–1954) was born in Memphis, Tennessee. When his family went to New York he entered the College of the City of New York and then did post-graduate work at Cornell University and later at Columbia University. Menken married Gretchen von Briesen, a member of a "socially prominent family." He began the practice of law in 1894 as a member of the firm of Ogden and Beekman, the firm being Beekman, Menken and Griscom by 1914. Menken was active in city politics in New York City and was a member of the Reform Club. In 1896 he was organizer of the Hall of Records Association, which enrolled 10,000 members. That same year he was a candidate for justice of the City Court of New York. In 1908 he was organizer of the Democratic League, of which he was chairman.[22]

An idea of the wealth in the Menken family came to light in an incident that had nothing to do with the National Security League. On a day in June 1931 three robbers broke into the home of Menken, tied up two maids and then forced Mrs. Menken to open a "vault" containing $150,000 in jewelry. They took the jewels and disappeared. That news item also noted, "Several years ago Mrs. Menken was acclaimed as the most richly dressed woman at the beaux arts ball [in New York City]. She wore a costume on which 250,000 precious stones were sewed."[23]

Part I—Preparedness, 1914–1917 (April 5)

The story of how the NSL came to be formed changed somewhat over time. Early in 1919 a news item remarked that the idea of forming the organization was conceived by Menken, "an attorney representing sugar, steel and other large interests," while Menken was in London on a visit to the British Parliament, in August 1914.[24] Thus, at the end of 1914 the cause—soon to be mania—for preparedness was taken up. A number of items were at play in the fueling of this somewhat sudden and dramatic desire for a much greater military force in America, both in terms of a much bigger regular Army and Navy, and of a much bigger National Guard, or something equivalent as a home force, preferably federalized, as opposed to being run at the state level. World War I, underway in Europe from July 1914, was, obviously, an important factor.

The eyes of the capitalist class lit up at the thought of such huge profits as would come their way, but there were problems involved. One was that the workforce left behind to toil for their capitalist masters might be physically not up to the task. One response from the overlords could be seen, for example, in the National Security League's move to get the home population involved in physical training. There was also a worry that labor at home would recognize the advantages it had in wartime. The gains to be had from strikes, and so forth, could be great. Thus the National Security League, for one example, beat the drum of patriotism, loyalty, and so on, very loud and very long in an effort to keep the working class quiet, tractable and obedient. It was one thing for the capitalist class to make extortionate profits; it was quite another thing for the working class to reap any sort of minor benefit.

Another worry for the capitalist class at this time was the "bad example" being set by the Russian Revolution, the successful one of 1917. The first, unsuccessful one of 1905 had already stirred things up and the 1917 success threatened to spread the "disease" of socialism/communism to America. And that explained the National Security League's constant demand for a huge increase in the Army and a National Guard–like force. That demand was always pitched as needed for home defense. The chance that the United States would be invaded by a foreign power in this time period was zero. The real reason for an increased military at home was to be ready to counter any such rebellions or insurrections that might occur at home. A federalized National Guard was more easily able to respond to such events than was a similar force that was under 48 different commands.

One idea emphasized by the NSL was that the military was woefully inadequate, making the United States next to helpless. Yet the reality was the opposite. A page in Wikipedia lists a timeline of United States military operations. In the three decades from 1890 to 1919 there are 62 separate military actions listed, all over the globe. They ranged from a naval

Chapter 1. Formation, December 1914

party that landed in Argentina in 1890 to "protect" the U.S. consulate and legation in Buenos Aires to an action that lasted from 1918 to 1920 and involved Marines being landed in Vladivostok, Russia. Seven thousand Marines were landed as part of an allied occupation force (an early coalition of the willing) that was trying to bring about regime change in the newly liberated Russia. A few of the notable military incursions of those three decades included: the overthrow of the Hawaiian Kingdom in 1893; Korea, 1894–1896; war in the Philippines, 1899–1913; Panama, 1903–1914; Cuba, 1906–1909; China, 1912–1941; Mexico, 1914–1917; the occupation of the Dominican Republic, 1916–1924; and Cuba, 1917–1922. As of January 1917 there were about 2,000 United States Marines in Santo Domingo, Dominican Republic, and 800 Marines in Haiti.[25]

Notwithstanding the ludicrousness of the idea that the United States was almost militarily helpless, the constant drumbeat for more military bore fruit. The National Defense Act of 1916 (Pub. L. 64–85, 39 Stat. 166) was enacted on June 3, a U.S. federal law that updated the Militia Act of 1903. As well, the 1916 act included an expansion of the Army and the National Guard and the creation of an Officers' and Enlisted Reserve Corps and a Reserve Officers' Training Corps. An expanded authority to federalize the National Guard was given to the United States President. That act was passed in the midst of the "preparedness controversy" and authorized the President to mobilize the Army in case of war or "other emergency," and for the duration of the event. Previously the National Guard was limited to service within each state, although federal activation within the United States could be authorized for up to nine months, in certain circumstances. That legislation of 1916 authorized an expanded Army of 175,000 and a National Guard of 450,000.[26]

The NSL constantly touted the patriotic aspects of war, of a person doing his bit for the homeland, and so forth. But for the capitalist class war was, and is, about one thing only—money. At the end of August 1914, with the European part of World War I then underway for just one month, it was reported that Wall Street interests were taking advantage of the conflict, which had closed stock exchanges, by buying up stocks and bonds in order to strengthen and consolidate their control of capital and credit. At the same time those Wall Street interest were lobbying federal authorities in Washington, D.C., for items such as ship subsidies. Noted a reporter: "Capital in America is making hay while the war clouds hang over Europe."[27]

An article that appeared also in August 1914 observed the sharp rise in America in the cost of items such as sugar and meat and reported that the packing industry and sugar refiners were under scrutiny. At a hearing, warehouse men testified about vast amounts of sugar being stored following the outbreak of the war. In a bizarre example of logic being inverted, it

J. P. Morgan, 1910. An angry Morgan is seen here threatening a reporter with his cane.

was reported, "Big retail dealers blamed the small stores for the increase in price, saying that they had forced it and the big fellows merely followed suit."²⁸

About a year later it was noted that "The war trust, to which war means staggering profits, is tightening its grip on America." The stock of Bethlehem Steel had sold at $30 a share at the start of the war (July 1914) and was then (October 1915) selling at $450. Observed the journalist, "It is not in the interest of these men [Wall Streeters] that the European war is brought to a speedy close. The more war, the more profits." As of September 1915 the market value of the listed stock of 13 representative manufacturing companies in America—companies directly benefiting from the European war— had increased by $492 million from January 1, 1915. The preferred stock of the "steel trust," after the war orders for munitions for the Allies came to the Morgan and Company banking firm, had increased over $40 million in market value.²⁹

An idea of the amount of money involved in war could be seem in a report which observed that from the time the war started in Europe until July 1915, the banking firm of J.P. Morgan and Company had handled contracts totaling over $500 million for the account of foreign governments for war munitions and supplies. Of that amount, $400 million was for the British government and $50 million was for the French government. Commissions on those contracts to the Morgan firm began at 2 percent and decreased, by size of the contract. All of those contracts were placed with American firms.[30]

A couple of months later a different newspaper specified, in a list, the nine ways that Morgan made "war pay" from such contracts. Of course, all other U.S. financial firms profited in the same way as did J.P. Morgan. (1) The Allies paid him for transacting their munitions business in America. (2) The manufacturers paid him for giving them their share of that business. (3) He owned much of the stock in the factories that handled large war contracts. (4) He dealt in margin in the stocks of the firms that were going to get the contracts. (5) He owned stock in the railroads that took the finished products to the seaports. (6) He got bonuses from the proving rounds where American-made munitions were tested. (7) His steamships charged extra rates for taking the munitions to Europe. (8) His London branch (Morgan, Grenfell and Company) made money out of the distributing agencies. (9) He got enormous fees from England for raising the money in America to pay all those profits to himself.

Thus, extra fees and commissions (called bribery in some circles) came to Morgan and the Morgan firm from the likes of Carnegie's U.S. Steel for being given those lucrative contracts. Because he could trade on the stock exchanges on margin he was able to increase potential profits by a factor of ten. Only the wealthy had deep enough pockets to stand the risk of margin investment. All of the insider knowledge the firm had by way of receiving such contracts (as middlemen) and then awarding them to whomever they wished could also be used by bankers to increase their own income and that of their firms. Also, such insider information could be easily passed—freely or for "consideration"—to other members of the plutocrat class. Another aspect of excessive profits came from the production of shoddy, inferior goods to fulfill those contracts, a problem that plagued governments during all wars.[31]

In August 1917 an official statement was made in the British House of Commons that revealed the purchases of war munitions and supplies from America had reached $10 million daily. An American newspaper commented that the banking firm of J.P. Morgan and Company "had to handle a large share. In no previous year had all the foreign countries of the world combined taken any such quantity of American product."

Edward R. Stettinius was described in this account as the "biggest buyer in the world." He had been president of the Diamond Match Company but at the beginning of World War I he went to work as a partner for J.P. Morgan where he worked as chief buyer of war supplies for the Allies, overseeing a work force of about 150 people. When the United States entered the war (April 1917), he went to work for the United States War Department, in charge of procurement and production of supplies for the

U.S. Army. On April 6, 1918, he became Assistant Secretary of War. After the war, he returned to work with Morgan and Company, where he devoted his time to restructuring large companies. When this article was published Stettinius was with the War Department and, with respect to his procurement habits, he said, "Through the knowledge and experience and ramifications of those in the Morgan firm, we had a good idea of who was who and what was what throughout the manufacturing world."[32]

If the National Security League started off with a lie then a much cited reason for the U.S. entering the war was also based on a lie. On May 7, 1915, the British ocean liner *Lusitania* was sunk by a German submarine with a loss of 1,198 people, of which 128 were Americans. The public was outraged and that event has often been cited as one of the reasons why the Americans entered the war officially, although that entrance was just one month short of two full years into the future. Since the *Lusitania* was not a military ship the event was cited as an example of German ruthlessness. At the time the Germans claimed the ship was carrying munitions and that made it a valid target. That charge was vehemently denied at the time. However, decades later it was revealed that the ocean liner was in fact carrying war munitions, from America to the British.[33]

The threat of socialism/communism making its way to America, and the working class in general were very much feared and hated by the capitalist class. For the plutocrats there was little or no difference. Any worker, except the servile, obsequious and obedient ones, who dared to demand some improvement in conditions, no matter how minor, was by definition a socialist. A socialist or communist was anyone who fought, to whatever minor degree, to improve the lot of the workers. Socialism had to be stopped entirely and workers had to be controlled completely.

At the start of 1914 a federal Commission on Industrial Relations announced it would undertake an investigation of "great labor disturbances." Leaders of a miners' strike then underway at Trinidad, Colorado, defied the military authorities and declared that they would return "Mother Mary" Jones to that place from Denver despite her deportation by the troops. Jones had simply been abducted from the scene when she arrived to lend moral support to the strikers. Mother Jones arrived by train in Trinidad one morning at 8 a.m. but was forcibly placed on a train for Denver leaving at 9:30 a.m. that same morning, under guard by five soldiers. Jones was a well-known labor activist of the day and was then 77 years old.[34]

Also in 1914 George Pope, president of the National Association of Manufacturers, issued a statement in which he trashed unions, saying, "These unions take from men the right to bargain for themselves and are, therefore, lawless organizations and, because they are lawless, the courts, as well as the national guard meet with their enmity." Butte, Montana, experienced its first day of martial law in September 1914. On that day authorities raided the local offices of the I.W.W. (Industrial Workers of the World, known as the Wobblies) and arrested seven union men who were taken into custody for military trial. Later in 1914 an article in a West Virginia newspaper noted there were then four organizations in Huntington carrying the message of socialism to the working class, up from just one such organization a year earlier. Said the account, "No selfrespecting working man follows the banner of a capitalist.... These socialist locals are formed for the express purpose of overthrowing capitalism."[35]

One commentator considered the issue of "preparedness" and the supposed need for an increased military, in May 1916, and remarked, with respect to preparedness at home, "America needs no arms unless capital intends to crush labor." Later that year, according to a journalist, "Capital is putting up a more serious attempt than ever to combat the power of the labor organization." With respect to the fight for the eight-hour day E.P. Ripley, president of the Atchison, Topeka and Santa Fe Railroad, declared that the growing strength of labor would eventually demand everything in sight until a social revolution would result. In a different city a month later a different journalist stated, "The country is in the midst of an industrial turmoil. Employers are starting a concerted and determined effort all over the United States to crush labor forever." An opinion from the stock dealers/financiers J.S. Bache and Company stated, "The business of the whole country is menaced. The fault is with Congress, which has steadily refused to curb labor in the power of combination which the Sherman law is intended to control in all other industrial operations."[36]

The ruling class even had an ally in the form of the trade union movement that had been accepted by that class as no threat whatsoever to the capitalist class. That was the American Federation of Labor led by president Samuel Gompers. As a newspaper editor remarked in January 1917, "Mr. Gompers is a conservative. The type of labor organization he created is conservative.... A more radical unionism beats against the policies Mr. Gompers has reared.... He is the chief bulwark between the labor movement and the Marxian leaders who would seize, if they could, the American Federation and dedicate it to socialism." That editorial was written in praise of Gompers and the AF of L.[37]

The most obvious example of a radical union at the time was the Industrial Workers of the World. Also in 1917, some 1,200 members of that union were "deported" from Bisbee, Arizona, in cattle cars, across the state line. Their only crime was to be striking mine workers attempting to better their working conditions.[38]

In an article about an upcoming election in New York City for the position of Mayor a reporter noted, "It is not easily explained why both the old parties should become panic-stricken because of fear that the Socialists would carry the New York municipal election in November; yet that appears to be the state of mind of the political leaders of the campaign" of the Republican and Democrat candidates. A Socialist candidate, Morris Hillquit, almost finished second in that race. Of one of the candidates, incumbent Mayor John Purroy Mitchel, it was said that no candidate had ever entered a political campaign supported by more money and influence than Mitchel and that he was the candidate of the wealthy, the "monopolists of patriotism"—one of which was the National Security League, and the anti-peace crowd.[39]

In a lengthy article published in April 1917 in a labor newspaper, an account was given of many examples of state and capitalist class violence against workers engaged in strikes, and so forth. Some of those encounters involved the federal authorities and some involved various state militia. In some of those clashes women and children were injured or murdered. For one example, in a 1916 steel strike in Youngstown, Ohio, four people were killed and 37 injured. The grand jury found Elbert H. Gary and 113 other persons connected with the Steel Trust guilty but nothing was done to them. Gary was a key founder of U.S. Steel in 1901, bringing together partners J.P. Morgan, Andrew Carnegie and Charles M. Schwab. The town of Gary, Indiana, was named after him, as was Gary, West Virginia.[40]

Samuel Gompers, president of the American Federation of Labor and the best known labor figure of his time, spoke before a crowd of some 2,000 people in New York City. In that speech Gompers predicted that the American edition of the Bolsheviks "would be repressed before it could work America's undoing."[41] An editorial published at the beginning of 1919 declared, "There is a considerable group in the United States that professes to fear a revolution in America, accompanied with anarchy and bloodshed. This group represented by a powerful daily press is so much in fear of a revolution or professes to be, that it brands all movements springing from workingmen or farmers for political or economic reforms as 'Bolshevism.'" It continued, "The purpose is plain. It is believed by this group that, if a tradition can be built up in America that whenever the common people organize and ask reforms it is the first step in 'red revolution' and ultimate anarchy, then political and economic reforms, no matter how moderate or reasonable, can be discredited and blacked, thus preserving the present order intact and even defeating orderly, evolutionary reforms."[42]

"Regular" unions of the allied printing trades—meaning those affiliated with the American Federation of Labor—announced in September 1919 they were joining hands with the employers in waging a war to the finish against what they termed the "Bolshevist" organizations that threatened soon to force unauthorized strikes. Later that year 249 "anarchists" were deported from the port of New York City, bound for an undisclosed port in Soviet Russia. The most famous of those deported were Emma Goldman and Alexander Berkman.[43]

According to a November 1919 account from Assistant Secretary of State William Phillips, the Russian Bolsheviks "Have availed themselves of every opportunity to initiate in the United States, a propaganda aimed to bring about the forcible overthrow of our present form of government." Phillips relayed that information to Senator James Wadsworth (NY), chairman of the Senate Military Committee. Both Phillips and Wadsworth came from families of great wealth. The former was a graduate of Harvard; the latter, a graduate of Yale. Phillips stated that the Bolsheviks had large quantities of gold and the means to bring it to America "where it could be used to sustain their propaganda of 'violence and unreason.'"

Along the same lines was another 1919 account. This was in the form of a warning from Francis P. Garvan of the Department of Justice Bureau of Investigation who said he believed the Russians were pouring $2 million a month into the United States. Said Garvan, "Certainly. We have evidence to show that, and that is shown by the tremendous amount of money they are spending. The condition is serious throughout the country." No evidence was presented for any of Garvan's allegations. At the time Garvan was speaking, the United States military, along with the coalition of the willing from several other nations, had invaded Russia and were trying, unsuccessfully, to effect regime change. One of the subheads for this article was "Millions of dollars sent to United States to finance revolution." Another subhead, and one that would be very familiar 100 years later, stated that this move by Russia was an "attempt to destroy American democracy."[44]

Even at this early date the use of huge sums of outside money, dark money, in political campaigns was in evidence. And the National Security League may or may not have been involved in the best known such election campaign in that category. The NSL went on to target for defeat politicians that did not accept the League's ideas. One such person targeted was Henry Ford (see Chapter 16 for details). He was hated by the NSL. The event was the 1918 U.S. Senate election in the state of Michigan. Each of the candidates was a man of enormous wealth—Truman H. Newberry, Republican industrialist, and Henry Ford, Democrat and auto magnate. Ford had been asked to run by U.S. President Woodrow Wilson and the automaker entered both the Republican and Democratic primaries. Wanting to ensure that Ford, with his wider name recognition, did not win both primaries, the Newberry organization went into the Republican primary with an "unrestrained budget," especially to buy advertising. Newberry's campaign charged Ford with pacifism and anti–Semitism and said that Ford had made great efforts to keep his son Edsel out of military service. As a result, Ford won the Democratic primary; Newberry took the Republican primary and in the November election Newberry won the Michigan Senate seat. A large amount of protest erupted from many citizens offended by the Newberry campaign's "blatant spending," both in the August primary and in the November general election. Newspapers called for the removal of Newberry from the Senate. Nonetheless he took the oath of office on May 19, 1919, and took his seat at the beginning of the 66th Congress.[45]

Problems for Newberry began on September 17, 1918, when a resolution was introduced in the Senate calling for an investigation into the Michigan primary. That complaint was based on a report filed by Newberry's campaign committee stating it had received and spent more than $175,000 on the election—far in excess of the $3,750 limit imposed by Michigan law and by the Federal Corrupt Practices Act. Ford also filed petitions contesting the election. In due course all such petitions and complaints were referred to the Senate Committee on Privileges and Elections. On November 29, 1919, Newberry and 134 campaign associates were indicted and charged with violation of federal and state campaign spending laws. Newberry always asserted he knew nothing about any illegal contributions and disbursements.

Found guilty on March 20, 1920, Newberry appealed to the Supreme Court, which overturned the conviction by a vote of 5–4 on May 2, 1921. That ended Newberry's troubles in criminal court but not in the Senate. On November 18, 1922, he resigned his Senate seat and left politics permanently. He resigned, reportedly, because the balance between the two old parties had shifted, after the most recent elections, and Newberry feared renewed calls for his removal. The money expended by Newberry, $195,000 in total, was not from his own funds and, unbelievably, was said to have been "contributed by his relatives and friends without his solicitation or knowledge."[46]

Where did the money come from? One possibility was that it came from the National Security League, whose dislike of Ford was extreme. On July 30, 1917, the NSL issued a list of members who had entered active war service. Several people were listed by name. One of them was Truman H. Newberry. Most of the names on the list, it was said, had resigned from the National Security League when they entered war service, "for ethical reasons."[47]

This was the world that the National Security League helped to create and to reinforce, along with other groups. It was the beginning of the era of using large sums of money supplied by the plutocrat class to fund organizations to build a supposed groundswell of popular support for policies and actions that benefited only that plutocrat class, but were presented as being the will of the people. Groups that were funded in such fashion kept their sources secret, wherever possible, with the funded groups being led by, in the case of the NSL, well paid corporate lawyers and former military men who were all in the service of the plutocrat class.

Such tactics only became feasible from about the 1890s onward with the dramatic increases in literacy and changes in technology that brought in mass communication that could be spread throughout the nation relatively quickly. Mass literacy made mass advertising possible and a reality, and Wall Street and other financiers and capitalists quickly moved to engineer what Edward S. Herman and Noam Chomsky would much later famously describe as "manufacturing consent." For the National Security League that meant moving from preparedness (more military, bigger military) to patriotism (enlist, and if at home do not take advantage by demanding higher pay or striking, for example) to Americanization (those evil Russians/Socialists/Reds/Radicals/Wobblies/Anarchists/Unionists are trying to destroy American democracy).

Chapter 2

The Organization

The keyword for the National Security League from 1915 until the declaration of war by the United States on April 6, 1917, was "preparedness." It was the idea that the military capabilities of the United States were woefully inadequate to withstand any type of assault by a foreign power. And such an attack, if the NSL was to be believed, was imminent. So for a little more than two years the association beat the drums for a much bigger military—and that the increase had better come immediately. Aside from the regular military, an increase was urged in the home forces of militias, reserves, and the National Guard. One of the first orders of business, though, was the solidification of the organization itself, and the drive to establish branches anywhere and everywhere in America.

The NSL was formally registered with the Secretary of State, at Albany, New York, on January 14, 1915. It was established as a non-stock corporation with its main office to be located in Manhattan and a stated purpose of carrying out an investigation of the naval and military defenses of the United States and the organization of citizens to bring to public notice the results of those investigations. Directors of the National Security League were S. Stanwood Menken, Edward H. Clark, William T. Hornaday, Frederick Q. Brown, Charles E. Lydecker (NY), J. Bernard Walker (Brooklyn), Lawrence F. Abbott (Cornwall), Frederick H. Allen (Pelham Manor), and Herbert Barry (West Orange NJ).[1]

From the beginning the NSL moved to bring well-known people into its ranks, often to serve in "honorary" positions. For example, just days after registering the association in Albany, the group announced that Henry L. Stimson, former United States Secretary of War, had accepted the post of chairman of the National Security League's Army Committee. At the same time Beekman Winthrop, former Assistant Secretary of the Navy, was elected vice chairman of the Navy Committee, of which J. Bernard Walker (editor of the publication *Scientific American*) was chairman.[2]

Even at that early date the League insisted that the work of organizing branches in the principal cities throughout the country was "going

Chapter 2. The Organization

forward rapidly." Stanwood Menken, president of the group, added that branches of the NSL were being formed "in every state, county and congressional district of the United States." Purpose of the association, he said at that time, "is to arouse the country to the necessity of a better national defense."[3]

Reportedly, in February 1915, the National Security League had achieved so much success in New York City in that short time that a committee on extension (branches) had been appointed, with the following members: William Frederick Dix (secretary of Mutual Life Insurance Co.) as chairman; Lawrence F. Abbott (editor of *The Outlook*); A.E. Humphrey (executive secretary of NSL); John R. Iselin (lawyer); William R. Corwine (organizer); Rodman Gilder (of the *Century Magazine*); Elmer Thompson (Automobile Club of America); Fred A. Stokes (publisher); J. Beaumont Spencer (engineer); Albert R. Ledoux (physician); and John Winthrop Loveland (lawyer).

Henry Stimson, 1912. Stimson also moved through the revolving door. He was a former U.S. Secretary of War and then moved over to the NSL as chairman of the group's army committee.

That committee planned to send four representatives to Washington, Baltimore and Richmond to establish branches in those cities. From that initial start to establishing branch offices the group planned to extend the organization to all places in America having a population of at least 10,000 people. According to the journalist who wrote the article the NSL "has been organized by citizens who are convinced the United States is not adequately prepared for defense. They favor an army and navy with citizen reserves sufficient only for the adequate protection of the United States. They do not believe in a large standing army or in any form of militarism." Of course, the "citizens" who organized the group were a very narrow subset of that more general population. It was limited to wealthy, male, white citizens, and no other.[4]

Another high profile member was recruited in February when Judge Alton B. Parker accepted the office of honorary vice-president of the League. Parker had run as the Democratic Party's nominee for U.S. President in the 1904 election, losing to incumbent Republican Theodore Roosevelt. Parker also served as Chief Judge of the New York Court of Appeals

Alton B. Parker, 1906. Parker was very high profile, having been the failed Democratic presidential candidate in the 1904 election, losing to incumbent Theodore Roosevelt. He was appointed honorary vice-president of the NSL as a counter to Republican Joseph Choate who was honorary president of the League. Thus, supposedly, the League would appear to be non-partisan.

from 1898 to 1904. In his acceptance letter Parker wrote, "I am in full sympathy with the object of the National Security League … and am gratified to learn from you that its promoters are animated by the sentiment which prompted the Secretary of War to say, only the other day: 'The question of national defense should be approached in a non-partisan and purely scientific spirit.'" Circulars outlining the purpose of the association had been sent out "in thousands." Each contained a membership blank that could be filled out and returned. Those who believed in the NSL were invited to enroll "in order that the league may have the broad support of all classes of patriotic citizens from all parts of the country."[5]

Work establishing branches continued. A New England branch was established by early April 1915, with the headquarters located in Boston. Prominent members in that association were the Governor of Massachusetts (David I. Walsh), the Mayor of Boston (James M. Curley) and the former U.S. Secretary of the Navy, George von L. Meyer. According to his Wikipedia page Meyer was reared in "patrician society." A graduate of Harvard University, he was director of various trust companies, banks, manufacturing companies and public utility concerns. While managing his business concerns he also had positions in state and local governments. Meyer was U.S. Secretary of the Navy from 1909 to 1913, under President William Howard Taft. After retiring from national politics he joined the effort to reelect Theodore Roosevelt in 1916. As well he urged preparedness and "actively associated with the National Security League. As early as March 1915 the League was already publishing its own magazine, *National Defense*."[6]

When the National Security League set out to establish a branch in Keokuk, Iowa, it followed its usual procedure in going after the big names in the community. It was reported that Mayor D.B. Hamill would serve as chairman of that branch of the organization, when it had been "perfected." Philadelphia had a branch by the summer. Chairman of that group was Col. Theodore E. Wiedershelm. He saw the purpose of his branch as augmenting the efforts of United States Congressmen from Philadelphia "to obtain adequate increases in the standing army, the National Guard and the navy" at the next session of Congress. It was declared by this branch that after it had conducted a survey, a few days earlier, of the ground from Philadelphia to the lower Delaware Bay it found that there "were less than 200 men, manning inadequate forts, between Philadelphia and an enemy navy." Republican member of the House from Pennsylvania J. Hampton Moore then pointed out that an "absurd inconsistency" existed in the placing of 50,000 men in the Hawaiian Islands "to protect industry there and the safeguarding of Philadelphia and Camden with less than 300 men." Wiedershelm stated that NSL would direct work along two lines. One of those lines was to achieve an increase in the standing army until it "is on a footing adequate to meet eventualities." The second focus was to strive for a larger National Guard force.[7]

In the middle of August a news item observed that Minneapolis had "enlisted in a country-wide movement for national preparation against war." Thirty "representative citizens" at a meeting in that community had organized a National Security League branch. A campaign was to start with the goal at Minneapolis being to enroll 10,000 members. According to this account the national NSL "has some of the most prominent men in the United States enrolled." When an organizational meeting was finally held in Keokuk it was advertised as being open to "all men of the city who have at heart the protection of the United States against a possible aggression of foreign powers."[8]

An organizational meeting for an NSL branch took place in Topeka, Kansas, in September. Slated to address the meeting was William B. Brewster, National Security League field secretary. Since leaving New York City on an extensive organizing road trip he had established branches in

Cleveland, Detroit, Milwaukee, St. Paul, Minneapolis, Des Moines and Omaha. When asked about the association's aims Brewster asserted, "It is the purpose of the league to force Congress to heed the wishes of the people of the country." As was often the case when asked about goals, the NSL regularly declared the desires of a small number of wealthy white men were actually the desires of "the people." Brewster continued, "Already through our organization large employers of labor have been aroused and are encouraging their men to enlist in the state militia."[9]

A permanent organization consisting of 34 "prominent Richmond men" was formed on September 16, 1915, at the Business Men's Club in that city; it was the Virginia branch of the NSL. Henry L. West, executive secretary of the League and ex-Commissioner of the District of Columbia, addressed the group. West insisted his group "in no sense stands for anything like militarism." Since its formation some eight months earlier total membership in the group had reached 10,000 to 12,000. West went on to assert that many of the state governors had consented to serve on the national committee and that six of those governors had appointed committees on national defense in their own areas.

According to West, Samuel Gompers, president of the American Federation of Labor, was also "in sympathy" with the movement. At that time the NSL officers were: Joseph A. Choate (honorary president; he was a nationally known lawyer and a former U.S. Ambassador to the UK); Alton Parker (honorary vice-president); Stanwood Menken (president); Herbert Barry (secretary); E.H. Clark (treasurer); Henry L. West (executive secretary); E. Woodward Duke (assistant secretary). The League had three classes of membership; annual, dues of $1; contributing, $5; and life membership, $25.[10]

At a meeting held at the NSL headquarters in New York City early in October the group claimed it had won the support of governors of 10 states in its preparedness drive and that a total of 41 branches had been organized with 72 more then in the process of formation.[11]

The class nature of the League was very obvious in Philadelphia when the branch located in that city held a meeting late in October. Fifty-two men were present and after that mid-day meeting it was noted that "Men of financial, business and social prominence in Philadelphia to-day pledged themselves to support the purposes and aims of the National Security League, to aid in a membership campaign to start next week and to induce their employees to join."[12]

The relationship of women to the National Security League was non-existent in the beginning and later moved to something amounting to "affiliated" status, or tokenism. One woman attending an NSL conference in January 1916 in Washington, D.C., was Mrs. William Alexander of New

York City. She was the president of the National Special Aid Society, an organization that was described as "affiliated" with the NSL. The stated purpose of her group was to create and maintain an organization through which "the women of America may be prepared to do effectively the things that it is their privilege and duty to do in the event of war, and to increase the standard of efficiency and the unity of the nation at all times." Alexander's society had petitioned Congress "to take proper and sufficient means" to adequately prepare for the national defense of the nation. The society aimed to create a volunteer corps of women and arrange for their instruction in first aid and nursing, for service in times of national disasters.[13]

Women of the National Special Aid Society surfaced again in February when a number of them held a "patriotic rally for national defense" in New York City. The purpose was to raise money to help train aviators. Among the women in attendance and leading that rally

Every thoughtful American of to-day, whether private citizen, public servant, preacher or writer, is following George Washington in pleading that the Nation

Prepare for Defense Without Delay.

WHY? Because these men KNOW our country is in grave danger.

American honor, life and property require national insurance.

We believe America's continued existence requires obligatory universal military training for our young men and readiness for service by them for national defense.

Men and women of America you can help!

Help the campaign for National Preparedness by giving what you can to further the work of the National Security League.

Do your share. Don't expect others to do it for you.

The League Needs Funds

to give One Hundred Million People all the Facts–Facts known to Every Foreign War and Navy Office and unknown to most American citizens. Your contribution will be used for educational purposes through our Branches, as well as National Headquarters and other patriotic organizations, and will be carefully spent. This is a great work and merits the assistance of every man and woman in the country.

Congress will act only when there is a positive demand from the people. To impress upon Congress the necessity of action, the League is organizing branches to widen its influence and desires your membership.

Send your subscription at once to the
NATIONAL SECURITY LEAGUE, INC.
31 Pine Street, New York City

At last, an "I no n" member on the uncommitting nation. Send a two cent stamp for literature and membership blanks to distribute among your friends. We need your help.

OFFICERS	FINANCE COMMITTEE
JOSEPH H. CHOATE - Honorary President	Franklin Q. Brown, Chairman
ALTON B. PARKER Honorary Vice-President	Courtlandt Nicoll Samuel W. Fairchild
ROBERT BACON Chairman Board of Directors	Frederick H. Allen Walter E. Frew
S. STANWOOD MENKEN - - President	Sidney C. Borg John B. Langer
HERBERT BARRY - - - Secretary	Nicholas F. Brady Parker Sloane
E. H. CLARK - - - - Treasurer	Walter T. Rosen J. Kennedy Tod
	John D. Crimmins G. Creighton Webb
	George T. Wilson

Read This!

THE NATIONAL SECURITY LEAGUE is a non-political, non-partisan, absolutely neutral organization, which is conducting a nation-wide campaign to secure adequate preparedness for national defense. It has sixteen state committees on National Defense appointed by Governors and seventy-four Citizens' Committees appointed by Mayors, to co-operate in its work; 126 organized branches from Maine to California and a National Committee representing its 50,000 members.

The League advocates support of the Woman's Section of the Movement for National Preparedness, No. 1 Madison Avenue, New York City.

NOTE:—This advertisement is paid for by a friend of the League who believes that the American people will welcome an opportunity to unite in a single organization devoted to the service of the country.

THE NATIONAL SECURITY LEAGUE, Inc.
I desire to be enrolled as a member of the National Security League in the class designated below with a cross-mark X and I enclose herewith $........... in payment of dues.

MEMBERSHIP ..Annual....... $1.00
..Contributing $5.00
..Life .... $25.00   membership
..Founder ... $100.00   dues

Name ....
(Please write name and address with particular care.)
Address .... Street ....
.... City ....
Date ....191...   State ....
Make checks payable to The National Security League, Inc.
31 Pine Street, New York City.

Telegraph or Write Your Congressman!

This February 1916 ad from the NSL was looking for donations and new members. The ad also urged readers to contact their congressmen, to urge more militarism.

were Mrs. Alexander and Mrs. Menken.[14]

When the League held a meeting in New York City on February 16, honorary president Joseph Choate attacked U.S. President Woodrow Wilson for his unwillingness to be completely amendable to the NSL's militaristic program, declaring, "A President may change his mind, but the country may change its President." According to the reporter who attended the gathering, the crowd numbered about 600 and there were as least as many women as men in attendance. That was likely a gross exaggeration. Menken announced that in recognition of the services performed by the women in the league a number of females would be appointed to places on the various committees. Choate's outburst against Wilson came a week after Secretary of War Lindley Garrison had resigned his cabinet post due to differences with Wilson. Garrison was much more hawkish than Wilson and had, among other things, advocated for U.S. intervention into the Mexican revolution "to restore order." Said Choate, "The National Security League is organized for war, and let every man and woman in it be a soldier standing for defense until we have gained an adequate army and navy, organized by the best army and navy experts."[15]

Joseph Choate, 1914. He was another Harvard graduate and another wealthy corporate lawyer with many directorships in various companies. In short, he was a typical National Security League member.

When Pensacola, Florida, Mayor A. Greenhut called a meeting at city hall on February 23 it was with the purpose of looking to form a National Security League branch. He admitted that the gathering was "not as largely attended as desired," but went on to blame the sparseness of the crowd on "counter attractions." All of those who did attend were said to have been strongly in favor of preparedness. Mayor Greenhut had personally requested the chosen men (who mostly did not come, apparently) to attend; that is, there was no open call for a meeting that anyone could attend. Some 500 men had been requested. One attendee was B.S. Hancock, who asserted, "five hundred men in favor of preparedness in Pensacola will have a whole lot of weight with congressmen, in their consideration of any measure which might be put up to them to vote on." At the gathering

Chapter 2. The Organization

it was suggested that membership rolls be "opened" and that all patriotic Americans be invited. No dues were required to join the local branch but membership in the national NSL would cost at least $1 a year. However, it was not necessary for members of local NSL branches to join the national association.[16]

New York City Mayor John Mitchel spoke on the evening of April 18 at the Flushing, New York, branch of the NSL. During his speech he declared that he believed in universal military training as the "only solution of the national defense problem." He urged a citizen reserve force composed of "the entire manhood of the republic." Another change he urged was the federalization of the National Guard.[17]

A report from Menken around that same time indicated that the League had "upward" of 150 branches and 80 Mayor's Committees for Defense. He insisted that "our work has proceeded simply as advocacy of preparedness against war, and not as a plea for militarism in any form." Menken wanted to look at broader aspect of preparedness including "the menace to our country and the loss to the individual through inefficient government by the people, whether municipal, state or nation." It was also revealed herein that NSL branches gave money (from subscriptions and donations) to the national headquarters, and not the other way around. What percentage of money collected at the branch level to be sent on to headquarters was not stated.[18]

In that same month the League announced that it would soon form

A membership blank from 1917. At this time the original three categories, "annual," "contributing" and "life," had been expanded to a total of five, with the categories of "founder" and "donor" having been added.

a District of Columbia branch. The League also declared it then had more than 140 branches and a membership of 70,000. In July of the same year the NSL stated it had 225 branches. As well, the League executive council had voted that women "should" be eligible for membership.[19]

A newspaper ad placed by the NSL at the beginning of 1917 listed three levels of membership dues: $1, $5, and $25 upward. Reportedly, the branch total then stood at 280. That newspaper pitch requested "liberal" donations for its nationwide work and urged readers to write their Congressmen to support "universal service." Within the advertisement was the claim, "We are still unprepared." In general the pitch was directed at "Americans for America." Three points were emphasized in the ad. One was that military and naval forces were not sufficient for national defense. A second point was that universal obligatory military training and service for youths (between the ages of 18 and 21) was necessary. And finally, what was needed was the "Awakening and education of the people to the obligations as well as the privileges of citizenship."[20]

From time to time it was announced that a larger organization had been formed that encompassed a number of supposed patriotic and preparedness organizations, of which there were many at this time. The idea was the obvious one that a larger, umbrella group would have more clout than the groups working independently and singly. For whatever reason these larger societies never got off the ground and faded into obscurity almost immediately. One such grouping was the "Conference of American Patriotic Societies" which had supposedly grown out of a conference of delegates from such societies. They had at least one meeting, in January 1917, where they discussed coordination of plans for national defense. It was agreed to have a general committee, consisting of one representative from each of the organizations involved. Representing the National Security League was Raymond Price.[21]

CHAPTER 3

The Politicians

The National Security League's efforts to create a more militaristic United States and a more loyal and especially obedient society took many forms. They recruited "name" people to be figureheads, and often vigorous spokesmen; they held conferences and undertook various public relations campaigns to arouse the public in their efforts to convince people that what was not in their best interests actually was in their best interests. It was all a cloak, a disguise, a ruse by a small group of rich white men to maintain, and extend, that order. And, of course, the NSL spent much time and effort interacting with politicians, at federal, state and local levels. As early as the beginning of February 1915, when the League was only a month from its formal registration, League president Stanwood Menken had been in Washington, D.C., for several days conferring with U.S. Secretary of War Lindley Garrison, Senator George Chamberlain (Dem., OR, chairman of the Senate Committee on Military Affairs) and Senator Elihu Root (New York State, a lawyer whose clients included Andrew Carnegie).[1]

A concerted and determined nationwide campaign for adequate national defense was inaugurated in February 1915. Late that month every member of Congress received a letter from the NSL informing the member of the League's purpose to carry the battle for national preparedness into every Congressional district in the country. Simultaneously, the Merchants' Association of New York was moving along similar lines. Following the adoption of "strong resolutions" in favor of adequate national preparedness an announcement was made by that business group that it had launched a movement to get all the commercial organizations of America behind the demand for army and navy reform. An appeal was made by the Merchants' Association to the United States Chamber of Commerce to submit the matter to its entire membership with a view to bringing about concerted action. If that happened it would bring 600 commercial bodies representing 250,000 business establishments throughout the U.S. "actively into line." Action taken by the Merchants' Association followed a meeting held by the group at which addresses were made by Stimson and Leonard Wood (both favorable to the NSL). Reportedly, these two societies were working "in harmony." It was also stated that, with respect to the NSL, "Tons of literature already has been sent broadcast over the country warning the people ... of the inadequate state of the national defenses."[2]

Letter campaigns by the NSL were regularly directed at Congress members. One from them on April 7, 1915, went to every Senator and Representative in Washington and indicated the League intended to make an "aggressive" fight for national defense legislation at the approaching session of Congress. Declaring the letter contained "no threat," the organization asserted that it was in earnest. Signed by Menken, the letter started with a request that the recipient become a member of the League, the work of which was "strictly non-partisan." And, the letter continued, "If unable to give your personal support we respectfully ask you for a reply expressing your position as regards our program."[3]

The group also targeted politicians in lesser jurisdictions in their campaign for more military. A letter was received by Mayor J.E.T. Bowden in Jacksonville, Florida, in October 1915. That letter came from J. Beaumont Spencer, chairman of the League's Committee on Extension, and requested that Bowden appoint a state committee on national defense to aid the work of securing adequate preparedness. The letter stated, "A few days ago we wrote to the Governor at Tallahassee asking him to appoint a State committee on national defense to aid in the work which the National Security League is doing to secure adequate preparedness against war. Ten Governors have already taken this action." In reply Governor Park Trammell suggested the League write to Bowden and ask him to give the NSL names of persons so interested. That letter to Bowden ended by saying, "May we have your early reply and co-operation?"[4]

Two weeks later it was reported that Mayor Bowden was in receipt of two letters from president Menken of the NSL, requesting him to make the appointments to the citizens committee on national defense from a list "of the influential citizens in this city." Menken noted in the letters that the League was anxious to add Jacksonville to the list of cities organized and added, "We expect many cities will follow the example of Mayor Mitchel of New York, who today announced the appointment of a committee on national defense, of a dozen prominent citizens. This is the most direct way of crystallizing a sentiment for preparedness."[5]

The names of Speaker of the House of Representatives Champ Clark of Missouri and United States Senator James A. O'Gorman (NY) headed the list of Senators and Representatives whose names were made public in October by the NSL as being in favor of "adequate preparedness for national defense." Both were said to be enthusiastic supporters of NSL goals and positions. Some time earlier the League gave out a statement that included letters from nearly 100 Representatives and the names made public a day earlier added almost 50 to that list. Thus, the League insisted it had the support of about one-third of the entire membership of the House for its program. In this article brief quotes, all positive and favorable to the society, were provided from many named politicians. The names and replies of seven New York Congressmen who had previously not been on record were included in this round. Many of the replies from politicians were vague, such as from Representative John A. Sterling, who said, "I am thoroughly in favor of adequate preparedness for national defense." More enthusiastic were replies such as the one from Representative George S. Graham (Philadelphia): "I unhesitatingly advocate an increased navy and regular army and also the adoption of some plan to create a dependable reserve of citizen soldiers."[6]

Champ Clark, 1915. Speaker of the House of Representatives Clark was one of many members of Congress to come out publicly in support of the NSL's plan for increased militarism in the United States.

Other newspapers covered the same story, but in somewhat different manners. Another paper devoted half of the article space to a composite photo of eight legislators who supported the League. These opinions, seemingly shared by so many Congressmen, said the journalist, "have been formulated into a symposium on national preparedness of the National Security League, for use in a campaign to line up the views of all members of the coming congress on this subject." Said Representative Fred A. Britten (IL), "I shall do everything in my power ... to bring about a substantial increase in military as well as naval appropriations." Representative D.R. Anthony, Jr. (KS), was going to look for an increase in the National Guard to at least 250,000 men. He also wanted 12 fighting ships and 25 submarines added to the fleet. However, the article indicated that support for the NSL militarization program was not complete: "Letters from southern members of the new congress, while not strongly encouraging, indicate that sentiment in favor of a program of preparedness is slowly gaining strength in the south."[7]

If the League was to be believed, support for its program, that same month, ran deeper and included state and local officials. The governors of 13 states were said to have appointed committees of "citizens" for national defense that were ready to cooperate with the NSL in its nationwide effort to arouse public sentiment to adopt a program of vastly increased armaments. Those governors were: W.P. Hunt (AZ); Marcus H. Holcomb (CT); G.W. Clarke (IA); James B. McCready (KY); Emmet D. Boyle (NV); Charles S. Whitman (NY); L.B. Hanna (ND); Park Trammell (FL); James Withycombe (OR); R. Livingston Beekman (RI); Richard I. Manning (SC); Ernest Lister (WA); and E.L. Philip (WI). In addition, the mayors of 25 cities ranging from Boston to Los Angeles had already appointed citizens' committees.

"The purpose of these State and city committees, as well as the purpose of the National Security League itself, is not to interfere in any way with plans for increasing the system of defense," said a reporter, naively. Rather, as explained by NSL executive secretary Henry L. West, "the aim is to give Congress indisputable proof that the country as a whole deserves and demands an adequate system of defense." West told the reporter the whole thing rested with Congress: "Groups of men in one locality or another may get together, make speeches and pass resolutions favoring an intelligent and effectual plan of national defense; but nothing will happen unless Congress is convinced that the country insists upon action." Then action would happen, he believed. West argued the League then had more than 200 Congressmen on record in favor of "adequate national defense." He stated that the National Security League had formed, or was in the process of forming, branches in 70 cities. Massachusetts had 2,000 NSL members and the city of Chicago had 3,000 members.[8]

At the beginning of November 1915 a lunch meeting was held of the New York State Committee on National Defense, of the NSL. It was held in the dining hall of the Bankers Club in New York City. Speakers on hand were Governor Whitman of New York, NSL honorary president Joseph Choate and NSL president Stanwood Menken. Among the many "men of affairs" in attendance were ex-Governors Martin H. Glynn and Benjamin B. Odell, Mayor Joseph Stevens of Albany, Mayor Louis Fuhrmann of Buffalo, and others. Whitman dwelt particularly on the fact that when he appointed the state committee to cooperate with the NSL "nothing of a political nature in the partisan sense had or would enter into the workings of the committee."[9]

Later in November in New York City it was observed that Mayor Mitchel's appointment of a Committee of One Thousand, as his state committee for national defense was called, "has met with country-wide commendations." Mayors of many major cities from Massachusetts to

California, the reader was told, had appointed similar committees. Officials of the NSL at the local branches in many such cities had telegraphed their congratulations to Mitchel for his action in the interest of preparedness. In this article dozens of cities with such committees were listed, along with the names of the mayors. Since these committees were all part of the League it meant the organization was congratulating itself.[10]

Resolutions calling for adequate defense were adopted on the afternoon of December 17, 1915, in New York City, by the Committee of One Thousand that had been recently appointed by Mayor Mitchel. That was the first meeting of the group and attendance was reported at "upwards of 800." In his opening remarks Mitchel said, "No, gentlemen, I believe with all my heart that you have a national duty to perform in this matter. I believe that it will consist in bringing even more closely and fully home to the people of this country an appreciation of the facts concerning national defense and of the immediate pressing necessity for action."

Henry L. West (between 1915 and 1920). West was executive secretary of the NSL and worked on the campaign to get members of Congress to back the League in its demands, and for those politicians to come out publicly in support of militarism.

The mayor continued, "And I think, too, your duty will consist in part in bringing home to our Representatives in the Congress of the United States the fact that the people are not of two minds but demand that they shall now be made secure for all time against the possibility of successful attack upon their security or the breaking down of the great institutions of free Government that have been built up here." Note that the last part of the sentence in the quote was about internal dissent and any assault on the capitalist order. It was only rarely that such sentiments (which were the real ones fueling the NSL, along with greed for the money an increased arms industry would produce for that class) came to light, but sometimes they did. Major robber baron and plutocrat of the era Cornelius Vanderbilt was chairman of the executive committee on the Committee of One Thousand.[11]

Just before Christmas in 1915 Mayor John Lane of Honolulu announced the appointment of a citizens committee on national defense to cooperate with like committees appointed by the mayors of nearly 75 other cities and towns across America, all at the urging and the behest of the National Security League.[12]

The danger of relying on the National Guard as a means of defense in times of invasion, instead of providing for a force under the direct command of the Federal Government, was emphasized on January 7, 1916, by the NSL honorary president Elihu Root at the first business meeting of the Committee of One Thousand that had been appointed by Governor Charles Whitman to "co-operate" with the League for adequate defense in the drive for preparedness. Root thought the National Guard was too decentralized; that is, 48 different and unrelated forces, with 48 different state governors in command. Initially the NSL was after an increase in the Guard with the same vigor as they showed in pursuing an increase in the army and navy but eventually that decentralized nature of the Guard caused them to place less and less emphasis on the Guard, and to put increasing emphasis on creating a large reserve army, or militia, but only under a single Federal command.

The NSL apparently could not resolve the internal differences in the organization; some argued the Guard should remain a state prerogative while others thought it should be federalized. In order to quell that rarely mentioned dissent at home, to put down the socialists, communists, Reds, Bolsheviks, and so forth, the League understood what was needed was a large reserve force (separate from a standing army that would wax and wane in size with real foreign wars) that was available, and could quickly be sent anywhere within the U.S. borders from a single command, as opposed to having to control six or eight or more individual state governors to try and quickly establish a larger force than could be organized in one particular state, to address any problems in that particular state.[13]

One tactic the League used was to contact a Congress member, by mail or in person, and demand that person state his position clearly on some part of the group's plans for increased militarization and then defend himself. Often the NSL would publish positions taken by politicians, especially those viewed by the League as negative, and thus attempt to intimidate and shame the politicians. U.S. Representative Augustus Gardner spoke before what was described as a "large crowd" at a National Security League meeting in New York City on January 10, 1916. He was invited to attend. After he spoke for 15 minutes he answered questions from the audience. Gardner argued before his listeners the necessity of increasing the army to at least 250,000 men, instead of the 141,000 men called for in the plan advocated by U.S. Secretary of War Garrison.

One of the questions directed at Gardner came from Joseph Choate, chair of the meeting, who asked whether a warship from Germany or another nation could come and reach the city of New York. The politician agreed that such an event could happen and that there was the "threat" of warships covering the landing of foreign troops at Rockaway Beach, on the south coast of Long Island. At the meeting Gardner admitted that last year he had not favored the type of military increases he now advocated, noting that "I've made a mistake." Going even further to prove his patriotism to the League, Gardner also called for a bigger navy and he also wanted young men to be "compelled to serve at least one year with the colors without respect to their social condition in life."[14]

At an NSL meeting in New York City one month later, NSL member Frederic R. Coudert said, "The country is practically united on the necessity of preparedness. The only difference of opinion is how to get it. We won't receive it at the hands of the present Congress. The great danger is that Congress will trick the people, will palm off some sham project on them, making them think they are defended when they are not." He went on to add, "And then when this war is past, when our apprehensions are lulled, the people will lose their eagerness and we shall rest in a false security." Perhaps in that speech lay the seeds for the idea that Congress had to be changed in the 1918 election, as the NSL tried to do through buying and/or browbeating politicians it found unacceptable.[15]

The first meeting of the National Committee of Mayors, organized somewhat earlier by the National Security League, was held in St. Louis on March 2, 1916. That meeting was called by the mayors of 11 of the larger cities of American, headed by Mayor Henry Kiel of St. Louis and Mitchel of New York City. Prior to the gathering, the group had sent invitations to the mayors of 600 cities to attend personally or to send committees. A few females were slated to speak with a mass meeting to be held on the evening of March 3. It was a two-day session with featured speakers on the first day being Mayor Mitchel (New York City), Cornelius Vanderbilt (chair of the NY Committee of One Thousand), and many other city mayors, all of them named in this article. Mayor C.E. Sebastian of Los Angeles was to speak on "Protection of the Pacific Coast." Up to this time labor, trade unions, and so forth, had never been mentioned in connection with the League. It was as if no such thing existed. However, one of the speakers at this gathering was Owen Miller of St. Louis, described as the secretary of the American Federation of Musicians, who was scheduled to give a talk on "Labor and Preparedness." After that mention, labor would once again become almost invisible from the perspective of the League, except as a perhaps hostile entity that needed to be Americanized and to be controlled. At this time it was reported that the NSL had 75,000 members and branches in "many cities."[16]

Generally, NSL members did not directly enter the field of politics, but there were some exceptions. In August 1916 Robert Bacon, chairman of the executive committee of the National Security League, a member of "several other preparedness organizations," and a former United States Ambassador to France announced his decision to enter the primary contest for the Republican nomination for U.S. Senator from New York, against Representative William M. Calder of Brooklyn. Also he had briefly been U.S. Secretary of State in 1909 and earlier he had been in partnership with J.P. Morgan and Company. He was Morgan's chief lieutenant in the formation of the U.S. Steel Corporation.[17]

Petitions asking that the United States establish at once a system of compulsory military training, urging that immediate steps be taken to protect the country and calling for a special session of Congress, were distributed "wholesale" throughout the city of Philadelphia by the National Security League on February 17, 1917. When signed it was the intention of the NSL to forward the petitions to President Woodrow Wilson. The petitions would have Congress sit at a special session to "enact legislation that will provide for the adequate defense of the Republic."[18]

In March 1917 an inquiry was sent out by the League to the mayors of every city in America with a population of 5,000 or more. Questions were being asked as part of a program to canvass the sentiment of the public in every sector of the country on the subject of universal military training. Questions on the form included: "How do your newspapers stand generally?" and "Would your city endorse your senators and representatives for voting for military training?" This was possibly the start of the campaign that would be created to target certain politicians for removal from office in the 1918 election.[19]

At about the same time that the mayors were being canvassed, the National Security League urged New Jersey to make the preparations for national defense already adopted by other states. On March 12 under the "auspices" of the NSL a bill was slated to be introduced into the State Legislature at Trenton. That bill would empower the governor to take a military and industrial census of the state and follow that with whatever steps he considered necessary to equip New Jersey for war. It was also observed by a journalist that Massachusetts, Rhode Island, and Connecticut had formed "under the inspiration of the League, provisional committees of public safety, appointed by the Governors."[20]

Chapter 4

Conferences and Conventions

The National Security League regularly held conferences and conventions as a method of obtaining large crowds and of gaining a greater degree of media coverage. It was also another way to keep up the pressure on politicians with League pronouncements having perhaps a greater likelihood of being reported by journalists when delivered in the atmosphere of enthusiastic convention and conference attendees.

One of the first such events was held in New York City, under League auspices, in the middle of June 1915 and was called the Peace and Preparedness Conference. Among those who had accepted invitations, as of early June, were four former secretaries of the army and navy. There were Jacob M. Dickinson and Henry L. Stimson (former secretaries of the army), and Charles J. Bonaparte and George von L. Meyer (former secretaries of the navy). Others listed as having accepted invitations were the Rev. Dr. Lyman Abbott, Hudson Maxim, Alton B. Parker, Frederic R. Coudert and George Haven Putnam. It was more than a little disingenuous to say these men had accepted invitations to attend and to speak since virtually all of them were definitely NSL members in the first place. All sessions were to be held at the Hotel Astor, except for a mass meeting at Carnegie Hall, on Monday evening, June 14.[1]

Shortly before that conference was to take place a committee of the Central Federated Union in New York made arrangements to hold an anti-war Congress in New York City directly following the special peace conference of the executive council of the American Federation of Labor at Atlantic City. That convention was to be held in Carnegie Hall and simultaneous with anti-war demonstrations on the part of organized labor and citizens of New York City, in 15 sections of that city. Said the report, "The labor peace convention will come as an emphatic reply to the meeting of the National Security League, the [Theodore] Roosevelt organization." It was said that the peace sentiment was sweeping through the labor movement.[2]

One of those slated to speak at the peace and preparedness meeting was former Secretary of the Navy George Meyer. When the reporter wrote about the people who would be attending as delegates there was no doubt about the narrow and elitist range of those men: "Governors of states, mayors of cities and representatives of military organizations and former secretaries of the war and navy will discuss plans for alleviating the unpreparedness of the United States and its danger from attack."[3]

A few days before the conference opened an exhibit of some of the "modern implements of warfare" was installed in the Hotel Astor for display in connection with what a reporter called the "conference on preparedness and national defense." In this case the word "peace" was absent. On display were a torpedo, 14-inch shells, the tent life of an army, a hospital outfit, machine guns, modern rifles, and so forth, and a submarine display. All of it was, said the National Security League, an exhibit with an "educational" purpose—to show that war was no longer a matter of men so much as machines. And that was a huge benefit for the capitalist class because there were so many more implements of war with which they could satisfy their greed with enormous excess profits. An ad in the newspaper for the mass meeting aspect of the conference observed that admission to that Carnegie Hall event was priced at $1.50, $1.00 and 50 cents. Boxes that seated eight people went for $25 and $15. This was the only part of the conference that was open to the general public.

One newspaper article headline captured the weirdness of the conference, perhaps deliberately, perhaps not, with the title "War men to talk peace." In 1916 the cost of a movie ticket was 7 cents; the cost of a loaf of bread was 5 cents.[4]

Reportedly, 25 states were represented at that "Peace and Preparedness Conference." In the hotel room that held the military exhibits signs attached to the walls read: "Wars are sudden, and the ocean renders attack easy and the point of attack doubtful"; and "Do you believe in gambling with the national existence on the faith of a worthless aggressor?" and "We are unprepared against

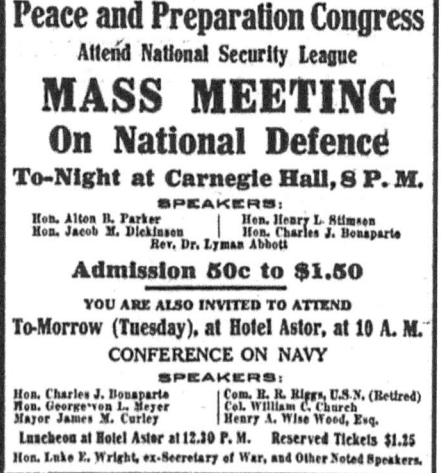

This June 1915 advertisement from a New York City newspaper touted the NSL's peace and preparedness congress to be held in that city with a line-up of "noted" speakers listed.

Chapter 4. Conferences and Conventions 45

attack. Present conditions of unpreparedness are intolerable." The U.S. Navy obtained permission to have the naval band at the mass meeting on June 14, augmented by navy musicians from three battleships. Secretary of the Navy Josephus Daniels, however, revoked that order. Rear-Admiral Strauss granted the use of a torpedo and a gun crew of six men to explain the working of the device to conference attendees. Daniels did not take away the torpedo but he ordered the crew of six sailors to return to their ship. At one session inventor Hudson Maxim read a letter received by him from former President Theodore Roosevelt. In that letter Roosevelt called pacifists "probably the most undesirable citizens that this country contains."[5]

Secretary Daniels had not been presented in a very good light in view of the above report. However, he declared that those press reports about him withdrawing the gun were false. Daniels said in a response to an NSL request that he had directed the New York naval yard to lend the shell and torpedo but nothing was said about a gun crew. Officials thought that perhaps a gun crew had accompanied the items to the exhibit and then returned to the naval yard. With respect to the naval musicians, Daniels remarked that naval bands were not permitted to play at civil functions because such events always brought adverse criticism from musicians' unions over the loss of jobs.[6]

One news account of the opening of the preparedness conference stated that "Soldiers, sailors, statesmen, clergymen and representatives of labor and business met today...." It was overwhelmingly just an audience of business men. Prior to the conference the letter sent by the organizing committee invited the labor unions to send representatives, saying, "The two classes that pay for the ravages of war most heavily are the laboring classes and the women of the country." The letter also stated that if called upon for the protection of the flag "conscription would be a national duty and labor would constitute an important element in the human bulwark of the nation." While women were mentioned in that letter there apparently were no women invited, although, of course, they were free to buy tickets to the event. Given the nature of the letter it was not surprising that labor representatives did not attend. In the letter that went out to women's groups it was stated, "Wives, sisters and daughters would live to see the annihilation of our unequipped men in the scientific attack of modern war. With a well organized, efficient and powerful system of national defense, the conscription and murder of our masses would not take place."[7]

At the conference itself the speakers echoed each other and reiterated the never changing themes about having a bigger military and to have it immediately. No attendance figures seemed to have been given, either for the mass meeting or for the daytime sessions at the hotel. No numbers except that 25 states were represented. Alton Parker declared that we need not fear militarism "but we must have an army and a navy large enough to protect us in our possessions." Again, this was one of the rare mentions of the real function of an increased military—to protect the capitalist order and the capitalists themselves, plus the excess profits gained from a military-industrial complex. Jacob M. Dickinson cited American military actions against Cuba, the Philippines and at Vera Cruz as "object lessons of pacific purpose...."

At another session the report of the Militia Committee of the NSL recommended the enrollment and military instruction of every able-bodied man in the United States between the ages of 18 and 45. It urged that national and state laws to that effect should be pursued immediately. That committee was headed by Charles E. Lydecker. He wanted to see courses in military education and field hygiene included in the curriculum of every college and the "huge enrollment" of citizens should be affiliated as a reserve, more closely with the regular army than the national guard is now affiliated. To worry people reading about this conference, the example of Belgium was often mentioned. Belgium was invaded by Germany, at the start of World War I. With such an inadequate defense, as seen by the NSL, the same result could befall America.[8]

An editorial in a New York newspaper, published at the time of the preparedness conference, agreed with the NSL aims: "The National Security League is doing a brave and patriotic work by its meetings, exhibits, distribution of literature and appeals for funds..." to continue its efforts. The editor stressed the "duty" of preparedness and concluded, "The movement is patriotic, and in no sense political."[9]

One of the speakers at the conference was George von L. Meyer, secretary of the navy under U.S. President William Howard Taft. He told his audience that of 33 battleships in the U.S. Navy, only 26 were fitted for service without delay. According to him the Navy lacked pretty much everything. Meyer insisted that the "navy is deteriorating for lack of men" and that Congress "is negligent." The subhead of this article stated, "Man who managed naval defense equipment under Taft assures the National Security League successor has let the whole works run down at the heels and indicates we are proud possessors of a bunch of a indiscriminate and futile junk." During his speech Meyer managed to criticize everybody, Congress, the people and the Democrats.[10]

One news account of the preparedness conference remarked that the National Security League got a huge boost from the gathering in the form of publicity with many, many press accounts of the June 14–15 conference. At the last session a resolution was introduced by Mayor James Curley of Boston, appealing to President Wilson to call the attention of Congress to "the primary need of prompt and efficient action" with regard to the national defense; it was unanimously adopted by the delegates to the conference. Delegates to the convention were said in this account to have been 1,000.[11]

Overwhelmingly the press was behind the NSL and its events such as this preparedness campaign. However, there were a few who were mildly against what was happening. Said one editor, "the assertions in regard to America's unpreparedness are vague, general and unproved. When we hear Mr. Gardner's and the National Security League's statements about our inadequate defenses we must not forget that both Admiral Fletcher and Admiral Dewey have testified that the 'efficiency of the navy has never been so high as it is today.'" The federal military expenditure at the time was $250 million per year; that represented an increase of $58 million per year over expenditures when Theodore Roosevelt was president, 1901–1909. The editor went on to argue that while the NSL was always stressing the need for an expenditure that would be a "real guarantee of safety," which the editor found to be vague, in any event, there was no such thing. England spent nearly 50 percent of her national income on defense and yet the country was still "unprepared." Finally, remarked the editor, an "armament increase does not in any way solve the question of how to prevent war."[12]

Another editorial that was very mildly critical of the NSL began by observing that, with regard to the problems in the world, World War I, and the border dispute with Mexico and the revolutionary Pancho Villa, "some of the agitators are overdoing the argument by grossly exaggerating the weakness of our defenses. At the recent meeting of the National Security League, the plight of Belgium was held up by speakers and a warning was sounded that the United States, despite her size and wealth, would be equally helpless in the face of an invasion." Among the advocates of preparedness, continued the editorial, "there are overzealous persons, as there are among the pacifists. But the trend of the argument for conservative preparation for defense is in the right direction."[13]

The first annual convention of the League took place in Chicago in late November 1915. One of the invited speakers was U.S. Senator James A. Reed of Missouri. After hearing arguments for preparedness, Reed insisted that there was no immediate need for preparation and no immediate danger to the United States. Said Reed, "There is no need of haste. Every power except the United States is quite busy in Europe. There are no hostile warships in our ports. No army threatens invasion. They won't." As might have been expected, those remarks provoked a furious response directed at Reed. Everybody in attendance disagreed and loudly attempted to refute him. At this time it was reported that there were 30,000 members in the League.[14]

A calmly, friendlier account appeared in a different press outlet. That piece opened by declaring that the most thorough organizational "campaign ever waged" in America was launched the day the convention started, in the interest of "adequate national defense." According to this article, "Every State in the Union, every shade of political opinion and every religion was represented by delegates who participated in the opening session of the first convention of the National Security League." Far reaching defense plans were laid out and showed the "unanimous support of the delegates and the sanction of the hundreds of organizations in every part of the country represented by them." Some 800 delegates attended, reportedly. While speakers suggested various plans for preparedness, "all agreed upon one point—that the nation today would be as helpless as an infant if attacked by any first-rate power in the world." There was no mention herein of James Reed, who was the featured part of the article directly above. This piece was so filled with cloying enthusiasm that it likely was not a news report at all, but simply a press release from the League that was printed verbatim and set into the newspaper to imitate real news stories.[15]

A third account of the convention (all three were published on the same date) gave a dramatically different delegate count, citing "over 200." When he addressed the gathering, NSL president Stanwood Menken said, "In our work we have no politics except preparedness, no creed but America. We believe we should prepare to fight, and if need be will fight to prepare." According to Menken, "It is clearly beyond discussion and established as true that in terms of modern war the United States is absolutely defenseless against any first class power." This article did mention James Reed, but only near the end. The NSL was then urging a bigger navy than President Wilson planned and he, Wilson, did have plans for big increases.[16]

National defense and the necessity for adequate preparedness were to be the topics for discussion at the National Security Congress, to be held in Washington, D.C., from January 20 to 22, under the auspices of the NSL. In its announcement the League claimed that speakers were chosen for the Congress irrespective of party affiliations, each having a "special fitness for discussion of the topic assigned to him by reason of his pre-eminence in his special field of investigation." Also in the announcement was the fact that the League had branches in all but three states of the Union and the governors of 15 states and the mayors of more than 75 cities and towns had appointed citizens' committees on defense to "co-operate" with the National Security League. Among the members of the NSL listed herein were former President William Howard Taft, John Hays Hammond (a mining engineer of immense wealth), Alton B. Parker and Oscar Straus (former U.S. secretary of commerce and labor).[17]

Ostensibly that conference was to "discuss" America's "vital needs," but in reality the sole purpose of the gathering was to argue for a bigger military and an expanded military machine to be put in place immediately. Among the big name speakers lined up were Robert Bacon (former U.S.

secretary of state), Dr. David Jayne Hill (former U.S. ambassador to Germany), A. Lawrence Cowell (president of Harvard University), Charles G. Curtis (president of International Curtis Marine Turbine Company), and U.S. Senator Henry Cabot Lodge. Theodore Roosevelt was not to be in attendance but he was scheduled to submit a paper that would be read at the gathering. Many other speakers were listed in the article. And finally, Miss Maud (also spelled Maude) Wetmore (chair of the woman's branch of the National Civic Federation) was to be a speaker. That seemed to have been the first instance of a female being granted anything remotely close to a position of note, in any of the NSL affairs. Maude was the daughter of George Wetmore, former U.S. Senator from Rhode Island.[18]

Even the buildup to the Congress was undertaken with a good deal of hype. A special train of five Pullman cars, and a dining car, carried the New York delegates from New York City to Washington to attend the Security Congress. New York City Mayor John Mitchel headed that state's delegation, which, said a journalist, "will consist of some of the most prominent men and women in New York." A delegation of 35 people from Boston joined that group in New York City and traveled down on the same train. Additionally, several delegates from Philadelphia joined that group when the train passed through the Pennsylvania city. According to the account, "The success of the congress is assured. The governors of Ohio, Indiana, Iowa, Michigan, Rhode Island, Delaware, and South Dakota have appointed delegates to attend and similar action has been taken by nearly 20 boards of trade and chambers of commerce. Also, practically all of the 112 'organized branches' of the National Security League have notified New York City that they will be represented by from 2–20 delegates." Reportedly, a letter from Samuel Gompers, president of the American Federation of Labor (AFL), would be read at the gathering. This article ended with an effusive outpouring from the journalist: "The broad scope of the program and the high character of the participants in the discussion will certainly make a deep impression upon Congress and the country and effectively advance the cause of adequate preparedness for national defense."[19]

On the day the conference began, one Washington, D.C., newspaper devoted a full page to an ad placed by the National Security League. That page consisted solely of the reprint of a speech given by Bainbridge Colby of North Carolina. Originally the speech had been given at Chicago on January 10, 1916. Colby would go on to become U.S. secretary of state in Wilson's cabinet, in 1920. He was best known for denouncing the communist regime in Russia.[20]

Another news account on the opening day of the Congress began by stating, "Another great group of prominent citizens of the United States came to Washington today … to voice an insistent demand for increased military preparedness for the country." Then the reader was given a list of the leading lights who would address the group. All of them, including Maude Wetmore, demanded the same thing: a vastly increased war machine. John B. Stanchfield (New York lawyer; in one case he won acquittal for prominent banker F. Augustus Heinze, accused of misapplying funds, and was paid $800,000 for his legal services) advocated the creation of a trained force in the U.S. to spy upon foreign spies and also charged that the *Congressional Record* furnished any foreign spy in America who read English "with all the important military secrets of the United States any enemy might need." Besides advocating spies Stanchfield urged a law prohibiting the publication or discussion of any facts or data concerning the national defense, except such as were expressly issued for publication by the government.

Frederic R. Coudert (New York lawyer and NSL member) was a principal speaker of the opening session. He said, in part, "We appear to be witnessing nothing short of a revolution in American public opinion. Eighteen months ago such a congress as this would have been an utter impossibility. Any attempt to have organized it would have been characterized as a byproduct of crankdom or, if taken seriously, as an outburst of unreasoned and absurd militarism." He went on to declare, "Even when our league was originally founded ... it was scarce believed that a group of honorable citizens could be found who would devote of their time, of their money and of their energy to the advocacy of a comprehensive program of military preparedness. Yet within a few months the President of the United States has himself declared to Congress in no uncertain words the need for military and naval preparedness."

Maude Wetmore spoke about "Woman's Duty Toward Patriotism." Man had fought since time began, she intoned, but his defense had not been of his own life; "this he sacrifices freely." His defense had been primarily of woman and her children—the home. Wetmore added, "The country is the collective home," and "Women must teach the young to lay down life at need for such ideals, which are more precious than life to the race."[21]

In his letter to the gathering, read at the NSL Congress, Theodore Roosevelt issued a demand for universal military service as the only solution to the national defense problem. Several other speakers urged the same thing. Pacific Coast Senators George Chamberlain (OR) and James Phelan (CA) delivered the same message and then added fear about the "oriental menace," citing danger of an attack from Japan. That outcome was even more bizarre than the idea that Germany might suddenly attack the United States. However, it may have been useful in rousing much of the western part of America to the NSL cause. Usually the focus was on the idea of a

Chapter 4. Conferences and Conventions   51

This January 1916 composite shows six committeemen of the NSL, for their security conference. Top (left to right): Philander Knox, Gov. G. W. Clarke, Stanwood Menken. Bottom: Theodore Roosevelt, Thomas Edison, Oscar Straus.

foreign attack force landing on the East Coast, as ludicrous as the thought was. Perhaps the NSL worried that people in the western part of the nation would not rally as enthusiastically to the cause unless some supposed fear was generated that endangered their part of the country.[22]

At that Congress a movement was reportedly underway to consolidate all of the organizations then advocating for a larger military machine together into one organization. It was all tentative at that time and it never happened in any meaningful sense, although it was often touted or tried. The other organizations with similar goals to the NSL at that time were listed as: the Navy League of the United States; the Army League of the United States; the American Legion (this was not the still-existing American Legion founded in 1919; that earlier version had Theodore Roosevelt as a prominent member and lasted from 1915 until 1917, its work being done when war was declared); the Aero Club of America, the military defense branch of the Automobile Association of America; and the women's section of the Movement for Military Preparedness (composed mostly of the woman's departments of the National Civic Federation and the NSL). Robert Bacon, of the NSL, was seen as the likely tentative president. Another movement reported to be underway was "for the league to send out through the country a great group of public speakers, especially through the middle west, to support the statements President Wilson is about to make as to the necessity for increased military preparedness for the United States."[23]

One negative comment came from a West Virginia newspaper editorial. At the opening of the gathering NSL president Menken solemnly declared that it was time to state facts coldly and clearly and, said the editor, "then the speakers who followed him proceeded to indulge in a flood of flannel mouthed oratory which would have done credit to a meeting of anarchists bent upon saying something to offend the finer feelings of the good people of the country."[24]

Plans for broadening the League's preparedness were laid at the closing session of the Congress. It was announced that St. Louis Mayor Kiel, with the cooperation of Mayor Mitchel of New York City, would hold a national defense conference of mayors and other representatives of American cities. That meeting was to be held in St. Louis on March 3 and 4. The nucleus of the gathering would be committees appointed by the mayors of more than 75 cities. An uproar at the Congress was briefly caused by Owen Miller, a delegate from St. Louis representing, he said, the labor element of the country. He aroused the attendees at one session by alluding to the charge that the preparedness movement was supported by munitions makers: "Only when he explained that he believed the charge to be false did the tumult subside," noted a journalist. Earlier that day NSL member Franklin Q. Brown of New York took occasion to deny specifically that the League received support from the munitions and armament makers.[25]

Another effusively gushing account of the Congress came at its close, from a New Jersey newspaper: "Of all the conventions that have been held in Washington this winter, where it is said, the sun never sets without shining upon one or more conventions, the meeting of the National Security League has been the most vital," declared the piece. "Men of all political parties have stood together in most serious discussion of the Nation's peril and present hopelessness against any third class power." It was noted that neither President Woodrow Wilson nor any of his cabinet appeared on the program or attended any of the meetings. However, it was remarked that "women too thrilled the large audiences with their patriotism and eloquence."

Chapter 4. Conferences and Conventions 53

The account observed that practically every speaker recommended adoption of compulsory military training of all boys between the ages of 18 and 21 and then to have them undergo drilling for one month a year for six years. All systems of volunteer service were condemned as unfair to the volunteers who would sacrifice time and earning capacity while the less patriotic or energetic could profit by their sacrifices, and "the influence in a democracy of thus breaking down all class distinction between the rich and poor who must stand on a common level in the ranks, is a powerful influence in maintaining the democratic spirit." In conclusion the story asserted, "Is it any wonder then that men with vision realize that the nation's peril is beyond exaggeration or that those who carry the responsibility of Preparedness, look upon the subject as the most pressing that has confronted the nation since the Civil War?"[26]

A banquet was held at the end of the conference and was attended by a reported 450 diners. Representative Gardner of Massachusetts was one of the guests. Among the guests, wrote a reporter, "were leaders of thought in industrial and commercial and financial circles from all over the country."[27]

Dr. Alexander Graham Bell, inventor of the telephone, was one of the speakers at the southern conference of the National Security League that was held in Charleston, South Carolina, on April 28 and 29, 1916. The purpose was to arouse in the South interest in the preparedness movement. Six governors attended, plus a group from the NSL headquarters in New York City, which included League president Stanwood Menken. That meeting offered nothing new as speaker after speaker echoed the old NSL refrains. Bell spoke on "Aerial Defense and Preparedness" and stated the entire United States Army and Navy air equipment totaled 47 machines, compared to 6,000 in Germany, 5,000 in Great Britain and 4,000 in France.[28]

Late in November 1916 yet another conference was held under the auspices of the National Security League. It was reported that "leading men" from all parts of the country would meet in Washington, D.C., from January 25 to 27. The name of the upcoming gathering was the "Congress of Constructive Patriotism, of Americans for America." Some months earlier the NSL was said to have determined that the "true basis" of national security was not to be found in the army and navy alone "which were merely expressions of a country's efficiency or inefficiency," said the League statement, "but in the united spirit of a people awake to the dangers inherent in neglect, vigilant of their rights and strongly united in the determination to achieve for their country its fullest moral as well as material development." According to the statement the Congress would be open "not only to the 100,000 members of the league, but to all members of learned and patriotic societies and commercial, labor and agricultural associations." Details of the Congress were to be worked out by four NSL officials, president

Menken, Lawrence F. Abbott (from the *Outlook* publication), Chase Mellen and Alexander Gordon (two New York lawyers).

At this date that committee had arranged for a preliminary discussion of certain fundamental questions by men of "recognized eminence." Included among the questions were: the scope and effectiveness of universal training and service; the function of education "in the development of a true American patriotism"; and "educational preparedness for Americanization and the question of Americanizing immigrants." The women's section of the Movement for National Preparedness, which had been recently absorbed by the NSL, had in its possession the signed pledges of 11,000 women in favor of national service and, with respect to the upcoming Congress, "Many women will attend the congress." Put another way, the Congress of Constructive Patriotism had as its objective the "development of a united American sentiment." Many names of the "eminent men and women" consulted as the Congress was planned were listed; 26 men were named as were two women, Maude Wetmore and Mabel T. Boardman.[29]

Professor Albert Bushnell Hart of Harvard University was selected, early in January 1917, to be chairman in charge of the educational features of the upcoming Congress of Constructive Patriotism. At the same time Menken announced that 14 governors of States of the Union would attend as would representatives from 50 colleges and universities and other defense societies. Reportedly there would be more than 1,000 delegates at the gathering. An objective was to set up a great national lecture system under the direction of experts who will present national topics "in a non-partisan and non-political way...."[30]

Questions of universal military service were a key part of the Congress of Constructive Patriotism. Plans were afoot to bring about a federal reserve army of 20 million men. A nationwide educational campaign to arouse American patriotism was to be undertaken, to convince people that universal service was necessary. Under the proposed plans a reserve force would be produced at a rate of practically one million men a year and would ultimately produce a reserve army of 20 million men at Uncle Sam's disposal; these would be men aged 18 to 45.[31]

Women's role in the NSL's grand scheme was given at least a little attention at this Congress. According to one account, "Definite plans for the co-ordination of woman's work in peace as well as war will be laid before the congress and a program for the women of America ... will be outlined." On the other hand, the report that of the 2,000 delegates "appointed" to the Congress, fully one-third were women from "all sections of the country" was almost certainly a lie. Some of the women who were in attendance included Frances A. Keller (National Americanization Committee); Maude Wetmore (NY); Anne Morgan (NY, of the Morgan banking family); Mrs.

Chapter 4. Conferences and Conventions   55

STIRRING UP PATRIOTISM AIM OF CONFERENCE IN WASHINGTON

Left to right, top: Governor Philipp, Robert Bacon and Frank Trumbull. Bottom: Joseph Choate, Luke E. Wright and S. Stanwood Menken.

Another conference under the auspices of the NSL was slated for January 1917. This photograph showed some of the featured speakers. Top (left to right): Gov. Phillip, Robert Bacon, Frank Turnbull. Bottom: Joseph Choate, Luke E. Wright, Stanwood Menken.

Barrett Wendell (Boston); Mrs. Philip N. Moore (St. Louis) and Grace Parker, who "under the direction of Morgan and Mrs. William K. Vanderbilt and other well known women spent several months in the warring countries studying the condition of the women there." Said Parker, with respect to that experience, "Are we women of America ready and willing to take advantage of the greatest opportunity which will ever come to a nation— an opportunity to study the elements which are at work in war-stricken Europe and evolve from it a program of 'Preparedness' which shall mean the development of women's resources—women's power, not only for the benefit of the individual but for the benefit and protection of the corporate

> WOMEN PROMINENT IN CIVIC AND SOCIAL SERVICE WORK
> WILL ATTEND CONGRESS OF PATRIOTISM AT WASHINGTON

Left to right: Frances A. Kellor, Anne Morgan, Maude Wetmore and (lower right) Mrs. Philip N. Moore

Four women who were to be featured at the Congress of Constructive Patriotism. Left to right; Frances A. Kellor, Anne Morgan, Maud Wetmore. Inset, Mrs. Phillip N. Moore.

life of the nation, and for humanity." Note that reality slipped in here with the use of the word "corporate" by Parker.[32]

An ad appeared in a Washington, D.C., newspaper to announce that because of the large expected attendance at the NSL Congress, opening session admission was to be limited to credentialed delegates and persons having admission tickets. Those admission tickets were to be had on application to the NSL headquarters at the New Willard Hotel in Washington—where that opening session was to be held. Also noted was that "This restriction does not apply, of course, to ladies accompanying delegates."[33]

At the opening session Menken urged Congress to convene in extra session to carry out "President Wilson's demands for adequate preparedness measures." Alton Parker spoke also and declared that the outbreak of the European war had shown to "thoughtful men the utter impotence of the United States to defend itself against a first-class power." A part of this article listed some of the "prominent men here," but in this list no women were included. The grandiose claim was also advanced that this conclave was "expected to be the largest convention in point of numbers ever held in Washington." There was even a new slogan coined, "Prepare or Perish." The NSL's Robert Bacon (now president of the NSL; Menken remained an executive, chairman of the board) laid stress on the two great objects to be accomplished by the National Security League—enactment of legislation for universal military training, and the "inculcation of patriotic spirit throughout the county be means of lecture courses on patriotic topics."[34]

While this Congress of Constructive Patriotism was underway an article appeared that had nothing to do with the Congress directly but contradicted any arguments that the U.S. was militarily weak. A rumor had surfaced that the United States was getting ready to withdraw its troops from Haiti and Santo Domingo (Dominican Republic) as well as from Mexico "to avoid all appearances of interference with the governments of those countries," noted a journalist. This idea of withdrawal was said to have stemmed from President Woodrow Wilson's recent declaration "that no nation should seek to extend its policy over any other nation or people...." No verification was made of the rumor because the Navy Department (responsible for the Marine Corps) stated there "was no prospect whatever of the early withdrawal of the American marines from either Santo Domingo or Haiti" where the United States had assumed military control, much to the "gratification" of the local populations.[35]

Another idea put forth at the Congress was a plan for the organization of a great country-wide league of women enrolled to aid the nation in time of war. It was tentatively going to be known as "The Woman's League of National Service" and plans for its formation and extension across America were being carried out by Maude Wetmore and Anne Morgan (daughter of the late J. Pierpont Morgan). Henry West, NSL executive secretary, declared that this potential new association was all the work of the NSL, which then had 15,000 female members, "who undoubtedly will be enrolled as members" of the proposed organization. West added that he had on file in his New York City office the signed pledges of 11,000 women (out of the 15,000) from throughout the nation to work for and support the idea of compulsory military training and service for the United States, "which idea will be one of the important ideas in the rules and regulations of the proposed 'Woman's League of National Service.'"

A letter read at the Congress, from Theodore Roosevelt, supported universal military training and service. Roosevelt characterized the Hay bill (then in Congress), which sought to federalize the National Guard as a second line of defense as being "foolish and unpatriotic." The former American President advocated a regular army of 250,000 men under the direct control of a general staff and observed, "Be it remembered that such a force as that for which I ask, while very powerful for defense, would be almost worthless for aggression." National preparation, wrote Roosevelt, "meant spiritual, material, civic, industrial and military preparedness and the thorough Americanization of the country."[36]

Another speaker at the Congress was Rear Admiral Robert E. Peary, who spoke on air power. He claimed that at that time, four foreign powers, probably six, had the men and equipment and knowledge such that any one of them could issue an order to destroy Washington or any other of our coastal cities from the air—they could do so in a single night two weeks from now. Former U.S. Senator Lafayette Young (Iowa) urged that every practice of accepting foreign fashions and views, from philosophy to music and women's dresses, be "discouraged." One resolution adopted at this Congress for Constructive Patriotism was to adopt a committee report that outlined a comprehensive plan for spreading knowledge "on the duty and privilege of citizenship."[37]

At a banquet to close the conference a dinner was held with a reported 800 people in attendance. Speaking at that occasion was U.S. Senator Chamberlain of Oregon who warned the American people that they were facing troubles "not only at home, but abroad, from predatory nations, who are banding themselves together for what purpose God only knows. I do know it behooves us to prepare." Chamberlain's speech was capped by Bacon with the cry, "Wake up America! The hour is at hand!"

A journalist in attendance remarked, "Some of the most distinguished men of the country were present, many having come long distances to take part in the proceedings of the congress...." Lafayette Young lashed out at immigrants who "could get along without acquiring the English language." He advocated that the waiting period before applying for citizenship be extended from the current five years and that every man be required to be able to read and write English before he could vote. Young would stop the practice of sending exchange professors to foreign universities and colleges and stop the inflow of such people from foreign nations. "The American professor going abroad for two years as a rule comes back un–American.... The European professor on this side advertises his own country before all his own classes and at every opportunity." Young added: "I would have American dresses for American women.... I would discourage everything which does not assist in laying the foundation of real Americanism."[38]

A few days after the Congress had ended, details of a controversy arose between Henry A. Wise Wood and the Rev. John Haynes Holmes, pastor of the Church of the Messiah. A series of letters between them, made public by Wood on January 29, revealed the refusal of the NSL executive committee, of which Wood was a member, to permit speakers from the American Union Against Militarism to appear before the Congress on Constructive Patriotism. In a letter dated January 13, Holmes complained to Wood and asked for a few moments of the latter's time for the opportunity to present his side. Wood replied on January 16 with a no to any meeting and declared in his letter, "I consider the movement damnably treasonable." Wood stated the same position at the NSL executive meeting which discussed the original letter received from Holmes. A January 18 letter from Holmes to Wood pronounced it "painful" to have himself and his fellows branded as "traitors." The final letter that was released was dated January 19 and was from Wood to Holmes. "I class you among those who are well meaning but misled, and emphatically condemn your activities as being exceedingly dangerous to the body politic," said Wood. "You and your association I regard as among the most pernicious undermining of our nationality, and as such I feel it my duty to attack you relentlessly and expose the insidious danger which lies in your patriotically poisonous propaganda."[39]

Chapter 5

Fear, Weirdness and Public Relations

Fear was a standard practice for the National Security League as an organization and for the individual members as they spoke out relentlessly for an expanded military machine. That is, the practice was to put forward unlikely or impossible situations, such as a foreign power attacking an impotent America and overrunning the country. From time to time such fear-producing illusions wondered into the twilight zone, becoming laughably weird and bizarre. Much work of the League was also concentrated in the area of public relations. Genuine reporters regularly accepted items from the NSL in a non-critical way. Still, though, when they produced work based on their own filter of critical intelligence the result was, perhaps, overly gullible and naive. However, the League was also skillful and successful in getting their own press releases accepted and published verbatim in newspapers, looking exactly like news items that had been generated, somewhere, by journalists. These were inserted specifically to fool the readers into thinking they were reading real news and not self-congratulatory press releases. It all helped in the relentless and remorseless drumbeat of noise created to dramatically increase the war machine.

One of the weirdest pronouncements came from Frederic R. Coudert, a member of the NSL described as a "specialist in international law." On the evening of March 18, 1915, in New York City when he was addressing a gathering in the Columbia University Club on the topic of "National Defense Needs," he solemnly declared that New York City would be forced to pay $5 billion in tribute 10 days after war was declared upon the United States by any first rate power. He followed that statement with figures of the nation's military and naval deficiencies and showed how an invading force could overrun New York City and its vicinity "almost regardless of the forces America could offer in opposition under present military conditions."

Said Coudert: "It has been announced by the general staff that 200,000 men could be landed in the vicinity of New York in ten days. There are

Chapter 5. Fear, Weirdness and Public Relations 61

at least four large countries which are so supplied with merchant marine facilities and transport service that they each could ship 250,000 to our shores at one time." Those troops, he argued, could be landed without serious opposition at Southampton, Long Island, Buzzards Bay, Massachusetts, or on the New Jersey coast. "New York would be held up for at least $5,000,000,000 the first thing. What would our army and national guard be doing all this time? You may ask. Precious little, you can be assured." This was another example of how true motives often surfaced from a chance remark. Coudert revealed the real reason behind wars; that is, it is now, and was then, always about money and things. It was never about honor, or patriotism, or protecting the homeland, and so forth, it was always about the capitalist class greedily fighting over money with each trying to get more, trying to get a bigger share.[1]

On May 10, 1915, the NSL issued an open letter announcing the results of the so-called investigations by its committees into the military situation and appealed for public support for a program for better national defenses. Trying to induce fear into the public the report claimed there were "barely" 20,000 mobile troops in the continental United States; that they were so widely scattered as to make their rapid mobilization "impossible"; that those men who were available were short of officers, ammunition and equipment; and that there was no organized reserve. (If that was true one explanation was that large numbers of the American military were then stationed abroad in the quest to impose American capitalist imperialism on other nations. Military personnel were then in Haiti, Dominican Republic, Mexico and the Hawaiian Islands.)

The National Guard was found to be below its paper strength in men, equipment and efficiency. Coast defenses, the NSL announcement continued, were inadequate and fortifications were insufficiently manned. Also declared was that the U.S. Navy was neither adequate nor prepared for war, inadequately manned, short of ammunition, and with no organized reserves. As well, the American submarine flotilla existed "chiefly on paper," plus there were deficiencies in fast scout cruisers, battle cruisers, and so on, and target practice had been neglected or omitted. In short, the letter closed, more of everything was needed, and soon, very soon. That letter was signed by organization president Stanwood Menken, honorary vice-president Alton Parker and chair of the naval committee Henry Stimson.

That letter was sent to present and former members of the U.S. Cabinet, members of Congress, governors of the state, clubs and alumni associations of colleges and universities, all women's clubs, chambers of commerce, boards of trade and mercantile associations. Those groups listed above were part of the upper classes and perhaps upper-middle. Absent were any groupings that might have represented the views of ordinary men or ordinary women. No trade unions were mentioned; that was at a time when unions were more powerful and had more influence than they do today. Another account of the same NSL open letter declared in its subhead, "National Security League in proclamation to 'all American citizen' says we are utterly and hopelessly helpless."[2]

Another part of that open letter was an appeal for an "American army" of one million "volunteer workers" for national defense because the U.S. had to "adequately prepare itself against any possibility of attack or invasion."

When the NSL spoke of this letter being for "all American citizens," and it did, the League meant those ordinary citizens had access to it from the press; everybody that really counted got a personal copy mailed to them. Briefly, the NSL wanted the following: legislation correcting the present wasteful methods of military appropriations and disbursements, adoption of a definite military policy, a larger and better equipped National Guard, and the creation of an organized reserve for each branch of the military service. Demands from the League were always vague; achieving efficiency through reduction of waste was a cliché even back in that time period. Keeping demands somewhat vague meant that whatever the government did, the NSL could argue it was just not enough. And, of course, the organization wanted "a stronger, better balanced navy," and "an effective, mobile army." The media release also actively solicited names from any readers who wished to be volunteers in that army of one million volunteer workers. Interested readers were urged to send their particulars to the NSL headquarters at 31 Pine Street, New York City.[3]

Frederic R. Coudert, 1914. One thing made clear by Coudert's bizarre ramblings was the real reason for wars, any wars and all wars. To the capitalist class it was all about money, and only about money.

Commenting on the NSL open letter, an editor remarked that

his newspaper had recently produced an article by Cleveland Moffet that detailed the ease with which an invading army could capture the eastern part of the United States: "As a result of that story, what is known as the 'National Security League' has been formed and much progress is being made in enlisting." Other NSL members involved in those "investigations" which led to the open letter were Benjamin F. Tracy (former U.S. Secretary of the Navy), Col. William C. Church (editor of the *Army and Navy Journal*) and General Frances V. Greene, all of whom were on NSL advisory committees. Said NSL executive member J. Beaumont Spencer: "The Moffett article will go a long way toward crystallizing 'preparedness' sentiment in the United States. No adequate defense could be made if we were attacked as he outlines ... [his account] bears every appearance of having been based on expert opinion." According to Moffet, "if the U.S. naval fleet were in the Pacific, an enemy could land 150,000 men near East Hampton, New York, and the United States could oppose its [sic] march to New York City with just 30,000 men."[4]

A few days after the release of the open letter, Secretary of the Navy Josephus Daniels, in a speech at a dinner in honor of officers of the Atlantic fleet, defended the Navy as efficient and prepared for war. It was reported in the account that he answered critics of the navy, "particularly the National Security League...." That perhaps indicated the growing influence and power of the League, then only some six months old.[5]

That dinner was attended by 250 Navy officers and 500 civilian New Yorkers. With respect to Daniels' remarks, one journalist reported, "His attack upon the National Security League for its comment upon the efficiency of our fleet fell flat, and was greeted by only a few scattered hand-clappings." His applause in general was "not vociferous. Once or twice in the course of his address he received hearty approval when referring to prospective increases in the strength of the navy." At the conclusion of his address Daniels read a letter from Admiral Dewey, expressing regrets at his absence and praising the morale and equipment of the fleet. Dewey recalled his own triumphant return to the U.S. in 1899 from the Philippines. Another speaker was Major General Leonard Wood who was greeted with "vociferous cheers." Wood was a major supporter of the League. Wood urged growth of the navy and army and laid especial emphasis "upon the necessity of instilling into the young a full appreciation of the military needs of this country, and criticized the 'anti-war movement' existing in some New York public schools."

Said Wood: "We must build in the child a sound realization of his military duties, just as broad and deep as his appreciation of his civic responsibilities. No government can exist in which a respect for things military is lacking." Daniels said, with respect to the NSL open letter of May 10, "If the gentlemen who signed the above libel had known the real truth, their signatures would never have been appended." He considered those signers to have been "misled and misinformed." At least one of the signatories to that letter, Alton Parker, was at the speakers' table that night at the dinner. One other comment of note from that dinner was that the *Lusitania* (a UK owned large ocean liner sunk at sea by the Germans on May 5, 1915, with a large loss of life) incident had driven home to the American consciousness the necessity of adequate national defense and emphasized the inadequate condition of our army and navy.[6]

Perhaps the weirdest of all National Security League outpourings came from a meeting on the evening of July 22, 1915, in Philadelphia at which, noted a reporter, "prominent business and professional men formed a local branch of the National Security League." One of those in attendance who addressed the group was John Wanamaker. He had been United States Postmaster General in the early 1890s but was better known as the founder of a huge department store chain, Wanamaker's. When he addressed the gathering he suggested that the United States should purchase Belgium (invaded and occupied on August 4, 1914) from Germany. Later at that meeting Wanamaker was elected president of that newly formed Philadelphia branch. Wanamaker suggested that $100 billion be loaned without interest to the United States government for the purchase of Belgium and later the government of Belgium could be turned over to its own people. That suggestion also brought up the real reason underlying war, any war—money. Also at the meeting

John Wanamaker 1915. He was famous for his department store empire, based in Philadelphia. However, he did not take a back seat to Coudert in the "crazy" sweepstakes. He concocted the novel idea of buying Belgium (occupied at the time by Germany) for $100 billion and then, later, turning the government of Belgium back to its own people. His plan also emphasized the real and only reason for wars, from the capitalist class perspective—money and "stuff."

Chapter 5. Fear, Weirdness and Public Relations

were the NSL national president Stanwood Menken and national field secretary William McComb.⁷

When Menken spoke at that Philadelphia meeting he warned the audience that utterances from them as a group, and as individuals, should be "extreme in their conservatism as to statements of fact and policy." He added, "We must not let the people feel that we want to impose upon this country a large standing army nor that we are ignorant of the burden of taxation." Elaborating on his idea, Wanamaker felt that wealthy Americans could lend, at no interest, that $100 billion to the United States, without interest for five years to fund the proposed purchase of Belgium.⁸

As might have been expected, a storm of protest arose after Wanamaker suggested that America buy Belgium. So great was the protest, in fact, that Wanamaker was forced to resign his leadership of the NSL Philadelphia branch, just a few days after attaining that position. He explained that he was quitting because he felt the controversy "might embarrass the progress of the organization." However, Wanamaker did retain his NSL membership and declared he would continue to support the League "morally and financially."⁹

Around the same time that Wanamaker resigned his NSL executive post he was offered the presidency of a company called the World's Liquidating and Refining Company, a "huge" insurance concern that had just been organized in Bridgeport, Connecticut. One of the promoters of that firm was David Beach. He wrote to Wanamaker and offered him the presidency and declared that his firm could raise the $100 billion proposed to buy Belgium. The idea of no interest loans had disappeared in Beach's proposal, which was to sell bonds in denominations of $1,000 to $10,000 carrying an interest rate of 4.5 percent per year. Beach enthused over his idea, calling it "the financial peace club of the world," and "a profitable investment for everyone to join and take part it." Explained Beach, by saving 10 cents a day for 20 years the United States with its 100 million people could raise $110 billion, with $100 billion handed to Germany.¹⁰

One stunt the National Security League used was the employment of an armored vehicle equipped with a Colt automatic machine gun, one airplane gun of heavy caliber and a crew of three officers of the U.S. Army. The vehicle, a 1912 Reo truck, set off in May 1916 from New York City on a trans-continental tour ending up in San Francisco. It stopped in various cities along the route and was part of the National Security League's program of increased militarism.¹¹

CHAPTER 6

The General Campaign

As early as the beginning of March 1915 the NSL was said to have been rapidly extending its work throughout America and generally awakening people to the military needs of the country. Secretary of War Lindley Garrison and former Secretary of War Henry Stimson had recently given speeches in New York City before "strictly nonpartisan audiences," noted a journalist, and this "greatly stimulated" the movement. Many organizations such as the Civic Federation, the Economics Club, the Republican Club, the Union League Club and the Merchants' Association of New York had approved the demand "for the immediate consideration of our military needs." It was an approval for an increased militarism, not for some neutral "consideration." Those organizations named had a reported total membership of 10,000 and "This is more than the total membership of all the sixty peace-at-any-price societies in the United States." A.R. Humphrey, an NSL executive, had been in Washington for several days conferring with "prominent" men in and out of Congress. Humphrey observed that his group, in addition to its campaign for membership and its distribution of literature, proposed to conduct a nationwide speaking campaign and for that purpose the League was calling for volunteers in every state and city in the country. He added that his organization would form a "strong branch" in Washington but had refrained from undertaking the organizing work while Congress was in session "so there might not be even a suspicion of our motives!"[1]

Around the same time the NSL, which was, said a journalist, composed of some of the nation's "most prominent men," such as Joseph Choate, Alton Parker and Henry Stimson, had conducted its own investigations into the American military situation. According to their work they found many "significant facts." With respect to the U.S. Army the League found it to be composed of only 30,000 men in the United States and noted that "It is widely scattered and cannot be speedily mobilized." As well they found it short of officers, short of ammunition, and having no organized reserve; and reported that coastal defenses were inadequate and fortifications

Chapter 6. The General Campaign   67

were insufficiently manned. The National Guard was found to be below its proper strength in men, equipment and efficiency. The U.S. Navy was found to be in as woeful a state as the army.[2]

In April 1915 Augustus P. Gardner, the U.S. Representative from Massachusetts and known as a strong advocate for increased militarism, remarked, "Six months ago I should have been a mighty poor politician if I had preached about our lack of national defense; today I should be a mighty poor politician if I were to drop the subject." And that, perhaps, was indicative of how quickly the movement for a dramatically increased war machine was moving and gaining support.[3]

The Navy Committee of the League issued a report at the start of May 1915 fully endorsing the recommendation of the General Board of the Navy that called for "a stronger and better balanced navy." Supposedly the League had spent three months researching and writing their own report and not just rubber-stamping the Board of the Navy's inflated request. National Security League members on that committee were J. Bernard Walker, R.W. Neeser, W. Butler Duncan, R.P. Forshew, William S. Lloyd, William McAdoo, Roland R. Riggs, Herbert L. Satterlee, Benjamin F. Tracy, Beekman Winthrop, Henry A. Wise Wood, and Cushing Stetson.[4]

A letter to the editor was published in a New York City newspaper in May 1915 from William T. Hornaday, a member of the NSL although he was not directly identified as such. According to him, during the previous December and January he "begged and implored" the League to back a committee in demanding of the U.S. Congress $100 million worth of national defense bonds, for the extra expenditures that should be made on our national defenses in 1915. Said Hornaday, "The executive committee of the league was literally scared out of its wits by the idea, and it is equally so to-day." Then came the sinking of the ocean liner *Lusitania*—with more than 100 American lives lost—that was said by Hornaday to have led to a great awakening in the people for an increased military. In December 1914 he said he started with a request for $100 million a year for five years but the *Lusitania* sinking showed a need to increase that request to $200 million a year for three years. Concluded Hornaday, "The safety of Americans on the high seas and in Mexico, the Monroe Doctrine and the honor of the nation among the civilized nations of the earth, all are now at stake. Will we defend them or not? We must now name our figures and either put up or shut up."[5]

Also in May, here and there in New York City could be seen small posters pointing out to citizens that the United States was unprepared for war and asking them to join an organized movement "toward placing the nation in a condition of preparedness." According to this article the results from such a campaign could be seen at league offices at 31 Pine Street, New

York City—in the form of many letters and callers arriving at headquarters. "There is a steady stream of visitors bringing words of encouragement together with subscriptions to membership in the league, which can be had from a dollar a year up, according to the patriotic zeal of the subscriber." The most expensive membership listed was a life membership for $25 but there was also a special donation list. Heading that list was the New York Stock Exchange, which gave $1,000.

Other names on the list had given amounts of $500, $200, $100, and so forth. "In short there is a boom on at 31 Pine Street, and the enthusiasm thereof is growing daily. It seems like a spontaneous expression of public feeling excited by the incidents of the European war culminating in the sinking of the Lusitania and by the naval review, but it is in reality the outcome of months of organized hard work by a group of business men who determined last year to arouse public attention...." According to Henry L. Stimson, former secretary of war, the United States was then spending roughly $100 million annually on the U.S. Army and about $140 million on the U.S. Navy. The previous November it had been reported by Secretary of War Lindley Garrison that after excluding the troops in our foreign "possessions" our mobile army in the U.S. consisted of fewer than 25,000 men.[6]

Still in May, a composite photo of six "famous men," all League members, was published and the reader was informed that those men declared the U.S. must get ready for war. Those men were Choate, Parker, Stimson, Menken, H.L. Satterlee (former assistant secretary of the Navy) and William McAdoo (former assistant secretary of the Navy). Said the item, "They have seized on the situation that has arisen since the sinking of the *Lusitania* to further the aims of the league." From their appeal to the public came the warning "That if any nation saw fit to attack us our immediate fate would be that of Belgium."[7]

Governor Samuel Ralston of Indiana, on May 27, 1915, endorsed the war leadership of President Woodrow Wilson and refused to participate in a movement for a larger army and navy engineered by the NSL. That rejection of the NSL occurred when the League was planning its peace and preparedness congress and had asked Ralston to personally attend or to send representatives. Ralston replied by telegram, "I am averse to taking any steps toward making preparation for international war that does not have the sanction of Pres't Wilson. Movements of this character might become more embarrassing than helpful to the president and the country."[8]

During the summer of 1915 it was reported that the NSL had been sending letters "broadcast" to the clergy asking them to speak on the subject of "National Defense" and suggesting several topics. Frederick Lynch, editor of the publication *Christian Work*, received one of those letters. An annoyed Lynch declared in the opinion of the ministry of the nation, "if there ever was a time when great nations as well as great men should be thinking of what they can do for the rest of the world rather than taking care of themselves it is now." Lynch also stated that a referendum he had recently taken showed that 29 of every 30 were opposed to the movement for an increased armament. One specific request from the League to the clergy was that ministers preach sermons on July 4 urging the nation to adopt an adequate national defense. One reply to that request came in a letter issued by the American League to Limit Armaments in which several clergymen of New York City expressed the idea that the United States needed a "spiritual preparedness" rather than the sort advocated by the NSL. A general, more secular pitch was made to Americans in the form of a newspaper ad on the occasion of July 4 for readers to support the idea of increased militarism by joining the League or donating money to the organization.[9]

Later in July the League announced it had begun yet another nationwide campaign. This program was to urge corporations and other employers to induce their employees to join the National Guard. The League argued that employers were part of the national defense problem and were a "serious obstacle" to that development as they were reluctant to see employees join the National Guard, feeling winter drills and summer tours of duty might interfere with their regular work. According to the National Security League, cases had emerged (no details were provided) of employees having been discharged for that reason. To deal with that situation the League was then sounding employers out with regard to their attitude toward the National Guard "in the belief that once the matter is brought to their attention they will adopt a patriotic course." Employers who did just that and encouraged their employees to join the National Guard were requested to write to the NSL with details. At the time this article was published four companies had done so: United States Rubber; New York Telephone; General Electric; and American Express. All four of those concerns declared that positions would be kept open for employees absent on National Guard duty.[10]

Also in July 1915 the Militia Committee of the NSL, headed by Charles E. Lydecker, released its report. That report urged the development of the National Guard to the full limit of efficiency, making it serve as an effective school for officers. Also recommended was a course of study in the public schools calling attention to the need of public service; sports and physical drills for school children; theoretical training in the art of maneuvers as a part of the college curriculum; an official classification of all those fit for military enrollment; and a requirement of some military duty from all persons between 18 and 45 years of age.[11]

That report by the Militia Committee stopped short of recommending the giving of military instruction to American children in the public schools. However, it did urge courses in "manly sports" to make boys fit. The object of all these recommendations in the report was to prepare "proper material" out of which, when required, a greater army and navy could speedily be created. The first step in such a plan was the enrollment, by the states, of all men liable to service—those from 18 to 45.[12]

A report from the Army Committee of the NSL, chaired by Henry L. Stimson (former U.S. secretary of war), was released shortly after the Militia Committee's report. That report characterized the military defenses of the nation as "woefully insufficient," and endorsed the recommendations of the general staff of the Army "made repeatedly to Congress" for a reserve army of half a million men. According to this report the total defensive mobile force then consisted of about 25,000 regulars and 60,000 militia for the protection of many thousands of miles of sea coast. "Quite aside from its weakness in numbers, this force would be poorly trained, hastily and ineffectually organized, ill balanced, incompletely equipped and lacking in such essentials as light and heavy artillery and ammunition to serve it," declared the Stimson report. "With ordinary fortunes of war the probable outcome is so apparent that it need not be stated."

Stimson's report wanted to see a reserve force of 500,000 men. According to the report, "The great armed nations of the world have sufficient merchant shipping to transport to our shores in a single expedition a much larger force than we can possibly concentrate against it."[13]

A more detailed breakdown of military numbers was to be found in another July 1915 article. According to this piece the strength of the U.S. Army was then 4,572 officers and 88,444 men. Thus, the army was 154 officers and 7,533 men below its authorized strength. The "mobile" army was said to consist of 30,481 men in the continental United States and 20,863 men in America's "foreign possessions." Of the enlisted men on the mobile army in the United States, 18,954 were in the field in Texas and on the Mexican border (this was during the time of the Pancho Villa rebellion in Mexico); 1,665 were in the field in Colorado (dealing with labor strikes); 245 were temporarily in Montana; 300 were in Arkansas; and only 9,317 were at their home or permanent station. Total strength of the organized militia was 8,233 officers and 119,087 enlisted men. No source was given in the article as to how the numbers were obtained but they most likely came from the NSL. The article carried no dateline, with both place and date of origin absent.[14]

At the end of July it was reported that the NSL was not satisfied with its efforts to date. League President Menken stated that he and his organization would welcome suggestions from people that would "put dynamite into the league." George C. Cochran, a Brooklyn member, suggested that all "patriotic citizens" of New York join in an immense demonstration. Said Cochran, "Instead of circularizing the public, let us organize the public."[15]

A short-lived craze that appeared in the summer of 1915 involved the elite class taking what was euphemistically called "military training." Likely it was done to show that our "betters" were also willing to get down in the dirt, rub elbows with, and generally bond with the great unwashed masses. Noted one account, "Nearly 100 men prominent in business and professional life in this city [Philadelphia], including many well known athletes, polo players and former collegians," left on August 9, 1915, for Plattsburgh, New York, where they would undergo a four-week course of instruction under regular army officers. The vanguard of the local contingent had already left for camp where they joined more than a thousand other recruits in undergoing elementary training in military maneuvers. Other Philadelphians, including George Wharton Pepper (vice-president of the NSL Philadelphia branch), had arranged to go to the camp directly from their summer homes in various parts of the country.

Other cities were also involved. New York City Mayor Mitchel was one of the volunteer recruits from his city, which was composed of 1,200 "business and professional men" who began their month's training under United States Army officers at Plattsburgh on August 10. Mitchel expected to remain in camp for only two weeks instead of four as that was all the time he believed he could spare from the city's business. One of his stated reasons for going was "to set an example" for other New York men because he approved of Leonard Wood's plan for the military training of civilians. In preparation for his service in the camp Mitchel equipped himself with an outfit of army clothing, provided his own transportation and placed a $30 deposit at the camp to pay for his food and other necessities. Two special trains had been laid on to carry the volunteers to the camp. The journalist who wrote the article then stated a conclusion that could not possibly have been believed by anyone: "For two weeks the mayor expects to dig trenches, study military hygiene and march when ordered to do so."[16]

A different account about the New York contingent destined for the military camp began by asserting that the "cream of New York's young manhood, 500 strong, will alight from twenty-two Pullman sleepers this morning [August 10] at Plattsburgh...." Because today "the business and professional men's camp opens." Gathered together at New York City's Grand Central Station on the evening of August 9 to catch their special train were "bankers, lawyers, doctors, artists, policemen and clerks" and "former gridiron stars, steeplechase riders and polo players" to dig trenches and do practice hikes. It was acknowledged that "A few valets carried the baggage of their young masters, who on the morrow may be washing their own shirts. Perhaps the valets were smiling on the inside, but they never showed it." Wives and sweethearts were at the station for farewells, some with tiny flags. "The scene was gay, and the event savored more of the drawing-room then the military. Among those of the way to the camp were Hamilton Fish, Jr., Rhinelander Waldo, and Alderman H.H. Curran. Other contingents from such cities as Baltimore, Chicago and Philadelphia were also on their way. George Wharton Pepper, although he was 50 years old, led the Philadelphia group, as an example to the younger men. With him were W.J. Clothier the banker 'and a number of polo players.'"

From the moment all those men got off the trains at Plattsburgh, said this reporter with a sardonic twist, "all social and business distinctions will be wiped out in the democracy of khaki." Those men all paid $30 to cover board of 50 cents a day and a deposit against any breakage of equipment. All paid the $6.80 train fare to Plattsburg, plus $2 extra for a sleeping berth. Others who attended were P.J. Roosevelt, Magistrate Daniel Murray, Lewis Stuyvesant Chandler, Jr., C. Oliver Iselin, W.S. Van Renssalaer, and Bronson Winthrop.[17]

The League released more of what they called "military statistics" in August 1915. According to the National Security League, for the United States the total expenditure for army and navy and pensions when World War I began was nearly $487 million a year, not including some $10 million paid by the states for militias; supposedly that was more than any other nation on earth then spent for military purposes. In 1914 Great Britain spent $230 million for its navy, $120 million for the army and $20 million for army pensions. That year Russia spent $285 million for the army and $122 million for the navy; Germany spent $300 million for the army and $114 million for its navy; France, Italy and Austria-Hungary were all reported to be well behind those numbers. In 1913–1914 the U.S. Army cost was $173 million, equal to that of Germany before the Imperial Army Act of 1913, in preparation for World War I. America's navy that year cost nearly $140 million, second only to Britain's expenditure. Regarding the American military pension bill of $173 million, the League said it had no comparison and that "There was nothing like it." In conclusion the account asserted, "For years we have been spending more than any other country for war purposes, past and future, without getting the worth of our money. It is time for a change."[18]

Late in August the NSL issued a report based on a "comprehensive review" of its nationwide campaign for increased militarism or, as it preferred to call it, preparedness for national defense. The tremendous interest awakened throughout the country through the activities of the league is reflected in "the favorable attitude now being shown by members of Congress irrespective of political affiliations toward national defense

Chapter 6. The General Campaign

SCENE AT THE PLATTSBURG, N. Y. TRAINING CAMP

August 1915, the training grounds of the Business Men's Camp. Note the confusion in the ranks as the men there, "prominent" ones according to the caption, were experiencing trouble as they try to march.

legislation." The work of the League, said the review, "is based upon the realization that Congress is the pivot upon which more adequate national defense finally rests. The recommendations to Congress of the general staff of the army and the general board of the navy have not received in the past the consideration which they deserve, nor has the money necessary to carry out the various projects been appropriated." Yet only days earlier the League had pointed out the vast sums of money that had been spent, and appropriated, on the military. With respect to the recent letter sent to all members of Congress the organization declared that the replies received "indicate that the work of the league is not only thoroughly appreciated but is regarded as a patriotic and necessary endeavor." Then this lengthy report went through the country state by state listing by name the various Congress members supporting the NSL positions. The most "important" expression of support from Pacific Coast politicians was that of U.S. Senator George C. Chamberlain of Oregon. He said, "The people of the country can best be educated to the necessities of our government by agitation of the subject by associations such as the National Security League, that have no other purpose than our country's defense." The article listed dozens of names of "supportive" politicians.[19]

A lengthy article appeared in a small town newspaper on August 26, 1915. It was a plant by the NSL of public relation material masquerading as news. The articles had no dateline. Most of these plants, perhaps all, were placed in small town papers and were simply verbatim printing of NSL press releases and other NSL general nonsense. This particular example was likely one of the first such efforts, but it would be a tactic employed by the League throughout its existence. The piece looked just like a regular news stories except that it lacked any aspect of a byline. Another way of recognizing it as a plant by the League was the effusive, glowing praise that was always heaped upon the National Security League. This piece took up one third of the page.[20]

The NSL even got involved in motion picture promotion. An ad for the film *The Battle Cry of Peace* appeared in September 1915. The story line of the movie was "A call to arms—against war." At the bottom of the advertisement was a sort of sponsor line with credit given to the NSL, Navy League, Army League, American Red Cross and the American Legion.[21]

In September 1915 the National Security League announced it had launched a campaign with a view to organizing branches of the NSL in every university and college in the nation. The League's membership in New York, said the item, already included a "'large number of graduates of Harvard, Yale, Princeton, Cornell, Dartmouth and other institutions" and "assurances of support had been received from these alumni in establishing college branches." It was felt that by spreading "the gospel of preparedness" among young men the movement would receive "tremendous momentum."[22]

Another strategy used by the League was to conduct essay contests. The first example was announced in October 1915 when Jules S. Bache, New York City broker, had offered, through the NSL, a prize of $500 for the best essay or article "demonstrating the necessity and wisdom of reasonable preparedness against war of the United States." There were no limitations on sex or age with respect to who could enter the contest; the essay was to be limited to a maximum of 500 words. The winner would be selected by a committee of five "persons of national prominence, whose names will be announced later." It was hoped by the organization that "The value of the article in awakening popular appreciation of our national peril and necessities will be considered as well as literary merit."[23]

An editorial in favor of the organization that appeared in October discussed an upcoming NSL meeting and declared, "Real public service will be performed at the meeting ... under the auspices of the National Security League, if it places Richmond [VA] sentiment squarely behind a sane and conservative scheme of national preparedness." The editor declared public sentiment clearly favored a regular army of 125,000 to 130,000, a navy "abreast of the time," and a National Guard doubled or tripled in size. He called such meetings and conferences held by the NSL as "valuable agencies" in informing the public as to "the real situation's real needs."[24]

One of the sillier speeches that came from the mouths of NSL people was one delivered by William Brewster before an NSL branch of a university in Minneapolis. Brewster called national unpreparedness "criminal negligence" and declared that William Jennings Bryan, Andrew Carnegie and Henry Ford were doing more to undermine the moral fiber of American citizens than any other single force. Said Brewster, "They are doing more to make the nation look silly and to weaken our national defense than any other agency. They have a half-million dollars a year to spend creating the sentiment of pacifism, which muffles the voice of patriotism using soft speech where strong action is needed." He also declared, "We want a nation invulnerable as well as invincible. We want nations to fear our strength. We love peace and want to throw about it our arms of defense."[25]

When President Wilson released the number in the fall of 1915 for the expenditures he wanted in the coming time period it was revealed that he planned to ask Congress for an increase of about $140 million for national defense over the previous year's expenditure of about $260 million. Wilson wanted to see an army of at least 120,000 men, up from the current 87,000 men. As well, Wilson proposed a five-year naval building program to encompass 15 to 20 new fighting ships in that period. He had recently delivered a speech in which he said American people were convinced the United States "should be very adequately prepared, not for war, but for defense." In response to Wilson's proposals the National Security League stated that many Congressmen from all over the country would support Wilson in the fight for the increased military expenditure, as shown by letters received by the NSL from Senators and Representatives. However, the League felt any increase would be fought by an organized group of Representatives (naming Representative William Worth Bailey from Pennsylvania) and added, "The league gets letters from a long list of congressmen all over the country favoring the president's defense course."[26]

Henry L. West, the NSL executive secretary, penned an article that took up two full pages in a Richmond newspaper under the headline "Criminal Neglect of National Defenses." In the piece West outlined a scary situation about Japan and its supposed threat for the invasion and conquest of America's Pacific Island "possessions," and the nation's West Coast. This was another article in contrast to the scare stories about the hordes of foreign military men landing on the East Coast and taking over without breaking a sweat. So, from time to time, a scare story had to be positioned directly at the other coast to arouse the patriotism and preparedness fever in them. Were it all an East Coast problem then the West Coast people might not get too involved. Henry L. West was identified in the byline as an NSL member but he was also described as an "expert," although in what topic he was expert was not mentioned. West bemoaned that there were no battleships on the West Coast and said of a potential coming war, "It will not be a war of aggression. We do not covet with envious soul the possessions of any other nation. It will be a war of self-defense." There goes Hawaii. There goes San Francisco.[27]

One of the few articles that questioned the idea that the U.S. was militarily unprepared appeared in the *Commoner* on November 1, 1915, in response to many such NSL claims, including the above Henry West article. Pointing out that for the year preceding World War I Germany spent $293 million on her army and navy and the U.S. spent about $312 million for the same purposes, the editorial wondered, "Does anybody believe that the nation is in any such state of unpreparedness as the eastern press would have us think or as the paid traveling organizers of the navy league and the National Security League and similar organizations assert?" In another editorial on the same page of the same issue of the *Commoner* came the remark, "Congress will convene early in December. Weather note: Watch out for war clouds from Japan and strong winds from the eastern munitions factories."[28]

The editor of the *Commoner* returned with another poke at the NSL in a December 1 editorial. He pointed out the United States was expending annually on its navy from $20 million to $30 million more than Germany or any other nation, except Great Britain. For the 10 years preceding World War I the U.S. expended on its navy over $300 million more than any other nation, again except Great Britain, expended on their navies. The U.S. plan then under consideration proposed a naval program expenditure increase of $500 million, at a rate of $100 million per year. The four-year plan for the army demanded a total increase of $450 million. At the beginning of World War I Germany was spending on its army and navy (for past wars and for the future) 55 percent of the total revenue Germany collected; Japan spent 45 percent; Great Britain spent 37 percent; and France spent 35 percent. At that time the United States was spending 60 percent, and if the Wilson proposal was implemented that number would move to 70 percent.[29]

When several hundred people met later that month in New York City at an NSL meeting to consider plans for national defense one of the speakers was former U.S. Senator Lafayette Young of Iowa. With respect to naysayers, Young said, "I believe in fastening your heart on the old U.S.A. and forgetting everything else. And when a citizen doesn't stand by the United States there isn't a steer big enough, with a hide large enough, to make a boot great enough, to fit a foot hard enough to kick that man far enough." When Joseph Choate rose and asked those in favor of Young's sentiment to say "aye," the response was said to have been "a thunder of 'ayes' mingled with cheers."[30]

Another contest was announced by the NSL at the close of 1915. An unnamed member of the League had put up $250 as a prize to be awarded to the author of the best essay on the subject "National Security as It Involves the Preparation and Use of the Citizenry." This essay was to be

Chapter 6. The General Campaign

4,000 to 5,000 words long, with the envelope containing it to be marked "Militia Essay." The prize was to be awarded upon the recommendation of a board consisting of "three suitable persons," to be chosen by the NSL Executive Committee. Deadline for entries was February 1, 1916.[31]

The reach of the NSL with its militarism pitch even extended to the Automobile Show held annually in New York City at Madison Square Garden. Wednesday, January 5, 1916, was Society Day at the Auto Show. That followed a custom of former years in having one day so designated in the week the show was running. However, the admission for Society Day was not raised that year, as it had been in the past, instead, the regular admission of 50 cents was charged. Thursday the 6th was Military Day with representatives from many organizations to be there, including the American Woman's League for Self-Defense; the Automobile Reserve Corps; the American Defense Society; the National Security League, the National Committee of Home Defense Motorists, and other organizations. That Thursday evening there was to be a banquet of the Society of Automobile Engineers with the main address being delivered by U.S. Secretary of the Navy Josephus Daniels.[32]

One of the sillier articles from early in 1916 concerned female fashion and the arrival of the "gunboat" hat. It was gunboat gray in color, crowned with "a fashionable turret and bristles with guns—dozens and dozens of them." But it did have a usefulness, at least according to one journalist, who was probably being sarcastic: "The business man hurrying to his office sees it and is reminded that he has not subscribed to the National Security League as yet." Nothing was mentioned in the article about the origins or designer of the gunboat hat.[33]

An ad for a speech to be given in Topeka, Kansas, by

GUNBOAT HAT JOINS IN NATIONAL PROPAGANDA FOR PREPAREDNES

Included in the propaganda for preparedness was this silly piece of fashion. The gunboat hat is shown here in August 1916. Note the "gun turrets" above the hat brim.

journalist Frederick Palmer, in February, stated he was to talk about World War I. He was described in the ad as an "Officially accredited representative of the entire press of the United States with the British Army." That speech was given under the auspices of the National Security League with reserved seats selling for 50 cents, 75 cents, and $1. Unreserved seats, at the back of the second balcony, went for 25 cents.[34]

Critics of the NSL policies sometimes argued not so much against increased military expenditures but that any increases and munitions expansion in general should be made by the government in its own plants. That, of course, infuriated the capitalist class, especially given that such contracts, when given to private plants, were often awarded as no-bid, cost-plus contracts—a recipe for huge financial enrichment. No-bid contracts were often justified on the ground of supposed emergency in war time or near war time, or some other "emergency." In this article Hudson Maxim (NSL member and executive, but not identified as such), explained "how our safety in war depends on having many large private factories equipped and ready to turn out enormous munition supplies which no government plants could possibly provide." Then he cited NSL president Menken as having advocated the nationalization of the manufacture of munitions of war; that is, Menken wanted to take the profit out of it. Said Menken: "This work of actual manufacture should be under Government control. Let personal profit be taken out of preparation insofar as it can be done without impairing efficiency of preparedness."

Then Maxim stated, "If the National Security League, as a body, were actually to work for the nationalization of the manufacture of munitions, that body would be working shoulder to shoulder with the pacifists to bring upon us the red hell of war." Maxim went on to speculate Menken's intentions may have been good, but he was a misguided, good-intentioned person. Maxim never identified himself for what he was, an NSL member and owner of a munitions plant himself.[35]

In February 1916, twin brothers 80 years old supposedly walked into an NSL office and enrolled themselves as members of the League. They were said to be the only surviving twins to have fought in the Civil War. John F. Grayson and Frederick T. Grayson lived in Newark, New Jersey. Both fought in the same New Jersey regiment and both were wounded in the knee at the Battle of Gettysburg.[36]

A city-wide campaign of speech-making to arouse enthusiasm for adequate national defense measures among the people of Philadelphia was being planned by the Speakers' Bureau of the Philadelphia branch of the National Security League. That campaign was slated to begin in March 1916. More than 100 volunteer speakers were to be enrolled in the bureau and "instructed in the gospel of preparedness, and furnished with all the

Chapter 6. The General Campaign 79

statistics, facts and even their speeches, if they want them." No specific meetings were to be arranged, but only the supplying of orators to a group that requested a speaker.

"Politics will be avoided by all the speakers. It is said that no one will be attacked, there will be no such thing as putting the blame on the Administration, and there will be strict observance of neutrality." Preparation for that campaign had been underway for two months by the Speakers' Bureau, of which George Wentworth Carr was chairman. Of the 100 or so male orators, 25 came from the debating society of the University of Pennsylvania. Plans were to have the orators address "hundreds" of meetings over the course of the campaign that was expected to last perhaps six weeks. "The speakers will endeavor to invade banquets, church organizations, meeting of business men's associations, and both men's and women's clubs. An effort will be made to interest both sexes in the movement for adequate preparedness."[37]

One month later another article on the Philadelphia Speakers' Bureau noted that 149 "missionaries, mobilized by the National Security League, will spread the theme of preparedness and carry its message ... wherever men and women gather. Work was to begin on April 3rd and 'continue so long as anyone wishes to hear them.'" Those 149 orators attended a pair of NSL gatherings and "all pledged their efforts to make the proposed educational campaign an aggressive, sympathetic and profitable movement, one with a punch and a purpose."[38]

Stretching further afield for support, the League sent out inquiries addressed to "prominent members of the Baseball Players fraternity" throughout America seeking support for their policies. Telegrams received, the League reported, indicated that "all favor the movement for national defense." However, no details were provided except that Bill Donovan, manager of the New York Americans, was cited as declaring his team were not only in favor of a larger army and navy, and believers in compulsory military service for one year of all youths attaining their majority; they were also for a federalized militia.[39]

Another physical demonstration of the NSL's dedication to its campaign could be seen in the announcement from its New York City headquarters, on April 1, declaring that business men "representing all trades and industries" would march in that city on May 13 in favor of national preparedness. Reportedly this was to be accomplished by an organization formed of "prominent citizens" and while the affair was endorsed by the NSL it was supposedly not an NSL organization. This other group was known as the citizens' Preparedness Parade and planned to extend the movement to all large cities in the nation with the idea of having simultaneous parades throughout the nation. Charles H. Sherrill, former U.S.

ambassador to Argentina, had agreed to be grand marshal of that proposed parade. Emphasized was the idea that the parade was to be "non-partisan." That parade was to be reviewed by New York City Mayor Mitchel and Leonard Wood (both NSL supporters) and the commandant of the New York Navy Yard.[40]

An editorial that appeared on April 19, 1916, in an Arizona newspaper began by declaring, "The industries of the country are as deficient for national security as are its arms for national defense. This has been shown in the work of the patriotic organizations which have been alerting themselves to national preparedness." The editor continued: "In the organization of the National Security League, and its investigation of the matter, the industrial aspect of preparedness is closely associated with that of military and naval defense." The piece spoke of an awakening to that need all across America and stated that the Chamber of Commerce of the United States (300,000 members) had recommended increases in the army and navy and "the industrial resources so co-ordinated as to make fully available the military and industrial strength of the Nation."

With respect to industrial unpreparedness the editor noted that if a huge mobilization took place the military could be supplied with, say, surgical supplies, but soon problems would emerge in clashes with civilian demand. The Businessmen's League of Kansas City, Missouri, was actively organizing a military training camp while the Pennsylvania Railroad, the Western Union Telegraph Company, and the Postal Telegraph Company were encouraging their employees to attend military instruction camps or to join the National Guard.[41]

Mrs. A.J. George, director of branches for the NSL, urged students at a military training camp at Chevy Chase, Maryland, to learn the discipline that subordinated selfish interest to the state.

She spoke to them about preparedness, stressing that "it comes only from the determination of a people to face the duties imposed upon them by new occasions. Military preparedness, industrial preparedness—these are questions for experts, but the will to serve, the self-denial of the individual, the subordination of personal ambitions and of class interest to the common weal, these are the foundation stones of national defense, these make for social preparedness."[42]

An ad for a public meeting in Harrisburg, Pennsylvania, on the topic of preparedness appeared in a local newspaper on May 17, 1916. Both speakers were NSL people. The ad listed all of the organizations that generally popped up as being in favor of a militarism that meant bigger, and bigger immediately. The list included the usual seven organizations as well as a couple of engineering societies.[43]

A major New York City newspaper devoted a full page to the subject of

Chapter 6. The General Campaign

preparedness on May 21, 1916. It looked at preparedness groups all over the country, broken down by state. A subhead of the article declared, "Citizens throughout the country organize military training schools and camps—business corporations urge employees to join." The article provided a state-by-state summary of the "Preparedness Movement," remarking that "the data [had] been supplied by secretaries of the National Security League in various cities." Then a statement that the summary did not represent the "full strength or full scope of the movement." Wrote the journalist, "New York's parade of May 14 was an expression of the sentiment that is sweeping the country. Congress refuses to provide for a volunteer army, but here is proof of the fact that a volunteer army is forming despite Congress."

States summarized in the review numbered 17. Numbers for NSL membership were sometimes given for the various states, but usually vaguely. The California branch of the League had just formed and "expects a membership of 10,000 by the following year." The Los Angeles branch had

A company of the recently organized girls' regiment, composed of employees of the Wanamaker Philadelphia Department Store, drilling on the roof of the store.
International Film Service.

This photograph from May 1916 shows girls drilling on the roof of a Wanamaker's department store in Philadelphia. It was but one manifestation of the mania for preparedness that was then sweeping the country. The League was among the principal movers behind that craze.

500 members while Sacramento had 500 members of "patriotic organizations [i.e., more than one]. In Colorado the NSL and the Navy League had a combined total of about 800 members. In Indianapolis the League branch had 100 members."[44]

In Massachusetts the NSL was said to have 4,600 members while the American Legion had 2,000, the League to Enforce Peace had 3,200 and the Special Aid Society, a women's organization for preparedness, had 2,500. A number of business men's schools had been receiving military instruction under the National Guard with some of them being the Cambridge Business Men's School (75 men), Plymouth Business Men's School (75) and the New England Telephone and Telegraph Company (100 men). That training consisted of one drill a week and started back in October 1915. The NSL branch in Detroit had 540 members with the Detroit Business Men's Training Battalion numbering 240 men and having begun back in January 1916. That group was under the supervision of regular U.S. Army officers and under the direction of National Guard officers this battalion completed a schedule comprising of a drill and a military lecture one night a week for 16 weeks.

Within Michigan, it was said, "Most of the large business houses here have adopted resolutions permitting their employees to go to the United States training camps for four weeks without loss of salary. Many of the companies have notified their employees that hereafter no promotion to positions of responsibility will be given to any man who is not an American citizen, or who has not taken out his first nationalization papers." The NSL branch in St. Louis had 1,500 members while the Kansas City Missouri branch had 808 members. That branch had tried to secure a citizens' training camp at Fort Leavenworth but the reply received was that the federal government could not spare the money or the officers.

In Nebraska the Omaha branch had 200 members. Rhode Island had 2,585 members in the League branch and, it was said, "Many business concerns are granting generous concessions to encourage Plattsburgh and National Guard enlistments among their employees." In Texas the San Antonio branch of the NSL had 133 members and, in that city, "Individual citizens past military age are volunteering to pay the expenses of young men in the civilian instruction camps." Also in that Texas city, "Heads of business houses are offering leaves of absence to a percentage of their employees for military training and have guaranteed to hold positions for young men volunteering in the National Guard for service at the President's call."

Milwaukee had an NSL branch with 2,500 members. The women's section of that Milwaukee branch had 200 members. In Pennsylvania the state NSL branch had 10,000 members while Pittsburgh had 1,500 people enrolled. Reportedly, the total amount of money expended by individual citizens and organizations involved in preparation in Pennsylvania was $133,000. The largest contributor was Pennsylvania State College, which gave $55,000. The NSL gave $20,000. The amount spent for the same purpose in Pittsburgh was $26,500. Three different organizations, one of which was the National Security League, each gave $5,000.[45]

An editorial from a Virginia newspaper was enthusiastic over the prospect that a preparedness parade might be in the works for the city of Richmond: "If the people of Richmond believe in preparedness, as we think they do, it is proper and necessary they should show the faith that is in them." Added the editor, "There is no aggression in the heart of America. We shall never fight save in self-defense. There is no possibility, even, that we shall adopt a policy of aggression. Adequate preparedness, so far as this country is concerned, makes not for war, but for peace."[46]

By late in May 1916 the NSL believed the interest taken by Americans in various organizations operating for national defense indicated that people of the country "are aroused to a sense of the danger of unpreparedness." It found the organization of military training camps and the introduction of military instruction in educational institutions had become nationwide and that industrial and commercial establishments were generally extending to their employees the opportunity for military training without loss of time or pay. It was said that more effort was being made in almost every state to introduce military training in schools. Recently the Massachusetts Legislature had enacted a law transferring all organizations and departments of the state volunteer militia to the force of the United States, thus placing it under federal control "in case of threatening trouble." The Board of Education of Springfield, Ohio, had adopted military training as part of the high school curriculum. New Jersey had appropriated $159,999 for the expense of military training in the state's public schools and provided for two hours training each week.[47]

Theodore Roosevelt was a big booster of preparedness and when he spoke in Kansas City, Missouri, he declared, with respect to the volunteer military camps, "'I believe in these camps with all my heart and soul. They are supplying by private initiative what our government representatives have not the foresight to provide for everybody.' He also urged the adoption of universal military training."[48]

A major New York City daily paper, the *Sun*, devoted an entire page to the topic of preparedness, on June 18, 1916. There were many signed articles on the page. One was by NSL president Menken. Another article was by Dr. W.C. Rucker, Assistant Surgeon General of the U.S. Public Health Service; the topic was on military training camps for volunteer citizens benefiting the entire nation. Edward A. Moree, director of the Atlantic Region of the

American Red Cross, wrote an article in favor of increased militarism. Joan Peters, described as a private in Company D, at the Chevy Chase camp, wrote on the need for women in the preparedness movement.

Outside of the various articles on the page the only other material was four ads. One was for a New York City gunsmith, which featured "Maxim's silencers accurately fitted." Hudson Maxim was an NSL member who also owned a munitions factory. Another ad for a sporting goods store in New York City featured a price list for parts of a "regulation uniform" needed by those civilian volunteer military camps ($2 for a shirt, $1.35 for a hat, and so forth). A third ad offered a complete military outfit for $14.95.

A fourth ad was from the L. Maass company of New York City that was hawking a watch fob called the "All American Fob" at prices ranging from 35 cents to $1.50. Separately, in the text away from the ad itself, as though it were news, it was called a "patriotic watch fob" and especially recommended by the makers for wear at "Plattsburgh" camps (as those military camps were often called, in honor of the first one held there in 1915). The fob carried the slogan "Peace, Preparedness and Prosperity." A casual reader of this page could be forgiven for drawing the conclusion that the whole page was a setup and a plant that had nothing to do with news and was simply intended to fire up enthusiasm for militarism in its many aspects.[49]

By August 1916 it was claimed that a movement in favor of universal military training and service "is growing rapidly throughout the county, according to reports received by the National Security League." Supposedly it was growing everywhere and sprang up from almost nowhere, since November 1915; and it was asserted that "the real opposition to obligatory training and service is very limited." Every canvass or vote had shown strong sentiment in favor of universal service and training. A vote by the U.S. Chamber of Commerce businessmen was 889 in favor and 56 against. A referendum vote taken by the *Chicago Tribune* newspaper showed just 75 votes against, out of 6,255 votes recorded. And a poll conducted by the *Baltimore Sun* paper recorded 8,186 votes for and 1,055 votes against. Those results encouraged the NSL, said the news account, to continue its campaign for that very thing and "this necessary system of national defense."[50]

One negative comment on universal military training came from a labor publication, in January 1917.

The report noted that a statewide and nationwide campaign for compulsory military service was then underway, "thanks to the machinations of the National Security League, one of the most powerful and richest of the propaganda organizations for militarism. Bills have been framed by the central headquarters and will be introduced this winter in every state of the union. At the same time moves are under way to force the same kind of

Chapter 6. The General Campaign 85

legislation through Congress." That information came to the labor publication from a "confidential" bulletin of the NSL. Parts of that bulletin were leaked to a correspondent for the labor paper. It said, in part, "as legislation for physical and military training in the schools is purely a state matter, legislation to this end can be secured only through state legislatures, and therefore it is suggested that a committee be appointed to frame a bill for such training which should be introduced in each of the forty-one legislatures which meet this month." Another part of the bulletin declared, "It is also recommended that a committee be appointed to consider the advisability of introducing in Congress at the next session a bill providing for a referendum vote on the subject of universal military training at the election which occurs two years hence [November 1918] for members of congress."[51]

An article in support of compulsory military training appeared in a West Virginia newspaper in late January 1917. It was signed by Frederic L. Huidekoper, who was described in the author credit line as "Founder of the Army League and one of the founders of the National Security League." This editorial was clearly another one of the planted articles by the League; it was just printed verbatim from the NSL but was set into the paper as though it were news. It began by bringing up the country of Argentina that adopted compulsory military service back in 1901 and stated that even those who had originally opposed the system liked the result: "The rich man's son ceased to be an idler, the employers discovered that the man who had had military training was physically fitter, more obedient, more courteous and respectful because of his recognition of authority and therefore a better employee than the men who had received no such training." And, the editorial said, "The government became more stable, the men—many of them sons of European immigrants—were improved physically and morally and molded into clean law-abiding Argentinians instead of being permitted to cling to their foreign customs and traditions."

While the example may have been, ostensibly, Argentina, the country in mind was America. This explained, indirectly, why the NSL loved the idea of universal, compulsory military training. It produced a physically fitter workforce and, more to the point, an obedient, genuflecting workforce. The League had a belief, accurate or not, and an enthusiasm for what, say, a year of compulsory military training could do in the way of producing tractable automatons. No more restive employees attacking the capitalist order, no more socialists and Bolsheviks running amok. It was all part of the League's desire for huge profits from militarism and, as an added bonus, a slavish workforce. Well, a capitalist can dream.[52]

Huidekoper was back about six weeks later in the same newspaper with another planted public relations article from the NSL. It was another screed on the immense value of compulsory military training and service.

Frederic L. Huidekoper was one of the founders of the National Security League. He is shown here at the Business Men's Military Camp in Plattsburgh, New York, in August 1915 where he was "playing soldier."

After a brief mention of the Argentina story, he argued that if a similar result could "be achieved in the United States it would more than justify a system of military training and service, quite apart from the security which it affords to the nation from a military standpoint." Note that he did not spell out what the result would be, except to observe that it had nothing to do with national defense. Equally telling was the title of this so-called editorial, "Making Americans."[53]

Another media ad for the NSL campaign appeared in a newspaper in March 1917, regarding Germany's threatened invasion and "dismemberment" of the United States, which had recently been uttered. Readers were urged to send to their Senators and Representatives in Congress the following: "I pledge you my loyal support in any immediate action in defense of American rights menaced by Germany and urge that such action be taken forthwith." The NSL was worried, said the ad, because "German agents and their allies, the pacifists" were sending telegrams to Washington asking the Government to do nothing and "they are richly endowed with funds."[54]

Louise Bryant was a well-known feminist, political activist and journalist during this time period. She was known for her sympathetic coverage of Russia and Bolsheviks. She wrote a sarcastic article in March 1917 about her day spent with "lady militarists": "Among the various manifestations of Preparedness the women's military organizations loom large. From the daily press you'd think half the feminine population of New York was ready to rush into the trenches along with the Roosevelt family regiment at the first rumors of war." Therefore Bryant went to the NSL headquarters in New York City and met an obliging stenographer who gave her a list of "special friends of ours" to start on. At the offices she visited she found, in the first place, the contact was out but in the second place she spoke to Theodora Booth, president of the Girls' National Honor Guard. She told the journalist how they carried rolls and hot coffee to the militia men guarding the bridges "and her eyes sparkled with excitement."

At the National League for Woman's Service the national commandant, Grace Parker, was ill but Mrs. Coffin Renssalaer spoke to her: "I think the pacifists are dangerous because they have that spiritual quality we all adore. And then we all live the idea of the Brotherhood of Man but that's purely utopian, and won't work." She also visited the Woman's League for Self-Defense where the dues were $3 a year and infantry outfits, without rifles, cost $12, and cavalry outfits sold for $16. That group had 700 members in New York City alone, a branch in Milwaukee and one being formed in Boston. At the end of the day Bryant said she had learned some definite things, one of them being that there were more anti-suffragists than suffragists in the women's military organizations. Bryant concluded, "most of these organizations have absolutely no connection with one another, and indeed are mutually scornful—though they all fervently believe that war or some other catastrophe will bring them together in one great league of militant womanhood."[55]

In March 1917, as an indication of the widely spreading interest in the subject of preparedness for national defense and universal military

To Vigilant Americans!

In view of the announcement of Germany's threatened invasion and dismemberment of the United States, published today by the Associated Press and confirmed by the President, we ask you to appeal to your citizens to send the following telegram to the President and to their Senators and Representatives in Congress:

"I pledge you my loyal support in any immediate action in defence of American rights menaced by Germany and urge that such action be taken forthwith."

We urge you to act immediately because German agents and their allies, the pacifists, are sending thousands of telegrams to Washington asking the Government to do nothing. They are richly endowed with funds.

This appeal is made as our only available means of obtaining an expression of patriotic American sentiment. It is vital to impress upon Congress that the American people are determined and vigilant in the assertion and maintenance of national security and national rights.

THE NATIONAL SECURITY LEAGUE.

The above telegram has been sent by the National Security League to the Mayors of the principal cities of the United States and to the 280 League Branches and Committees. The League urges all citizens, whether members of the League or not, to send similar telegrams and to induce their neighbors to do likewise.

Join the National Security League
31 Pine Street, New York City.

This ad from March 1916 was another call from the NSL for more members and a plea for all patriotic and vigilant Americans—and likely more fearful Americans after reading the piece—to contact the authorities to urge more militarism.

training, the NSL cited quotes from many requests sent from all parts of the country asking for information on the topic that could be used in speeches, addresses and debates. Supposedly those requests came from colleges, high schools, YMCAs, doctors, lawyers "and representatives of every trade and industry." Young women, the reader was told, asked for the literature "almost as frequently" as did young men. In Indiana, Washington, North Dakota, and South Dakota, UMT (universal military training) had been made the topic of discussion in the state high school debating leagues. Requests for literature reportedly came from all over—Indiana headed the list with 83 inquiries. However, no total number was given, nor was the reader told over what period of time those requests were received.[56]

In the middle of March Stanwood Menken, NSL president, delivered a screed in favor of patriotism. "Drugged by prosperity and pacifism, our national sense of honor is blunted.... We want to bring home to every man and woman in the United States the fact that patriotism is a vital condition of national permanence," he exclaimed. United States entry into World War I was only a few weeks away and this must have been obvious to everyone who followed politics. Thus, the NSL was getting ready to shift into phase two of their campaign—preparedness would be dropped and patriotism substituted.[57]

That a large percentage of newspaper editors throughout the United States were in favor of UMT was shown by a compilation of editorial expressions on the subject, according to the League. There had been 1,193 such editorials since the introduction of the Chamberlain and general staff of the army bills in Congress, some two years earlier. Those appeared in 476 different papers, 270 of which were "enthusiastic" supporters of the UMT idea. There were also 157 papers that were described as non-committal and 49 newspapers "principally socialist, labor and religious papers" that were opposed. Were all supporting newspapers "enthusiastic" or were some just mildly in favor?[58]

In March an ad for a "patriotic mass meeting" appeared in the New York papers. The NSL was mentioned as one of four places where reserved seats could be purchased for $1; general admission was free. The list of speakers indicated that most of them were involved with the National Security League at some level.[59]

Near the end of March a new film from Vitagraph appeared in film theaters. It was called *Womanhood, the Glory of the Nation*. That movie grew out of a suggestion made by former president Theodore Roosevelt to J. Stuart Blackton, director general of the film studio. The film's story was written by Blackton and Cyrus Townsend Brady and depicted what would happen if a "powerful foe" landed on American shores. Following the movie's Philadelphia opening the Daughters of the American Revolution, the National Preparedness Society, the American Defense League, the National Security League and the Navy League outlined plans for a country-wide campaign to aid *Womanhood* in every way. Womanhood was described as "a powerful preachment for preparedness. The propaganda note does not, however, overshadow its dramatic story." Production was done with the cooperation of the U.S. Army and the U.S. Navy. Theodore Roosevelt appeared in a few scenes, as himself.[60]

A full page advertisement taken out by the NSL and published in a Washington, D.C., newspaper on March 29, 1917, purported to show that the voice of the American press demanded UMT. That ad contained a list of the 501 newspapers so inclined, by state. A total of 43 states were listed, with at least one newspaper named—all of those endorsements of UMT were reportedly done through editorials that appeared in those publications.[61]

Just one day after that an editorial that was enthusiastically in favor of UMT appeared in an Indiana newspaper. That editorial pitched UMT to the parents as a choice between sending a disciplined soldier (through UMT) to the field of battle or a raw recruit—who was much more likely to be injured or killed. "Do you want your boy to die a perfectly useless and unnecessary death on the field or in the hospital, or do you want him to go forth with a reasonable chance of coming home to you? The choice rests with you," asserted the editor. Readers were urged to contact their Senators and Representatives and urge those people to pass a universal military training bill: "Act now! The future safety of your son rests in your own hands."[62]

As a first step towards UMT an organization of several hundred DC citizens came forward at the start of April to propose a military census be taken of DC to record the details of all men of military age and also record the details of women willing to give service to them in war, and also to register all aliens who were resident in DC or just passing through the area. Such a proposal was submitted to the District of Columbia Board of Commissioners by Frederic Huidekoper, William D. Hoover and Edward J. Stellwagen. It was noted that Huidekoper was a National Security League vice-president and one of the originators of the Army League and the Navy League.[63]

CHAPTER 7

Critics and Impugners

Challenges to the National Security League began to appear as early as February 1915 and continued throughout the next seven years or so. Some disputed the idea that the United States was militarily unprepared; that it was weak, inferior, helpless and hopeless in the face of foreign invaders who, if the NSL was to be believed—and it could not—were always on the verge of landing wholesale on American shores. Other challenges attacked the NSL for the fact that it was an organization of rich capitalists who were out to promote militarism because of the enormous extra profits that would accrue to their class, and used the sham of military ineptitude on the part of America to cover that fact.

And some wrote to expose the more deeply hidden and more sinister aspects of the League, and similar organizations—to control the masses of American citizens in the face of a rise in socialistic and communistic ideologies (real or perceived) and a general worry by the parasite class (as the challengers would say) that the workers of America might indeed rise up and attempt to throw off their chains. There was a great faith within the NSL and presumably, in the parasite class as a whole, in the value and power of military training, and especially UMT, to remove any and all such "radical" tendencies and thought from the masses. And some of the opposition attacked the League on more than one of these categories.

Just a couple of months after the National Security League was organized it was criticized by the American League to Limit Armaments. With respect to the NSL's purpose the latter group wondered if the NSL would show people specifically in what respects the United States was unprepared, whose fault it was and against precisely what danger the country was unprepared. The American League said they had been trying for two months to get those answers but the NSL only repeated "the same old general statements, statements varying the monotony only as they differ among themselves as to the extent of our unpreparedness, the identity of our enemy and the measure of preparedness we need." Members of the American League to Limit Armaments included Dr. Nicholas Murray Butler and Jane Addams.

Several NSL names were mentioned. One that had not surfaced elsewhere was Colgate Hoyt, who was involved in railroads and also was a New York investment banker in the firm Colby Hoyt.[1]

One month later a brief editorial appeared in an Oregon newspaper. "The National Security League advocating a large army and navy, have opened the usual press bureaus and are flooding the newspapers with ready-made editorials and news stories," declared the editor. "Some interest back of the movement evidently has money to spend with the idea of being reimbursed from some source. Possibly the manufacturers of war material may be interested in the patriotic (?) work."[2]

Also in March 1915 there appeared a challenge to the League from Dr. Frederick Lynch. Originally the piece appeared in the mainstream *Literary Digest*, but it was also reprinted in various newspapers. Said Lynch, "The enemy that is within our gates is the group of men who are leaving no stone unturned to urge the United States to follow in the footsteps of the Old World and base its civilization upon armaments, guns, a vast navy and a huge army." Lynch went on to outline the classes who would "turn the minds of our people from industrialization to militarism and the preparation for war."

In his mind there were four such classes; the first was officers and ex-officers of the U.S. Army and Navy. Their business was guns; that was all they saw. The second consisted of the people who profited by war and the preparation for war—the manufacturers of powder, guns, armaments, the builders of battleships, and so forth. "Their activities are illusive, but after the revelation in Europe which have shown how fervently this class of men worked to bring on this present war—willing to plunge Europe into this hell to make a few dollars, there can be no doubt of their activity here," Lynch explained. In class number three were the politicians who were taking part in the fight against President Woodrow Wilson's peace policies simply to discredit and embarrass his Administration. And the fourth group urging the nation to arms was composed of "hysterical people" who had been stampeded with fear by the present war.[3]

An editorial in a Washington State newspaper declared the NSL had omitted something: "This thing they've submitted to the administration and us sounds like the roar of the jingo, the whine of the contractor and the solicitation of the prostitute war expert." If the American people were in favor of adequate armament for self-defense, the editor argued, those people were opposed always to preparation under existing methods; "No more millionaire families from villainous armor contracts! No more millionaire families from private powder monopoly! No more robbing of the people by private contractors for war supplies!" That, declared the editor, was the vital thing the NSL had omitted. "What the league presents is the same, old, emasculated proposition that trots to the front, with its 40 per cent, private profit feature leering through a mask of patriotism, every time we have a war issue bigger than fighting the fleas in U.S. uniform at the El Paso camp." The editorial concluded, "We need full security against foreign invasion of our country no more than we need full security against domestic invasion of the U.S. treasury. The security that robs us while securing us against robbery by foreigners is not good." This editor urged that all the arming done for the United States should be done by itself, for itself, and in its own factories and plants. That is, no private munitions production.[4]

Some indication of the money involved for the capitalist class could be seen in a July 5, 1915, report. According to that report from the time the war began in Europe (July 1914), J.P. Morgan and Company had handled contracts totaling more than $500 million for the accounts of foreign governments, for war munitions and supplies. Of that amount about $400 million was for the British government and $50 million for the French government. Commission paid to the Morgan banking firm on those contracts began at 2 percent and decreased in proportion to the size of the contracts. All of those contracts were said to have been placed with U.S. firms. And, of course, it was likely that J.P. Morgan and Company received some sort of "commission" or consideration from those U.S. firms, for placing the contracts with them.[5]

Thousands of people gathered in Carnegie Hall in New York City on July 9, 1915, to hear Jane Addams tell of her "peace pilgrimage" through war-riddled Europe. She argued that the vast majority of people in Europe were opposed to war but each country involved had a "military party" which prevailed. "Neither the masses nor the Government wanted the war, nor want it to continue now. But in each country a military caste has a fast grip on the people and on the governments, and the thing that makes it impossible for the peace advocates to reach their 'comrades in mind' is the censorship."

After her speech socialist Meyer London spoke. He exclaimed, "Frank Holt is dead. He was a dangerous man. But he was no more dangerous than living organizations such as the National Security League." He received no applause for that remark, but silence, plus some subdued hisses. Frank Holt's real name was Eric Muenter. He was a German-American activist and would-be assassin. For a time he was a professor at Harvard University and while an instructor there he murdered his wife. He moved to Cornell University and taught there, under a different name. He even managed to shoot Jack Morgan, son of J.P. Morgan the banker. He was, of course, notorious in this time period.[6]

Following his two unsuccessful political campaigns for the U.S. presidency William Jennings Bryan founded the publication *The Commoner*, which he edited and published out of Lincoln, Nebraska, from 1901 to 1923. That publication printed a criticism of the NSL in September 1915, which was a reprint from another paper. It was titled "Another insidious lobby." The background to that was that in 1913, soon after taking office, President Woodrow Wilson "electrified" the country when he charged that the nation's capital was infested by an "insidious lobby," which he was determined to smoke out. But, said this 1915 editorial, that lobby was "a negligible force in comparison with the more insidious lobby which now infests the capital." That 1913 lobby was "frankly selfish.... It made few if any pretensions of patriotism. It was not saving the country. It was not buttressing our shores against a threatened invasion. It was not particularly anxious about the flag. It was troubling itself little with the Yellow Peril or the German bogey. It was there merely to get all that was to be had for the railroads, for steel, for sugar, or glass, for ship yards, for powder mills, for gun factories, for lumber and for all the other pets of privilege which republicanism had been nurturing for so many years."

Meyer London, between 1910 and 1915. London was a New York City politician and one of only two people from the Socialist Party of America elected to the United States Congress.

In this editor's opinion Wilson had a good deal of success in sending that lobby away and that the hotel business in Washington was never as poor as it was in 1913 and 1914. But now, in 1915, there was a new lobby—"an infinitely more dangerous lobby infesting the capital of the nation today. It is a purely 'patriotic' lobby, a lobby which has wrapped the flag about it,

Chapter 7. Critics and Impugners

a lobby profoundly concerned over the welfare of the nation and the perpetuity of our sacred institutions, a lobby which is in deadly fear of some imaginary foe, a lobby that thinks in terms of air ships, submarines, dreadnoughts, 16-inch guns, torpedoes, shells, a huge standing army and a navy greater than a Hobson ever dared to propose."[7]

The editor continued his article by noting that even the railroads, in their successful lobbying campaign to force the U.S. Government to raise freight rates, "flooded the mails with no such deluge of literature as that which the preparedness lobby is today disseminating. Never before in the history of the country has an equal activity in any behalf been witnessed. Evidently this lobby is richly endowed."

All of that was in a campaign in which the American people were being asked to approve of vast expenditures on the national defenses—the implications being that American shores were menaced by some powerful oppressor. The ramifications of that lobby were said to be widespread: "Scores of leagues, societies, clubs and associations have been formed to push particular phases of the general campaign." Schools, churches, political organizations, the magazine and newspaper press, chautauquas (an early 1900s adult education movement mostly in small communities, in tents, in warmer weather, with lectures, displays and some entertainment), the lyceum, everything that contributed to the "molding of public opinion, is being used by this lobby as far as possible in spreading the gospel of preparedness and in dragooning popular sentiment into an acceptance of the fantastic notion that preparation for war is a guarantee of peace."

As far as this editor was concerned the 1913 lobby was minor in comparison. "But the lobby of which the Army and Navy league, the National Security League, the National Rifle Association, the National Aero Club of America are the visible expressions, is of the very essence of false pretense. It is greed masquerading in the vestments of patriotism. It is militarism cloaked in the garb of peace. It is selfish ambition posing as disinterested public spirit." He continued, "It is imperialism of the sordid sort whose democratic habiliments do not conceal the iron hand or the two-edged sword. That it should indefinitely pursue its sinister work unchallenged seems unthinkable. The president and congress should both call it to account and force a revelation of the secret springs of action and the secret sources of supply."[8]

A letter to the editor of a Philadelphia newspaper mentioned the scare stories about America's "useless" navy and the "dreadful peril" of a Japanese invasion. J. Augustus Cadwaller's letter continued, "Now the second invasion of our dear city occurs. This time by the National Security League. They do not intend to let you forget the awful lessons which their paid publicity agents spread out for you in the papers. They are here to scare you out of your wits by telling you it is all but up with you unless you heed their advice." And, he added, "They announce that they want 20,000 signers from this district to petition Congress to carry out the carefully prepared and useless plan known as national defense which will put profits into the pockets of a few estimable multi-millionaires and provide the Government with a large quantity of junk to be disposed of in five to ten years as old iron."[9]

William Jennings Bryan delivered a signed editorial in his paper on November 1, 1915. He wrote, with respect to the NSL, "Investigate the activities of the business groups pecuniarily interested in increased appropriations for army and navy, which has become so active in pushing its selfish demands. Congress ought to at once appoint a committee to investigate. It is more than a lobby. It is a concerted attempt to misinform the whole nation with a view to the securing of enormous profits at the expense of the tax payers." Bryan continued by writing, "Publicity is the surest weapon with which to meet an evil of this kind. Let the people once know the real motive back of this movement for preparedness and it can not succeed. Exposure will kill it. Turn on the light and let the country see the fraudulent character of the pretended patriotism which is now being paraded before the country by men who claim a superior attachment to the nation, but are in fact nothing but leeches and parasites. The investigation ought to begin at once."[10]

A few days later, officers of the Philadelphia branch of the National Security League called "false and absurd" the assertion of William Jennings Bryan that the NSL was a paid agent of the ship builders and ammunition makers. When Bryan gave a lecture November 3 on "universal peace" he attacked both the NSL and the Navy League saying they "have programs that call for an expenditure by the Government of about half a billion a year for 10 years on the army and navy." Robert Morris, secretary of the Philadelphia branch, called Bryan's assertions "malicious slander without any foundation."[11]

National Security League president Menken also denied Bryan's charges about his organization being in thrall to the munitions makers and the ship builders. He did release what he claimed were "the names of all persons who had contributed more than $25 from January 31, 1914, to July 31, 1915." Some 84 names were on that list with the biggest donation being $1,000, from each of five people—Anna B. Bliss, J.C. Brady, Clarence H. Mackay, H.C. Frick, and Nicholas F. Brady. Note that the list was of individual contributors; corporations were not mentioned. Also, no mention was made of donations in kind.[12]

Journalist Charles Collman began his piece about "Why the money trust wants war," which appeared on November 5, 1915, by telling about events he had witnessed back on August 15 at noon on Wall Street in New York. He observed mounted police leading and surrounding a convoy of 25 trucks—each with four armed men on board. It was that way that King George of England sent to J. Pierpont Morgan (the banker), his accredited agent, the gold in payment for bayonets, shrapnel and so forth.

As he observed the scene Collman asked himself whom those armed men threatened on the open street. Collman saw it as "the defense of Morgan and his Money Trust to the silent wrath of honest men." And, he added, "The pleasing masks these bankers wear had dropped, and there were revealed the hideous males, the primal brutes, conveying over the gold they had earned by the mangling of human flesh, gnashing their tusks in rage at the people whose sympathies they had thwarted, whose ideals they had crushed by the shameful trade in war munitions." J.P. Morgan and Company were agents of the British, French and Russian governments for the purchase of war materiel and were also interested in huge corporations making bigger profits from the manufacture of war supplies. United States Steel had been getting, and would get, orders for steel from concerns in the United States, which had taken orders for shrapnel and other war munitions. U.S. Steel, on August 3, got a Russian rail order amounting to $25 million. J.P. Morgan, Elbert H. Gary and Edmund C. Converse were all members of the Steel Trust board.

Henry Clay Frick, between 1915 and 1920. Frick was a major industrialist and union-buster. He was also revealed to be one of the League's major donors.

Lackawanna Steel Corporation had gotten $7 million in war orders for steel and rails—Cornelius Vanderbilt and Ogden L. Mills were directors of that company. National Surety Company estimated $1.5 billion in war material had been contracted for (based on the applications for surety bonds the company had received). Among its directors was Frederic R.

Coudert. The International Nickel Company was doing more business from the increase in nickel consumption. Westinghouse Electric and Manufacturing and General Electric were each described as "war stocks"—that is, firms that did well during wars. Charles Steele (of J.P. Morgan) was a director of General Electric. The Farmers' Loan and Trust Company was transfer agent for the General Electric Company. On the trust company board was Percy Rockefeller. Those were some of the people Collman found behind the preparedness idea of spending some $500 million on the U.S. military each year.[13]

Explained Collman, "For you see, the war in Europe some time will be ended, and the Money Trust's war munitions plants must not be idle. No, it is the duty of Wall Street patriots to organize Navy Leagues and National Security Leagues and the like, that the government may be urged by the great patriotic clamor to spend vast sums on war materiel." Collman then listed a number of U.S. manufacturers, involved to some extent in expanded war production. Then he quoted from the *Wall Street Journal*, "Will the demand for war materiel outlast the conflict? Will the great industry that has been established in so short a time end with the wars? It is noticeable that those concerns that are erecting plant extensions or new plants to take care of the war business, are not providing temporary and inexpensive structures. They are building modern and permanent structures of brick or concrete and steel. If the war continues or is followed by others, the munition makers will be in a position to reap enormous profits as a result of having the plants ready." He wondered if the ordinary Americans would continue to be "the dupes of Wall Street 'patriots.'"

At a meeting of the NSL on June 15 Charles J. Bonaparte (a former U.S. Attorney General and NSL member) was asked what he meant by "reasonable possible enemy" and he replied "any power except Great Britain." Collman's article only saw the light of day in obscure publications. One was the *New Ulm Post* (Minnesota). That was a German language newspaper but Collman's piece was published in English therein. He explained to his readers why the piece was published far removed from the mainstream by saying he could point out the names of men who were part owners of the great New York dailies, "who finance them, dominate them with their advertising. Small wonder that the Money Trust has poisoned the public mind with the tainted syndicate news services sent broadcast throughout our country. The New York newspapers know that what I write about the Money Trust is true, but they do not dare to print the truth."[14]

At a meeting on November 21, 1915, the Chicago Federation of Labor resolved to bring back a report and some resolutions in order to start a "counter agitation ... against the campaign for militarism now sweeping the country." Said Emmet Flood, general organizer of the American Federation of Labor, "Patriotism is emotional insanity. We must warn our people against the dope the capitalistic press is trying to give us. The ammunition makers and others who profit are trying to make cannon fodder out of us." Morton L. Johnson, of the Penny Phone League, discussed a chain letter that was being sent out by the NSL, advocating preparedness: "The workingman's war is against the capitalist. We are working people. All other people are our brothers and sisters." The reading clerk explained that the NSL campaign was endorsed by the Illinois Manufacturers' Association.

George Koop, former socialist candidate for Illinois governor, said, "The Schwabs and the Morgans want Uncle Sam to keep the newly-built factories manufacturing war munitions after the European war is ended by purchasing what they produce." Koop asked the audience to purchase copies of that month's *Pearson's Magazine*, which contained an expose of the preparedness campaign by Allan Benson. Captain Wilde, representing Electrical Workers' Union #134, asked for the passage of a resolution instructing the members of the federation not to see *The Battle Cry of Peace*, a propaganda film then running in Chicago. Said Wilde, "It is a suggestive picture full of misrepresentation. Organized labor does not stand for the kind of preparedness it advocates. We want a militia. Let the United States remove that strike clause from the militia law, which makes us shoot down our striking brother workers, and they will get 3,000,000 recruits."

Victor Olander, secretary of the Illinois Federation of Labor, noted that England was then training its young men physically to send them to war and that they "are stunted and dwarfed from industrial slavery." He added, "Why doesn't the Nat'l Security League and the Navy League take warning from the war in Europe? Why don't they say it is unpatriotic to work men to death in unhealthy occupations? That would be real preparedness."[15]

On November 24, 1915, Hudson Maxim delivered an address before the committee of 100 appointed to represent the NSL in St. Louis, and advocated for an increased military. On November 26 the following ad appeared in St. Louis papers: "The Maxim Munitions Corporation was formed to take over the important inventions of Hudson Maxim in aerial torpedoes, bomb-throwing devices, aeroplane guns, improvements in range-finding guns, position indicators to show constantly the geological position of submarines and other vessels, improvements in periscopes and many others. Further details in this space tomorrow. Full details on application." That was the $10 million Maxim Munitions Corporation, two days after the appearance of Hudson Maxim before the Business Men's League and about 10 days after the appointment by St. Louis Mayor Kiel of a committee of 100 to prepare a plan whereby the U.S. Congress might be influenced in its army and navy program; that ad caused much comment among members of the committee.

A canvass of members of Kiel's committee of 100 drawing their attention to those events was conducted. One of them, John H. Gundlach, declared that if the activities of the NSL, the appearance by Maxim and the appearance of the ad could be connected, then "it is treasonable." One man who refused appointment to the group of 100, because he was too busy, Henry S. Caulfield, said, "When any man connected with the manufacture of munitions declared himself for war, one can not help thinking he has some ulterior motive. I am for adequate national defense, of course, but I believe we ought to confer with some authority who will not profit by war, or who is not connected with the manufacture of munitions of war."[16]

Another article that discussed Maxim in St. Louis noted that, "He spoke in Saint Louis Wednesday as a representative of the National Security League. He advocated a navy as large as any in the world, and spoke with approval of Uncle Sam's 'matching dollars with any other nation as long as they want to play the game.'" And then on the Friday the morning papers carried the ad for Maxim Munitions Corporation. The piece then declared, "In the light of this advertisement we have no difficulty in understanding Mr. Maxim's buoyant optimism with respect to Uncle Sam's dollar-matching operations in the naval field.... It is not only an eye-opener, but it indicates that the 'Republic' is seeing more clearly than it did the real force behind preparedness." Concluded the article, "It ought to open the eyes of everybody. Who is so blind that he can not see the active special interest behind the propaganda for preparedness? Match dollars? Yes, the manufacturers of munitions will advocate this international gambling game just as long as they can spend Uncle Sam's dollars, but why should anyone else advocate it."[17]

Another editorial against the League and its programs appeared in a Missouri paper in December 1915. "A crowd of one-horse statesmen, near maniacs and general nuisances, dubbing themselves the National Security League, are storming every city in the United States, prating abut preparedness." If America stayed out of World War I, and it looked like it would, that meant to the editor that it would be a long time before big armies and navies would be needed again. There was no danger from Germany (often cited by the NSL as one of the foreign powers ready to invade American shores) as it was then at war itself, and depleted as then were all the combatants. "When there was a real danger, the United States maintained virtually no standing army. But now that the danger has been obliterated, it is going insane about militarism," fumed the editor. "An adequate army and navy are essential to the welfare of this or any other nation, but a fanatical desire to have the greatest army and navy in the world is neither profitable nor necessary." He felt that it was a contest like that which had precipitated the current war—to the regret of all the participants.[18]

When the National Security League offered a prize of $250 for the best essay on the topic of preparedness one editor was moved to comment, "In every conceivable way the preparedness propaganda is playing for publicity. There was never anything plainer than that there is a deal of commercialism behind and underneath this 'patriotic' movement."[19]

Arthur Capper was the governor of Kansas and the owner of some area newspapers, including *Topeka Capital*, the *Oklahoma Farmer* and others. In February 1916 he had a broadside fired at him by Col. William Conant Church (an NSL member). Church wrote to Capper

Hudson Maxim, 1916. A member of the NSL, he gave speeches urging increased militarism and the need for munitions production to be done in private factories and not in government facilities. Never mentioned when Maxim made such pronouncements was that Maxim owned a munitions factory.

and asked him to explain what authority he had for the following statement that appeared in an article over his name, printed in a New York weekly periodical: "We have quite apparently a well organized propaganda systematically and cruelly promoting this war hysteria in the United States. Manufacturers who see fat contracts looming ahead of them are deliberately playing upon the imaginations of the excitable and the fears of the timid. In order to stampede the nation into a campaign of extravagant expenditures, regardless of all other consequences." According to this article not a word was heard from Capper in response to Church's comments and "In his string of papers which keep him in touch with the rural voters of the middle West the challenge was not printed." After waiting for 17 days for a response from Capper, and not receiving one, Church printed his letter publicly "with a report by certified accountants showing for his enlightenment that the National Security League is not indebted to ammunition makers for its publicity fund" and went on to characterize Capper's charges as "a fair sample of the unfair, if not to say dishonest, methods pursued by those who seek to discredit patriotic efforts to arouse this country to prepare for defense."[20]

In an editorial from April 1916 it was noted that the publication had received a batch of tracts from the "Preparedness Headquarters." The editor refrained from commenting on the local committee of the NSL but said, "it is, however, fair to say that his is decidedly not a workingman's movement. It is a rich man's movement. The preparedness propaganda is being urged in this locality by the 'upper crust,' the folks who have an inborn contempt for democracy. Moreover, the gospel they preach is the gospel of suspicion, and fear, and hate. These people ought to be quarantined. Their ugly thoughts are worse than yellow fever or smallpox." He added, "Working people should avow that these rich organizers of fear and hate should pay by heavy income and inheritance taxes every penny of the cost of preparedness."[21]

Another editorial that same month started by declaring, "All workmen, particularly those who are members of organized labor, should stay as far away from the preparedness program of the National Security League as possible.... Do not be misled by the red-fire and brass bands, which are paid for by the enemies of organized labor." The NSL, and the other such organizations, circularize and call on a merchant or a workingman in an effort to get him to join the league; "they make a strong appeal to his patriotism on the ground that the money is necessary to support a lobby at Washington, D.C., in opposition to the efforts being made by Andrew Carnegie and Henry Ford, whom it is alleged are spending a great deal on money in the interests of peace, and the two mouthpieces of this organization are Wm. Jennings Bryan and Wm. Howard Taft...."

Another hint about a usually unmentioned aspect of the NSL agenda was the comment in an article attributed to William Cooper Procter, described as a capitalist and son of a rich father, who said, "The time will soon come when we will have to fight for our property." Henry T. Hunt, former mayor of Cincinnati, said of the National Security League, "It is undoubtedly true that dangers menace this republic and that preparation to meet them is urgent. These dangers are not only external, but internal, the fierce class antagonism which seems about to convulse our country, the ever widening gulf between the industrial workers and the business element." Hunt added, "The propertied class fear the growing strength and increasing bitterness of the industrial classes. They also fear the possible destruction of their property and ruin of their business, which would result from a German or Japanese invasion."

In regard to schemes such as those urged by the NSL, Samuel Gompers, president of the American Federation on Labor, stated that those plans "are organized by capitalists, in order to place their kind in command and force the working class to serve under them." Then Gompers said, "The workingman should repudiate preparedness unless given equal leadership and equal opportunity.... Organized labor has refused to endorse or subscribe to any scheme like the National Security League, unless equal opportunity for leadership, equal opportunity for education and prohibition of the use of the militia in strikes [are instituted], and these apply equally to the working classes in general."[22]

In April 1916 a full page article appeared in various newspaper; it was all text, with automobile magnate Henry Ford listed as the author. Nothing else was on the page except his text and it appeared in a number of newspapers besides this one; others including the *Evening Star* (Washington, on April 17), the *Washington Times* and the *El Paso Herald*. It was obviously a paid advertisement placed by Ford but was not identified as such. It was titled "Humanity—and Sanity" and stated, "For months the people of the United States have had fear pounded into their brains by magazines, newspapers and motion pictures. No enemy has been pointed out. All the wild cry for the spending of billions, the piling up of armament and the saddling of the country with a military caste has been based on nothing but fiction."

Ford then used many quotes, largely from various military men, as to the strength and efficiency of the U.S. military. "If there is no fear the preparedness proposition now before Congress for a vast army and a vaster navy will not become law. But to escape the burden of billions of taxes, an armed aristocracy, and ultimate subjection to the munitions makers and their financial allies backed up by a great army, the people must act. They must write to their congressmen, to their senators, to the president." Troops were then in Mexico, against Villa, Ford noted. After the order to get Villa it took them only a week to get started. The expedition into Mexico was police work, "But the president himself has discovered a capitalistic plot to bring us into actual war with Mexico."

Ford then derided the film *The Battle Cry of Peace* by Hudson Maxim, who was in the film himself. In Ford's opinion the purpose of that movie was to create more fear for the nation: "Now, Mr. Maxim was merely advertising his wares and playing on your fears to make a market for his goods. Mr. Maxim has something to sell—war munitions." Ford finished by remarking that there was then a proposal before Congress for the appropriation of $500 million for a great naval building program. That was first proposed by Robert M. Thompson, president of the Navy League and chairman of the board of directors of the International Nickel Company.[23]

It was reported in April 1916 that William Cutts, secretary of the NSL, had refused the challenge of George K. Kirkpatrick, candidate of the Socialist Party for U.S. vice-president, to debate the subject of preparedness. In a letter addressed to Albert F. Meissner, secretary of the Montana Socialist

Party, Cutts declared the NSL was not committed to any military program "involving either the regular army or the state militia in strike disturbances or any other purpose than national defense." Cutts believed the National Guard should be federalized and made a part of the regular army. In ending his letter of refusal to debate, Cutts said, "we must decline to furnish the entertainment for your little family gathering at the Auditorium (in Butte, Montana) next week."[24]

Journalist Thomas Levish looked at the influences behind the preparedness movement in a June 1916 article. He saw several different influences pushing the movement forward; firstly, "The manufacturers of munitions of warfare, who were behind the founding of the Navy League and National Security League and similar organizations who foresee a tremendous loss in profits after the European war unless the U.S. takes up the preparedness craze." A second group were the "professional militarists," officers of the army and navy who always wanted more. His third group was "The big exporters of American products, that is, big business in general, who want a powerful army and navy to back them up in the aggressive policy they are pursuing to seize the world's markets temporarily abandoned by the belligerent nations." The fourth group were "The employers of labor, who desire a large army to quell 'dangers from within,' i.e., strikes by workingmen struggling for higher wages and better living conditions."

The fifth group were those who saw in the widespread industrial disturbances an "omen of danger to vested interests and who think a war would be the surest means of uniting Americans of all classes and preventing a possible revolution. The latter is a more important factor than you might imagine. Not only was it responsible for the precipitation of the conflict across the seas, but I have been informed by a member of the citizens' training camp at Fort Sheridan, who fought during the Spanish American war, that the unrest of the laborers following the railroad strike of 1894 made the business men seize upon the Manila incident as a means of favoring the 'patriotism' of the unpaid toilers. He frankly admitted that such a course is necessary today to protect the commercial and financial interests of the country."[25]

Later in June, William Jennings Bryan spoke in New York City at Madison Square Garden before a large crowd of teachers at an education conference. He spoke against military training in public schools and the 6,000 teachers at the convention of the National Education Association reportedly applauded noisily. The invitation to Bryan to speak at that convention provoked a response from Menken of the NSL. Menken wrote to the National Education Association, "Mr. Bryan's career is evidence of the fact that he is incapable of hard reasoning or correct thinking." Said Bryan, regarding World War I, "What an idea—is it possible that a country that could not be frightened two years ago by solvent nations filled with able-bodied men should now be frightened by bankrupt nations filled with cripples! ... Shall we convert our nation into an armed camp and our public schools into breeding places for an army?"[26]

In March 1917 a letter from Amos Pinchot, described as a "well known publicist," to Samuel Gompers, president of the American Federation of Labor, was printed. That letter was mindful of the menace to American liberties in the proposed compulsory universal military training. "You take a boy of 18 or 19 when he is just beginning to build the permanent structure of his character; you put him in a uniform and drill him; you make his body automatically obedient to the orders of his officer (generally a member of the privileged class); you subordinate his will and conscience to that of another person...." What you got was "not only unthinking physical obedience to his officer, but unthinking obedience in general to authority, to that of the employer, the boss, the politician, the state...."

Pinchot then discounted any who put forward the argument that here in America the ultimate political power was in the people's hands. That was true in theory "but intelligent people all over the world have come to realize that popular political machinery does not, in fact, mean popular power. The main power in the world is the economic power; and it does not rest either in the hands of the general public, nor in the labor group." And, he added, "In spite of popular government, the moneyed class is, with us, still the governing class.... And the unresting demand for compulsory [military] service, which is filling the country with clamor, comes almost exclusively from this class; and it has a good deal more class interest in it than real patriotism." And: "These men, who are calling for the disciplining of the people through military service, are thinking more of defense of their own investments than of the country's borders."

The NSL, said Pinchot, informed us that universal military service was necessary to defend the nation but "This is pure, unadulterated bunk.... No one knows that better than the Wall Street interests that are behind the campaign for compulsory service." But those interests wanted something that could not be obtained in any way except by forced service, argued Pinchot, "and that is a meek and disciplined labor group that will make no trouble at home, and will fight obediently to defend the American dollar abroad." He declared conscription to be slavery, no matter if the master is a private individual or the state: "conscription is a great commercial policy; a carefully derived weapon that the exploiters are forging for their own protection at home, and in the interest of American financial imperialism abroad."[27]

The idea that the National Security League should be investigated by the United States Congress, along with other such preparedness groups, was first voiced in Washington on December 6, 1915, when the NSL was about one year old. On that day Representative Augustus P. Gardner of Massachusetts introduced a resolution for a "searching investigation" into the members, finances and activities of the Navy League, labor's National Council, the American Defense Society, and the National Security League. The resolution was referred to the Committee on Rules.[28]

One month later Representative Hensley of Missouri, a member of the House Naval Committee and of the opposition to the proposed naval increases, introduced a resolution for an investigation of organizations active for and against preparedness, including the four listed above. His proposed investigation included an inquiry into what, if any, interest members of such organizations had in the manufacture or sale of munitions.[29]

Gardner and Hensley and Representative Tavenner of Illinois appeared before the House Committee on Rules on January 19, 1916, to urge an investigation of various preparedness and anti-preparedness organizations of the United States, based on resolutions filed by Gardner and Hensley. The purpose was to find out who were behind the four previously named groups and to find out if any of the individuals involved had any connection with firms engaged in the traffic of munitions. The public, the representatives felt, had a right to know about any and all vested interests.[30]

Part II

Patriotism, 1917 (April 6)– 1918 (November 10)

CHAPTER 8

The Organization

With the formal entrance of the United States into World War I, the need for the never ending rhetoric from the NSL on the question of preparedness came to an end; only rarely was it mentioned again.

Very quickly the League switched from a drum beat of preparedness to a drum beat of patriotism, loyalty. One of the first things the League did was to organize a major new committee, the Committee on Patriotism through Education. Also, the group incorporated women to a greater extent, allowing them to become regular members, for the first time. However, female participation remained little more than token. Trade union people and other labor representatives remained virtually nonexistent. The NSL's idea of having "labor representation" in the League was to hire famed attorney Clarence Darrow, who sometimes defended labor people in court cases. However, he was hired to help remove a big city mayor who advocated nothing except to allow the practice of free speech for a group the NSL did not like and wished to muzzle.

On May 18, 1917, the National Security League announced that when Brigadier General John J. Pershing, who was expected to command the first U.S. expeditionary force in Europe, went to France he would do so as a member of the NSL. Pershing had just become a life member and, said the report, "is one of a long list of men and women prominent in many walks of life who have joined this great national defense organization during the last few days." Reportedly, "The league does not attempt to account for the recent important additions to its membership.... It is assumed that the emphatic non-political and non-partisan stand taken by the league in its recent activities is responsible."[1]

Vacancies in the NSL Executive Committee were filled by the election of the following: Professor Robert M. McElroy (Princeton University), Professor Thomas F. Moran (Purdue), Professor Henry W. Farnam (Yale), Menton B. Metcalf (Orange, NJ), J.G. White, Franklin Remington and George Hornblower (New York City), according to a League announcement on August 15, 1917. As part of that announcement it was also revealed

Chapter 8. The Organization 109

Major General John J. Pershing, 1921. Just before he left America to lead the first expeditionary forces to Europe it was announced that Pershing had become a life member of the NSL. He was one of many prominent people to join the League; the NSL was always quick to publicize any and all such high profile recruitments.

that steps were being taken by the NSL Executive Committee to remove Chicago Mayor William Hale Thompson from the executive board of the NSL Chicago branch because of his "pacifist activities."[2]

About one week later it was reported that Thompson was to be ousted from the Chicago branch on August 23 because of his "anti-American attitude." The National Security League's board apparently wanted to know how he got on the local board in the first place. H.H. Merrick, president of the Chicago NSL branch, said that Thompson "was made an ex-officio member of the local executive board merely as a courtesy which the society thought due the mayor of Chicago. He never has attended a meeting and has had nothing to do in any way with the affairs of the league."[3]

A report from Chicago on August 29 confirmed that Mayor Thompson was not re-elected as a member of the general committee of the NSL Chicago branch, when officials of the local organization were chosen on the 28th. Said H.H. Merrick, "The nominating committee did not include Mr. Thompson's name, because it was considered that the war policies he has expressed are not in accord with the policies of the National Security League."[4]

An indication of the "crimes" of Thompson could perhaps be seen in a report from Chicago early in September. With respect to the meeting of the Council for Democracy and Peace held under "orders" from Mayor Thompson before Lowden could get troops to Chicago to prevent the meeting, Illinois Governor Frank O. Lowden said, "The time has come to find out who are for the government and who are against it." A furious Lowden condemned that meeting. Apparently Thompson's felony was to come out in favor of free speech and freedom of assembly.[5]

The ouster from the League was not enough punishment for Thompson. On the night of September 4 the Mayor was hanged in effigy in Chicago on a downtown corner of Michigan Avenue. The scarecrow effigy dangled from a lamp post for about 20 minutes before a policeman cut it down.

Earlier in the day the NSL was pushing its demand that Thompson be indicted on grounds of "palpable omission of duty and malfeasance in office." Declared an NSL resolution, "In our opinion he is a disloyal citizen. In his words and actions since the outbreak of the war, he has adhered to the enemies of his country, giving them aid and comfort."[6]

A day later an editorial in a major New York City newspaper jumped on board and condemned Thompson. "There are times that try men's souls. There are also persons who have the same effect. The Mayor of Chicago didn't have to be one of them. But he

Chicago Mayor William Hale Thompson, September 1917. He drew the wrath of the NSL when he was willing to allow a group to hold a meeting in his city; it was a group the League did not agree with. That so angered the group that it tried, unsuccessfully, to have Thompson removed from office or indicted for something or other.

chose to be," fumed the editor, and "therefore good Americans will not be inclined to overblame anyone else for the consequences." This was to be, the editor added, a "stern epoch for citizens of the United States holding responsible public office who flaunt deliberate disloyalty in the face of City, State or Nation."[7]

Some members of the National Security League were, on the surface, unlikely soul mates with the League. One of those was attorney Clarence Darrow. On September 11 it was reported that Darrow "today is a member of the NSL" and that he was "appointed for the purpose of devising means to oust Mayor William Hale Thompson from office." Darrow was appointed, according to Chicago NSL executive Merrick, so that the local committee could have the benefit of his legal advice "and also to afford the labor movement, of which Darrow is one of the leading protagonists, representation in the organization."[8]

A patriotic rally was held in Chicago on September 14 by the NSL for the announced purpose of vindicating Chicago of alleged lack of patriotism. While Thompson was not mentioned by name he was clearly one of the targets. Keynote speaker was Elihu Root (former U.S. Secretary of State): "The men who are speaking, and writing and printing arguments against the war and against everything that is being done to carry on the war.... It is impossible to resist the conclusion that the greater part of them are at heart traitors to the United States." Samuel Gompers also addressed the rally. Judge Jacob M. Dickinson (an NSL member) presided as chairman. One day after that meeting, Elihu Root accepted the honorary presidency of the National Security League. Alton B. Parker remained honorary vice-president. Root succeeded Choate, who had been honorary president of the organization from its birth in December 1914 until his death in May 1916. Reportedly the League then had more than 100,000 members in 280 branches.[9]

A landmark moment was reached by the National Security League on November 19, 1917, when, for the first time since its beginning, at a meeting of the group's executive committee in New York City two women were elected to membership: Mrs. Thomas J. Preston, Jr. (formerly Mrs. Grover Cleveland), and Miss Maude Wetmore (daughter of former U.S. Senator from Rhode Island George Wetmore), head of the National League for Women's Service—itself an NSL organization, a sort of woman's auxiliary.[10]

Although the NSL's next annual convention was not to take place until February 21–23, 1918, in Chicago at which, according to an announcement, "100,000 men and women will be present at the sessions representing all sections of the country," the formal invitations had already been sent out, as of early November 1917. That meeting was to be "a congress of national service" and to be held at the La Salle Hotel in Chicago and at a number of other venues in the city. Invitations to that event were signed by the

Clarence Darrow, 1915. Famed attorney Darrow was widely seen as a labor proponent. The NSL hired him to assist the organization in its attempts to oust Mayor Thompson. Also, the League believed that by associating with Darrow it would give the labor movement "representation" in the NSL.

following: Theodore Roosevelt, William Howard Taft, Samuel Gompers, Jacob M. Dickinson, Judson Harmon, Dr. John Grier Hibben, Dr. Edmund J. James, Dr. Harry Pratt Judson, Governor McCall (Massachusetts), Samuel Mather, E.T. Meredith, John Purroy Mitchel, Mrs. Phillip North Moore, E.W. Nichols, Dr. Frank Mason North, Charles Edward Russell, Mrs.

Cordenio A. Severance, Dr. Anna Howard Shaw, Philip B. Stewart, Frank S. Streeter, Booth Tarkington, H. St. George Tucker, Festus J. Wade, Henry Watterson, Miss Maude Wetmore, H.A. Wheeler and Luke E. Wright.[11]

In a newspaper section called "Queries and Answers," one person asked about the NSL, its objectives and so forth. The NSL was said to be a "non-political, non-partisan league of American men and women" that had two purposes. One was to arouse the American people to a sense of United States naval and military weakness and of the national menace that such weakness involved. The other was to secure, through the power of public sentiment, such measures of preparation as would ensure the nation against attempted invasion "and enable it to enforce its rights and make its flag respected in every quarter of the civilized world. The league is also doing effective work in promoting patriotic education and universal military training and service." According to this piece, qualifications for membership were "American citizenship and a belief in the principles of the league." Membership costs were $1 a year for ordinary membership; $5 a year for contributing membership; $25 for life membership; $100 for "founder" status; and over $100 for "donor" status. Headquarters of the group remained at 31 Pine Street, New York City. The officers, as of November 1917, were honorary president Elihu Root (NYC), honorary vice-president Alton B. Parker (NYC), president S. Stanwood Menken (NYC), vice-presidents George Wharton Pepper (Philadelphia), George Von L. Meyer (Boston), Willet M. Spooner (Milwaukee), Luke E. Wright (Memphis), Frederic L. Huidekoper (Washington), Franklin Q. Brown (NYC), secretary Herbert Barry (NYC), and executive secretary Henry L. West (NYC).[12]

On January 1, 1918, a journalist who described the National Security League as "a pioneer organization in preparedness" was then at its new, and considerably larger, headquarters in New York City. It had been moved from 31 Pine Street (its home from its formation in December 1914) to 19 West 44th Street.[13]

Bringing more women into the organization, although always in a secondary and subordinate way, the NSL announced in February a new committee and the wives of four former presidents of the United States were members of that new committee. The first appearance of that committee was slated for later that month at the League's annual convention called the Congress of National Service, February 21–23 in Chicago. That committee had pledged itself "to conserve the food supply, to invest their money in liberty bonds and to inspire in every patriotic way the efficient service of the men who are fighting for them." Among the speakers at that February Congress were to be Elihu Root, James W. Gerard, former Presidents William Howard Taft and Theodore Roosevelt, and U.S. Secretary of the Interior Franklin K. Lane. The four wives of former presidents on the committee were Mrs. Thomas J. Preston, Jr., Mrs. James Garfield, Mrs. Theodore Roosevelt and Mrs. William Howard Taft. Mrs. Preston, widow of Grover Cleveland, was not only a member of the NSL's executive committee; she was also secretary of the Committee on Patriotism Through Education. She said, "I am happy in accepting this opportunity to work with the league. I can think of no way in which I could more surely contribute my share to the present needs of our country than by joining in the very important work which the bureau has undertaken." Miss Susanna Cocroft was the chair of the new woman's committee of the NSL and she presided at a meeting of the Chicago branch where plans for a loyalty meeting for women of all nationalities in Chicago were discussed; it was to be held in connection with the coming Congress later in February.[14]

A report released in May 1918 purported to show the activities of the National Security League during the previous year. A total of 20 million pamphlets had been distributed, in various languages. The *Bulletin* of the League was said to be read by 12 million readers. As well, more than a million signatures had been obtained from citizens in support of universal military training and 44 United States Senators along with 174 United States Representatives and 467 mayors of American communities were said to have been enrolled in support of universal military training.[15]

A report released in July 1918 gave a few lines about Charles E. Lydecker becoming the new president of the National Security League. It did not mention that S. Stanwood Menken had been forced out nor give any reason why the League had undergone such a sudden change in the top leadership post in the organization.[16]

According to one brief report on the League, much of the success of the organization in instilling throughout the United States the principles of preparedness and action in the war was due to E.L. Harvey, publicity director of the NSL: "He has spread the fame of the organization over the world."[17]

The most comprehensive listing of NSL officers appeared in the press in October 1918. Honorary president, Elihu Root (NYC); honorary vice-president, Alton B. Parker (NYC); president, Charles E. Lydecker (NYC); founder and former president, S. Stanwood Menken (NYC); vice-presidents, George Wharton Pepper (Philadelphia); Willet M. Spooner (Milwaukee); Luke E. Wright (Memphis); James W. Gerard (NYC), Myron T. Herrick (Cleveland); secretary, Franklin Remington (NYC); treasurer, A.J. Hemphill (NYC); directors, Franklin Q. Brown (NYC); H.H. Chamberlin (Worcester); C. Willing Hare (Philadelphia); Hayden B. Harris (NYC); Herbert Barry (NYC); Lawrence F. Abbott (NYC); Edward H. Clark (NYC and San Francisco); chairman, Congressional Committee, Charles D. Orth (NYC); Executive Committee, Lawrence F. Abbott (NYC); Dr. Ephraim D. Adams; Leland Stanford, Jr.; John G. Agar (NYC); Robert Bacon (NYC);

C.A. Bill (NYC); George M. Brown (St. Louis); H.H. Chamberlin (Worcester); Frederic R. Coudert (NYC); John Davis (Dallas); William S. Ellis (Philadelphia); Dr. Henry W. Farnam (Yale University); Alexander Fitzhugh (Des Moines); D.J. Haff (KC, MO); Edward Harding (NYC); C. William Hare (Philadelphia); Hayden B. Harris (NYC); Dr. Albert Bushnell Hart (Harvard University); Alexander J. Hemphill (NYC); Dr. John Grier Hibben (Princeton NJ); Dr. William H. Hobbs (U. of Michigan); Dr. Robert H. McElroy (Princeton U.); Cyrus H. McCormick (Chicago); H.H. Merrick (Chicago); R. Walton Moore (Fairfax CT); Guy Murchie (Boston); Herbert Myrick (Springfield MA); Charles P. Neill (Washington); John M. Parker (New Orleans); Mrs. Thomas J. Preston Jr. (Princeton NJ); W.E. Remington (Ridgewood NJ); Dr. William T. Sedgwick (MIT); Lewis B. Stillwell (NYC); Frank S. Streeter (Concord); Lloyd Taylor (NYC); August H. Vogel (Milwaukee); Dr. Claude H. Van Tyne (U. of Michigan); G. Creighton Webb (NYC); Miss Maude Wetmore (NYC); William H. Wiley (NYC); Lafayette Young (Des Moines).[18]

Within a few days of the end of World War I, Mrs. Thomas J. Preston, Jr., was reported to have assumed charge of the 2,000 volunteer patriotic speakers in all parts of the nation as director of the National Security League's Speakers' Bureau. She succeeded her husband, Dr. Thomas Preston, Jr., who resigned to become dean of the New York Homeopathic Medical College and Flower Hospital.[19]

CHAPTER 9

The Politicians

At the start of 1918, the NSL announced its plan for the election coming in November to "combat the various disturbing elements which threaten the preservation of a loyal war-congress." The League declared it was ready to carry the fight into every state of the union where action was necessary. Especially worrying to the NSL were several items: the National Nonpartisan League; the formal announcement that the national Socialist Party was about to undertake the raising of a one million dollar fund to finance the campaign of Socialist Congressional candidates; and the announced Congressional candidacy of Socialist Morris Hillquit, who polled an "enormous vote" in the recent New York City mayoral race "on a frankly anti-war platform." According to the NSL, "The well intentioned, but poorly informed farmers and laboring men of the country who are giving ear to the communistic program laid down by the organizers of the Nonpartisan League must not forget that it was this organization which held the meeting in St. Paul at which [U.S.] Senator La Follette [WI] made his notorious speech." The NSL reported that the Nonpartisan League claimed a membership of one million voters and were striving to enroll five million more before the coming summer.[1]

The League planned to start its campaign in Wisconsin because the "loyal" citizens of the state had organized the Wisconsin Loyalty League with 65,000 members and were fighting the anti-war elements. August H. Vogel was the leader of the Chicago NSL branch with Willet M. Spooner (son of former U.S. Senator John Spooner of Wisconsin) as a member. That Chicago NSL branch was cooperating with the Loyalty League. Its chief activity was to cover Wisconsin with speakers who explained "the real meanings of the war and the necessity for its efficient and aggressive prosecution" and revealed that "It has not been unusual for these speakers to be booed down by the audiences they have faced." That was a rare moment of candor with respect to the reception that sometimes greeted the League and its spokespeople. This seemed to have been the start of the National Security League's campaign against politicians that it did not like.

The campaign would intensify as the 1918 election drew closer in time. It was a campaign by the League, of naming and shaming, browbeating and bullying, and spending money to undermine the campaigns of those politicians.²

Some politicians drew praise from the NSL. On January 19 the League paid tribute to U.S. Senator George E. Chamberlain (OR) and U.S. Representative Julius Kahn (CA), referring to their efforts in Congress in the interest of national defense. They were strong advocates of universal military training. Chamberlain waxed eloquently about conscription asserting that "we take from all the walks of industrial, commercial and every day life young men of all classes, so that there is not the horizontal loss that I speak of [in volunteer enlistment], but neither a perpendicular loss, where the high and the low, the rich and the poor, the professional man and the artisan, stand shoulder to shoulder and when losses come, the loss falls on every social strata of life." Representative Kahn went on to denounce pacifists by declaring, "The strong arm of the government should reach out and get these people. A few prompt trials and a few quick hangings, would prove most salutary at this time."³

Morris Hillquit, between 1910 and 1915. Socialist Hillquit was one of many politicians of any stripe, not just Socialists, who were targeted by the NSL in the 1918 Congressional elections.

An editorial about the NSL's praising of Chamberlain and Kahn observed that both of those politicians advocated UMT in time of peace and the requiring of every male to register at 18 years of age and have at least one year's training. Kahn pointed out what the training in the volunteer camps for civilian had already accomplished "in the way of making rugged, virile men" and made it evident that a bill providing for this training would be placed before Congress. Former U.S. President Theodore Roosevelt was present at the luncheon honoring Chamberlain and Kahn and he urged the nation to stand behind those two in their efforts to bring about universal military training.[4]

Toward the end of January Senator Chamberlain delivered another of his militaristic screeds in the Senate. That caused an editor to comment, "It seems to have been more a case of swollen head with the Oregon senator than anything else, due probably to Teddy's [Roosevelt] encouragement coupled with the attention received from these hair-brained [sic] fanatics who compose the so-called National Security League...."[5]

George Creel served as head of the United States Committee on Public Information, a propaganda organization created by President Woodrow Wilson during the war. He generated a storm of controversy when he remarked, "I will be proud to my dying day that my country was inadequately prepared when it entered the conflict." He meant that to have been prepared for war before actually entering it and reaching out with one hand to attempt to reach a peace deal would have given "the lie to such attempts as being real." Creel's remarks were taken up by the NSL executive committee at one of its weekly meetings in New York City, in April. Not only was Creel personally censured by several members of the committee, but after discussion it was decided to ask Congress to abolish the entire Committee on Public Information as then constituted. A resolution was passed to that effect by the organization.[6]

Early in May 1918 the League announced it would be throwing all of its effort into the coming Congressional elections with the purpose of seeing that victory in those elections would go only to those who "can be relied upon to support a continuing policy of adequate naval and military preparedness." According to the NSL it had discovered "not only apathy and opposition to the war, but the existence of an alarming inclination by many people toward an inconclusive peace." And, it continued, "The menace to the Administration's aggressive prosecution of the war, due to this condition, is so great that unusual measures must be taken to ensure the election this fall of a Congress that will stand militarily behind the carrying of the war to a decisive victory. The league will begin its activities with a tabulation of the records of all the present members of Congress in their relation to the more important preparedness and war measures."

In preparing its table, the National Security League announced, it would go back six years, listing the votes cast by the Senators and Representatives. Wherever the result would indicate a "reasonable probability"

Chapter 9. The Politicians

that the attitude of a member could not be relied upon "with certainty," the NSL would call the matter to the attention of the national committees of the Republican and Democratic parties and would take "such other steps as may be deemed effective to prevent the renomination, or if renominated, the re-election of such members."[7]

Active participation in the upcoming 1918 Congressional election campaign by the National Security League was to commence shortly throughout the county, the League announced in June of that year. The NSL declared, "unusual measures must be taken to insure the election this fall of a Congress which will stand militantly behind the carrying of the war to a decisive victory." The entire force of the organization's 281 branches and its membership of over 100,000 "patriotic American citizens" would be thrown into that campaign. Creation of support of the movement outside of the League would also be undertaken by means of active propaganda among the leading citizens of every state in the Union, "irrespective of party."

That intense campaign was decided upon by the League's executive committee at a meeting attended by Alton B. Parker, James W. Gerard, S. Stanwood Menken, Lawrence F. Abbott (of the *Outlook* publication), "and other prominent men." Reportedly, the leading newspapers of the nation were expressing their approval and the piece then printed a brief supporting quote from each of five newspapers. A committee led by Charles D. Orth, "a prominent New York commission merchant," was to lead the campaign. As a preliminary step that committee had laid the matter before 25,000 "leading citizens" in all parts of the country, in a letter. In part that letter said that the NSL was "asking you to pledge your service for prompt action to prevent disaster which might follow the election of incompetent or disloyal men to Congress…. The remedy is for everyone to assume the personal obligation of speaking with or writing without delay to political leaders, newspaper men and others who form public opinion in their Congressional Districts."[8]

The Congressional records of the United States Senators and Representatives who returned to Washington on July 5, 1918, after celebrating the Fourth of July in New York City as the guests of William Randolph Hearst were looked into on July 6 by the National Security League. How they voted on the question of preparedness, which was the one issue on which the League came closest to agreeing with Hearst and their stand on other war measures, was revealed in a report prepared by the Congressional Committee of the NSL. Hearst and his newspapers were regarded as enemies by the League as it felt the Hearst-owned papers did not agree with the militaristic stance of the organization.

Charles D. Orth, chairman of that Congressional Committee, issued the following statement: "The National Security League is engaged in a country-wide endeavor to create a demand on the part of the people for the nominations at the coming primaries as candidates for Congress men of high character, who possess coordinated vision, judgment, ability and statesmanship." He added, "The presence in New York as the guests of Mr. Hearst invited an examination of the records of these gentlemen to see how nearly they conform to the standard which the league has ventured to suggest to the people for the United States, who are directly responsible for the selection of the men who are to administer the legislative branch of the government."

Work of the League before America entered World War I was largely confined to the issue of preparedness. In that connection a pamphlet was published in July 1916 and gave a tabulation of the way members of Congress had voted on the various preparedness legislation which came before it. Those issues were as follows: (1) The Kahn amendment to the Hay bill to increase the size of the regular army; (2) Brandegee amendment to the Hay-Chamberlain army bill for a U.S. army of 250,000 instead of 140,000; (3) Chamberlain "Section 56" providing for a volunteer reserve army under federal control; (4) A motion to recommit a naval appropriation bill instructing an increase in the navy.

Twelve of the 40 men who went to New York City were not members of the 64th Congress, before whom those four measures came. Of the remaining 28 legislators, 25 voted against and three in favor on the first, second and fourth of the above measures. On the third measure 26 of the legislators voted against and two voted in favor. Concluded the NSL, "It is a lamentable fact that only one of the gentlemen voted right on every measure of preparedness and war which came before him. The judgment of what was right and what was wrong is the public opinion of the people of the United States, and not the judgment of the National Security League."[9]

A couple of days later the NSL appealed to voters to make loyalty and not partisan politics their guide in the upcoming 1918 Congressional elections. According to the League's analysis a close vote was expected in 164 Congressional districts and in 14 of the 32 states that would be electing senators. Results of the primaries in Arkansas, Florida, Indiana, Iowa, Maine, Minnesota, North Carolina, North Dakota, Oregon, Pennsylvania, South Dakota, and Utah were not regarded as hopeful by the NSL's Charles D. Orth. Said Orth, "A survey of the candidates selected by these states reveals that neither the political managers nor the people have risen to their manifest duty. If prompt action and decisive action is taken now it is not too late to influence the selection of candidates in many states whose primaries do not take place until August or September."[10]

Oscar S. Straus, chairman of the Public Service Commission,

expressed a willingness to run for Congress if he could have the endorsement of both parties; that is, if he could become a fusion candidate. In the interest of the candidacy of Straus, Orth wrote to Charles F. Murphy of Tammany Hall (the Democratic machine) and Samuel S. Koenig, chairman of the Republican County Committee, and suggested that the two parties combine upon the nomination of Straus to defeat Meyer London (the Socialist Party candidate) in New York City's 12th Congressional District. However, Orth was forced to report that those two men had "completely ignored his suggestion." Earlier, on June 6, the National Security League sent a letter to about 15,000 "prominent men" all over the United States suggesting fusion nominations. Straus said he was willing to run if he was nominated by both parties or if he was nominated by one party and endorsed by the other. In the last election in the 12th District the Socialist candidate (London) had received 6,103 votes; the Democratic candidate got 5,763 votes and the Republican candidate received 968 votes.[11]

Orth and his NSL's Congressional Campaign Committee continued to express worry during the month of July. In the opinion of Orth and his committee unless there was a Democrat/Republican fusion in five New York City Congressional districts in the November 1918 election, the Socialist Party was likely to elect five Representatives from that city. According to Orth, the Socialists stood a good chance to carry the 10th, 13th, and 14th districts and were almost sure to carry the 12th and 20th districts. In the 1916 election the 10th, 14th, and 20th elected Republicans; the 13th elected a Democrat and the 12th elected an "anti-war" Socialist (London). Said Orth, "All men and women in greater New York and particularly in the districts in question, owe no greater or more imperative duty than to write at once to their political leaders and to the newspapers, demanding that coalition candidates be agreed upon...."[12]

The League's fusion efforts focused specifically on defeating London and also Morris Hillquit, also in New York City. In the NSL letter, signed by Orth, to the Democratic and Republican parties in New York City, the League wrote, "The National Security League does not feel that in having suggested fusion in these districts its duty is wholly discharged. If it appears to you that the help of the league can be used in assisting the election in these districts of the fusion candidates I will be very glad to request the authority of the executive committee to extend such assistance, which would be in the form of distributing literature and utilizing the services of the league's large corps of speakers."[13]

August 1918 saw the National Security League release ratings of 347 men who sat in both the 64th and 65th sessions of the United States House of Representatives. The League discovered that only 47 of those men "proved themselves" 100 percent "right" in their votes in the House on eight tests; which the NSL described as "critical" preparedness and loyalty measures that were voted on in the House preceding and following America's entry into World War I. Those were the conclusions drawn by the NSL from a chart that it issued on August 4 "for the future guidance of patriotic voters." The 64th session ran from March 4, 1915, to March 4, 1917, during the 3rd and 4th years of Woodrow Wilson's presidency; the 65th session ran from March 4, 1917, to March 4, 1919, during the 5th and 6th years of his presidency.

U.S. Representative Meyer London (NYC) was one of only seven men who, in the eyes of the NSL, failed to back up the wartime interests of the United States on any of the eight measures; that is, they voted "wrong" on all eight measures. The other six were Denver S. Church (CA), Benjamin C. Hilliard (CO), A. Jeff McLemore (TX), Adolphus P. Nelson (WI), Edward Keating (CO), and Carl Van Dyke (MN). Of these, only Adolphus Nelson was re-elected; he remained in the House until March 1923. London returned for another term in the House, 1921–1923; while Denver Church returned for another term in 1933–1935. When the NSL analyzed state results it found only Rhode Island had a perfect record of no "wrong" votes. Its three Representatives had each voted "correctly" eight out of eight times. New York State had a 15.11 percent of "wrong" votes cast by its House members. The worst state, from the NSL's perspective, was North Dakota which ran up 79.16 percent wrong votes while Colorado followed closely in second place with 78.12 percent "wrong answers."[14]

The eight measures used to rate the Representatives were as follows: (1) The McLemore resolution of March 7, 1916; this measure was to the effect that American citizens should forgo their national legal and constitutional rights to travel on the high seas. (2) The Kahn amendment to the Hay army bill of March 23, 1916, which sought to increase the regular army to 178,000 or more, approaching the recommendation from the U.S. Army General Staff. (3) The Brandegee amendment to the Hay-Chamberlain army bill of April 18, 1916, which provided for an army of 250,000 as against 140,000. (4) Section 56 of April 18, 1916, providing for a volunteer reserve army wholly under federal control (essentially a federalized National Guard). (5) A motion to recommit naval appropriation bill of June 2, 1916; that effort was designed to secure an increase in the navy beyond that provided in the original bill. (6) The Cooper amendment of March 1, 1917, designed to prohibit to American ships their legal right to carry arms or ammunition in their cargoes. (7) The declaration of war against Germany of April 5, 1917. (8) The Kahn amendment to the conscription act of April 23, 1917, which provided for the raising, by conscription, of the necessary army to give effect to the declaration of war.

The NSL chart rating the Representatives was issued to the nation's voters under the caption, "What are you going to do about it?" In summary, seven of the Representatives voted "wrong" on all eight measures, 22 on seven measures, 30 on six, and 58 "voted wrong" on five of the measures. With respect to those measures, six of them were introduced in the 64th Congress while the other two were brought forward in the 65th Congress.[15]

As a supplement to the above, the National Security League's Congressional Campaign Committee sent to all of the new candidates for the 1918 House elections a questionnaire asking for an expression of their views on the aggressive prosecution of the war by the United States. That query was sent out on August 12, 1918. That questionnaire plus the already released ratings list was said to allow the NSL to supply the voters in every part of the nation with definite information upon the war views of each man seeking election to Congress. That questionnaire inquired as to the candidate's opinion on the entrance of America into the war and whether that opinion had changed since the date that America entered the conflict. It also asked that each candidate state his viewpoint on the prosecution of the war to a conclusive finish and "that he state what qualifications he believes he has, outside questions of loyalty, which entitle him to sit in Congress."[16]

Explanatory material with the questionnaire outlined that the League would compile and publish nationwide the results from the query and went on to threaten that "If replies are not received within a period of time equal to mail-time plus ten days, it will be regarded as a declination to respond, in which case the Committee will send copies of the questionnaire to friends and opponents of the candidate for the purpose of securing the best available data."

Charles Orth, chair of the NSL's Congressional Campaign Committee, declared that it was all nonpartisan and that "The League believes that there are many men in the present Congress who do not measure up to the standard of vision, balanced judgment, sound common sense and broad general experience which proclaim the statesman. Every patriotic citizen should be willing to adjourn politics, and to decide the question of whom he or she will vote for, solely according to the merit of the candidates between whom there is a choice." Orth added, "If the Candidate for Congress in your district is a man who, by his votes or attitude on preparedness or war measures, has acquitted himself badly in the present Congress, it is your duty to vote for his opponent at the polls. In case your former Congressman has made a bad record on preparedness and war measures, but now proclaims himself to be loyal and in favor of a war until victory, it is better to supplant him with a man who has foresight instead of hindsight."[17]

Later in August it was reported that the work of the National Security League in its nationwide campaign to insure the elections of only such men to Congress as had demonstrated their "ability and loyalty" had been endorsed by Theodore Roosevelt and Judge Alton B. Parker. Not stated in the article was the fact that those two men were both NSL members, with Parker holding an executive office.[18]

Still in August, an editorial about the NSL ratings pointed out something that the League had neglected to mention; the editorial identified the party affiliation of the politicians who had been rated. Of the 47 United States Representatives who had voted "correctly" on all eight measures, 43 were Republicans and four were Democrats. Of the 17 Representatives who had voted right on seven measures and wrong one time, 13 were Republicans and four were Democrats. The editor concluded, "The analysis made by the National Security League confirms the statement heretofore made, that the Republicans have been better supporters of the war than the Democrats, and that the voters of the country can best stand by the government by sending Republicans to congress."[19]

In Washington on September 6 U.S. Representative S. Hubert Dent, Jr., of Alabama, chairman of the House Military Affairs Committee, made a speech in the House answering the attacks of the NSL. Declaring that propaganda was being directed against members of Congress "who fail to obey the edicts of this self-constituted National Security League," Dent referred to an editorial in the *Boston Transcript* newspaper of August 22 that denounced him as "an obstruction to the war program" and demanded his resignation as chairman of the House committee. Dent said the editorial in the Massachusetts paper was in line with the propaganda inspired by the NSL and that Dent had voted "wrong" on the League's list. He added that the same propaganda "was being used against other members of congress, both Republicans and Democrats whose course has been in accord with my own." S. Hubert Dent survived the NSL campaign. He served in the House from March 1909 until March 1921.[20]

Apparently some people took those NSL ratings seriously, as they used them as featured parts of their political advertising in the run-up to the November 1918 election. That politicians chose to use such material indicated that the League had a certain amount of power in the political arena, or at least some people seemed to think so. A September 12 political ad placed by Tom Scully, running for re-election as a House member from New Jersey, took up half of a page. That advertisement consisted of the National Security League name at the top of the ad in a prominent position and a copy of the letter the NSL sent to Representative Scully advising him of the rating system for politicians and announcing that he, Scully, had voted "right" often enough to be listed by the organization on what it called "The Roll of Honor." Scully also survived the 1918 election. He served as a member of the House from New Jersey from 1911 to 1921.[21]

Another sitting Representative lashed out at the League in September over its ratings system. Henry A. Barnhart of Indiana spoke in the House of Representatives setting forth his faithfulness and his patriotism. Referring to criticism from the NSL for his pre-war voting record, Barnhart exclaimed: "and for this we are criticized by a New York organization of military extremists, the National Security League, for not voting to amend bills which the war and navy departments considered safe and ample and which bills were signed by the president." Barnhart added, "This autocratic organization went so far in its enthusiasm for Prussianizing the United States with militarism before the war that it condemns me for not being present to vote to change an administration navy bill when I was away from Washington at a hospital at a bedside of my dying wife." Then he went on at some length to justify his past record, and so forth. Such a response, again, might have been indicative of the League's growing influence. Barnhart did not get re-elected and he ended his time in Congress in March 1919.[22]

Toward the end of October the NSL announced it would concentrate its efforts to allow "only 100 per cent Americans to be elected in the campaigns in ninety-four Congressional districts this fall." With regard to those 94 districts the League described 47 of them as being "close" while the other 47 districts had people nominated whose answers to the League's questionnaire "are regarded as unsatisfactory." Plans for an increased effort in those districts included the fact the League would circulate in each of those districts its report card on voting records on the eight measures the organization had deemed important, together with copies of the replies by the nominees of both parties to its loyalty test questionnaire.[23]

Another campaign ad that relied solely on a National Security League endorsement was placed late in October by Representative George M. Bowers of West Virginia. The only text in the ad touted the fact that Bowers made the list of 47 Congressmen who voted "right" all the time, on all eight measures—and thus was named to the NSL's "Roll of Honor." He went on to serve in the U.S. House until March 1923.[24]

A full page ad appeared in an Indiana newspaper at the end of October 1918, that touted not a single candidate but urged readers to elect the entire Indiana Republican slate to the Congress. Notes at the bottom of the ad observed that Republican members of Congress from Indiana received a rating of 75 percent correct voting from the NSL while for the Democrat members of Congress from Indiana the rating was only 26 percent correct voting.[25]

On October 29 the League announced that 17 United States Senators voted for all 10 preparedness and support of the war measures that the NSL was using to rate the senators. Five Senators voted against one measure;

When the "Boys Come Marching Home"

Congressman Geo. M. Bowers

will not have to apologize to them for any votes he has cast in the War Congress.

His name heads the list of the National Security League's "Roll of Honor," composed of the 47 Congressmen who voted RIGHT all of the time.

VOTE TO KEEP HIM ON THE JOB UNTIL IT IS FINISHED

Congressman George Bowers was another politician named to the NSL's "Honor Roll" and was proud enough of that accomplishment to run it as part of his ad campaign, as seen in this October 1918 advertisement. He went on to win re-election in 1918.

seven were against two measures; three voted against three; two senators voted against four; two were against five; one voted against eight measures and one voted against nine measures. Thus, a total of 38 Senators were rated. The ten measures selected by the National Security League were: (1) the Vardaman amendment to the 1914 naval bill; (2) section 56; (3) Brandegee; (4) the Norris amendment deferring until after the war the building of battleships; (5) the Kenyon amendment reducing from 10 to six the number of battleships to be constructed; (6) the navy bill; (7) declaration of war; (8) the 1917 Army bill; (9) the McKellar amendment to raise an army of volunteers before resorting to conscription; (10) the universal military training act. Senator Knute Nelson of Minnesota was the only senator to have voted "right" on all 10 of the measures. The other 16 were perfect in voting "right" on all the issues that came up when they were in attendance; that is, they each voted on a number of measures that totaled less than ten.²⁶

Thomas Scully, seeking reelection as a Representative from New Jersey, placed another ad that was limited solely to the NSL rating chart. In this full page advertisement Scully provided a detailed analysis of how his opponent voted, and found he failed the NSL standard on four measures out of the eight in total.²⁷

Congressman Henry A. Barnhart of Indiana resumed his attack on the NSL at the end of October. "In the first place the National Security League is opposing every candidate for congress who opposed or voted against the passage of measures of congress that would increase the profits of war profiteers." And "the secretary of the league admitted that some of its members are engaged in the manufacturing of war munitions and the secretary himself defines himself as an importer ... it is a well-known fact in Washington that he is an importer of material used in making war munitions." With respect to the League's honorary president Elihu Root, Barnhart declared that the man "made his reputation on telling corporations how far they could go in law evasion, and Alton B. Parker was defeated in his bid for the U.S. presidency by a popular uprising of the great majority of voters opposed to the interests Parker represents."²⁸

Yet another query went out from the NSL to politicians, about one week before the election. It was limited to politicians seeking election in New York State. Replies were received from 63 of them, although the number who received the query

Scott Nearing, 1916. One week before the election in November 1918 the NSL canvassed the candidates seeking election in New York State. Of 63 replies received, the League reported that 57 of them were in favor of the war being prosecuted on NSL terms. It noted that only six replies were equivocal or pacific, all of them from Socialist candidates, one of those being Scott Nearing.

letter was not stated. That query consisted of a single question in which the recipient was asked if he was for "war until Germany, Austria and Turkey concede the claims of the Allies?" Fifty-seven answered in the affirmative, including 27 Republican candidates for Congress in New York State; 25 Democratic candidates there; and five Socialist Party candidates (all in New York City). Only six replies were what the League described as "pacific or equivocal in tone," and all of them were from Socialist candidates, one of them being Scott Nearing. In conclusion the NSL stated, "Many of the other candidates went further in their affirmative answers than was required and pledged themselves to a war for unconditional surrender."[29]

A large advertisement was also placed in the papers by Edward E. Browne, running for re-election as a Republican candidate for the House, from Wisconsin. His ad featured six paragraphs of text, each dealing with a different issue. One was about the League. That ad stated, "The National Security League of New York, that is now under investigation by Congress and charged with using millions of dollars to defeat a majority of the present Congress, assails all but 47 Congressmen." It went on to declare, "Yet 40 per cent of the Congressmen that this League approves of voted against the taxation [increase] bill, one of the great war measures. Does this look as though Loyalty was their real reason? Big business is attempting to select the next Congress and control the taxing power of the Government." Browne was re-elected in 1918 and served in the House until March 1931.[30]

Even men who have never been elected to the House sometimes used the NSL ratings, against an incumbent. An ad for a candidate named Leiby, running to unseat incumbent Representative Benjamin Focht in Pennsylvania, was devoted to the NSL rating of Focht, who had fared poorly in the League's report card. The advertisement asked the reader, "Are you going to be satisfied with hindsight Focht? Roosevelt and Root are against his type. Why not try Leiby?"[31]

One of the stranger ads appeared in a West Virginia newspaper on November 4, 1918, just one day before the election. That ad was also devoted to nothing but the NSL with the reader urged to vote for a Republican because the Democratic incumbent, M.M. Neely, only voted "right" on four of the eight NSL measures. Thus, voters for the First West Virginia District were urged to elect a Republican to the House. What was strange was the fact that the Republican candidate was not named in the ad. Neely was re-elected.[32]

National Security League pressure for fusion candidates seemed to have been successful, at least in New York City. Results from the election showed that all 12 of the Socialist candidates for Congress in Manhattan were defeated, including Meyer London, running for a third term. He was successfully opposed in the 12th District by former Representative

Henry Goldfogle, a fusion candidate. London was first elected to Congress in 1914 and was the first Socialist ever sent to the House of Representative. While he went down to defeat in 1918 he was returned to the House in the 1920 election, but only for one more term. London would defeat Goldfogle in 1920. According to the news account: "In those districts in which the Socialists had a fighting chance, their defeat was insured by a fusion of Republican and Democratic strength arranged by the National Security League." In the 20th District Socialist Morris Hillquit was defeated by Republican incumbent Isaac Siegel, also fusion. In the 14th District Fiorello LaGuardia (fusion) beat Socialist Scott Nearing.[33]

Vote to Re-elect
EDW. E. BROWNE
Republican Candidate for Congress

Prosecution of the War

There is no difference in the attitude of the Republican and Democratic party in the prosecution of the war. Both believe in the vigorous prosecution of the war and the bringing the same to a speedy and successful termination.

From the time of the entry of the United States into the war, April 5th, 1917, I have stood as strongly for every war measure as any Republican or Democrat in Congress. Before that time I either supported the Administration's preparedness program or was for greater preparedness than the Democratic Administration.

The Patrioteer and the Profiteer

There are two by-products of this war;—the Profiteer and the Patrioteer. The Patrioteer is a person who is continually trying to apply the acid test to loyalty. He wants people to think that he is a greater patriot than his neighbor. He exploits his loyalty as a Political, Social and Business asset. He is fast becoming as despised as the profiteer.

National Security League

The National Security League of New York, that is now under investigation by Congress and charged with using millions of dollars to defeat a majority of the present Congressman, assails all but 47 Congressmen. Yet 40 per cent of the Congressmen that this League approves of voted against the taxation bill, one of the great war measures. Does this look as though Loyalty was theirreal reason?

Big business is attempting to select the next Congress and control the taxing power of the Government.

This 1918 campaign ad was from Edward Browne, seeking re-election to the House as a Republican from Wisconsin. One of the paragraphs in his ad attacked the NSL; he was re-elected.

Chapter 10

Loyalty and Education

Once the United States officially entered World War I the National Security League dropped, to a large extent, the subject of preparedness. They might have even faded away entirely, but they did not. They continued to pursue their militaristic agenda; they shifted focus from preparedness to patriotism and mounted many of what they called education campaigns. The war would end and with it there might have been a sudden decrease in militaristic sentiment. But the NSL remained vigilant to see that the fervor and the fever for bigger and more encompassing militarism would not fade away. The League scheduled a meeting for May 2, 1917, at the Hotel Astor in New York City. Readers of the ad announcing the meeting were urged to "Come and show your patriotism" while the top line of the advertisement read "Rally 'Round the Flag!"

In one of the ads for this meeting Robert Bacon was listed as president of the League with S. Stanwood Menken listed as chairman of the League's Executive Meeting. Bacon was president for a brief period before he resigned to seek political office. When he resigned, Menken resumed the presidency of the League. He had remained as chairman of the board during Bacon's brief tenure as president. At the meeting J. Bernard Walker was to speak on the "submarine menace" while Professor Albert Bushnell Hart (Harvard University) was to lecture on "Patriotism through Education." Grace Parker was to deliver a talk on "Woman's Work in the Preparedness Program."[1]

In tandem with pushing patriotism and loyalty, the NSL launched an attack on the education system, eventually targeting both children and adults. At a meeting on May 12, 1917, of the NSL's Committee on Patriotism Through Education the decision was reached by the League to spend more than one million dollars in a campaign of education. That plan, as tentatively laid out, would consist of sending volunteer speakers to every part of the United States "to address labor bodies, religious organizations and chautauquas." They planned to target not just big cities but also villages and hamlets. Main subjects to be taken up by lecturers would include: the cause

Chapter 10. Loyalty and Education

of the war; the ideals for which America was fighting; compulsory naval and military training and its uses "in protecting not only the country but the individual who might ordinarily find objections to it." Members of that Patriotism Through Education Committee included Albert Bushnell Hart, Arthur E. Bestor (president of the Chautauqua Institution), S. Stanwood Menken (chair of the NSL executive committee), Thomas F. Moran (Purdue University), and Calvin W. Rice (secretary of the American Society of Mechanical Engineers).[2]

Later in May the League announced it had inaugurated, through its 280 branches, "a campaign to counteract the active propaganda of the pacifists." First step was to hold a mass meeting at the same time as a gathering of the "First American Conference for Democracy and Peace and Terms of Peace" was to be held—May 30. The League wanted to counter what it saw as a pacifist gathering. In a statement the NSL declared, "In spite of all our efforts there still remains a large body of citizens unconvinced and half asleep…. Quietly, by underground methods the pacifists' propaganda, coupled with that of those who would weaken the United States and benefit Germany, is being spread broadcast." The statement went on to condemn a number of anti-war groups by name, such as the "No-Conscription League" and the "Emergency Peace Federation."[3]

Several weeks later the League explained its education program by asserting it was "to combat the activities of various pacifist organizations against the aggressive prosecution of the war, conscription and the Liberty Loan." After its "investigation," which lasted some weeks, the NSL said active steps were needed to counter the influence certain organizations "are exacting along these lines, which has been dangerously insidious although not actually illegal." In pursuance of its program the League sent a letter to all 280 of its branches: "Our country being actually engaged in war and the government being occupied with all sorts of war measures, including conscription, a great many people are of the impression that the National Security League has attained its object and that we have no further work to do. Nothing could be further from the truth."

This was all part of the process by which the National Security League re-invented itself, moving from preparedness to patriotism, loyalty and education. It insisted there still remained a large body of citizens unconvinced: "These persons are daily receiving encouragement from various so-called pacifist organizations. It is true that they are not so loud-spoken as they were, but there is no evidence of a cessation of their activities."[4]

Albert Bushnell Hart was a professor of history at Harvard University and chairman of the NSL's Committee on Patriotism Through Education. He had a lengthy by-lined piece in a major New York City newspaper in which he explained "why we fight and why we're sure we're right," as well as detailing for the readers the "Wake Up America" campaign.[5]

At the same time six people were members of the NSL committee at work on the plan to send orators over the entire United States to arouse the people to a better understanding of "war and its needs." Final plans for that campaign were to be arranged at a conference of all the organizations engaged in a patriotic education and a speakers' training camp at the Chautauqua Institution, Chautauqua, New York, from July 2–7. Those six people were Henry J. Allen (editor of the Wichita *Beacon*), Albert Bushnell Hart, Mrs. Philip N. Moore (St. Louis, president of the National Council of Women), Arthur E. Bestor (president of the Chautauqua Institution), Stanwood Menken, and Professor T.F. Moran (Purdue University).[6]

A letter to the editor from Stanwood Menken was printed in a New York City paper on June 26, 1917, in which the NSL executive explained that in order to carry forward the NSL message it would hold a training camp July 2–7 to train the speakers that would then go across America relating the NSL program. Menken wrote, "An unusual group of speakers will be present, representing various governmental activities to explain to the speakers exactly what the government is doing in connection with the war and what message the speakers should carry in their future addresses." Among those people to be in attendance at the training camp to instruct the volunteer, future orators were U.S. Secretary of the Interior Franklin K. Lane, George Wickersham (U.S. Attorney General under President Taft), Senator James Wadsworth, Jr., Franklin D. Roosevelt, and Frederic R. Coudert. Additionally, "A campaign handbook for speakers has been prepared by Professor Albert Bushnell Hart, of Harvard. One of the objectives of the speakers' school was to coordinate the work of patriotic education 'and define the methods to be adopted by the speakers.'"[7]

J. N. Elvebach, secretary of the Commercial Men's National Patriotic League, was one of the people who attended that speakers' training camp. When he returned home he explained to his home town newspaper that invitations were sent to the governors of all the states and to all colleges and universities in America asking them to appoint official delegates to the conference. North Dakota was one of the very few states not on the roll call for the event; Elvebach was the only person from North Dakota to attend. He was quoted as saying, "It would be impossible to plan a week that would promise greater results in the development of patriotic impulses." Franklin D. Roosevelt, Assistant Secretary of the Navy, told his audience about the submarine menace and warned against too great an optimism as to the task ahead.[8]

The League's campaign to arouse enthusiasm in the war began on July 16, 1917, throughout 18 states. Other states were expected to join the movement. That work was the outcome of the gathering at Chautauqua, where the representatives of 22 states had been present. States in which the campaign began were these: Vermont, Pennsylvania, Ohio, Iowa, Wisconsin, Kansas, Washington, Tennessee, New Jersey, New York, Kentucky, Michigan, West Virginia, Maryland, Louisiana, Virginia, Indiana, and Illinois. A speech-making campaign in New York City began that night. Each evening during the week volunteer speakers addressed the audience at the Globe Theatre. Reportedly, those talks began at 9:30 p.m. and lasted for 10 minutes. Professor Robert M. McElroy of Princeton University began the series that evening. As well, outdoor addresses were delivered at various points in the city.[9]

The plan of the NSL to have German societies and citizens of German ancestry declare their loyalty at

This June 1917 photograph showed the six people behind the Wake Up America campaign, which envisioned sending speakers all over America in order that people should better understand "war and its needs." Top row (left to right): Henry J. Allen (Kansas newspaper editor), Albert Bushnell Hart. Middle row: Mrs. Philip N. Moore (president, National Council of Women), Arthur Bestor (president, Chautauqua Institution). Bottom row: S. Stanwood Menken, Professor T. F. Moran (Purdue University).

mass meetings and by similar public action did not meet with a cordial response from those groups and individuals, according to one newspaper at least. However, the editor of another paper praised the effort: "These objections under conditions of war lack the force they might otherwise have ... these very conditions accentuate the need of some impressive public expression of German-American devotion to the American cause, which could not fail to be highly beneficial to that cause and to our loyal German-Americans themselves."[10]

Dr. Robert C. McElroy, head of the department of politics and history at Princeton University, accepted membership, on July 25, on the League's Committee on Patriotism Through Education, "which is conducting a nationwide campaign to educate the public to a realization of the duties of war." A full list of members was listed.[11]

One day later it was reported that, with respect to the volunteer speakers, over 400 university and college presidents and professors had already volunteered to actively take the field in carrying on "this great campaign." The presidents of 100 universities and colleges would either personally make addresses or had suggested members of their faculties who were willing to donate their services. The leading chautauquas were adding patriotic addresses in their programs. At the numerous annual conventions of fraternal, business and educational societies and associations that took place in the summer months, particular sessions would be devoted to the campaign. Slogans in the campaign included "Wake Up, America!" and "Tell the People."[12]

An article signed by Robert McElroy soon appeared in a New York City newspaper that outlined America's war ideals and, according to the article subhead, "explains the aspiration that stir this polyglot community to fight for dreams instead of profits." Bizarrely, McElroy declared that a Frenchman could reside for years in England or Germany or Russia and no matter how many papers of citizenship he had he would remain a foreigner. An Englishman could spend a lifetime in Italy but he would die an alien. A Russian could rear his family in Holland but they would never become Dutch. However, let that same Frenchman, Englishman or Russian come to American "and the great moving force of Americanism transforms him into a true American."[13]

Dr. Charles S. Hexamer of Philadelphia, president of the German-American National Alliance denounced the sending of a "creed" by the NSL to the editors of 450 German-American newspapers for their signatures. Hexamer denounced the creed as an insult to intelligence. There were nine paragraphs in that creed. One paragraph denounced the Kaiser "as a menace to the world." Another part of the statement to which the editors were expected to affix their signatures was to the effect that they believed the statements of the "German monarch and of his Prime Minister as to German aims and purposes in the war to be false." Reportedly, those

Chapter 10. Loyalty and Education

efforts by the League to have German-American individuals and organizations attest their loyalty to the United States brought forth a number of replies that ranged from "simple acknowledgment to violent abuse." The editors of those 450 German language papers were asked their position on the war and all were asked to subscribe to the League's "Confession of Faith."[14]

"Instead of welcoming the opportunity to make public a collective declaration of their loyalty to this county, many German-American organizations resent the suggestion of the National Security League...," declared a bewildered editor of an American newspaper. This editor regarded the League's request as "timely" and added, "It is our belief that the German-American people are more loyal to the United States than the German language press of this county; but even this comfort is taken away from us when they will not seize every opportunity to acknowledge their allegiance."[15]

Shailer Mathews of the University of Chicago, described as an author, editor, clergyman and educator, delivered a newspaper article on why America was fighting Germany. Mathews was also described in the byline as a member of the NSL's "committee organized to spread throughout the United States information on the causes of our war with Germany. The committee was formed because of a prevalent belief that many Americans were unfamiliar with the extent of our grievances and the reasons why war could not be avoided." Basically, in the article Mathews cast Germany as the great Satan and America as a benign, peace-loving, naive, innocent, and so forth, country dragged reluctantly into a war.[16]

Reporter William Black produced a large article about chautauquas on August 19, 1917, events that were held in tents and one Black described as a "nationwide instrument for social organization." The chautauqua movement had originated some 15 years earlier as an independent offshoot from the stationary Chautauqua Assembly at the lake of that name in New York State, and had within the previous four years "swept over the entire country." He said that England had spent some $25 million during the first two years of her war teaching, entreating, and promoting the "will to war." But in America there was an institution (the Chautauqua circuit) controlled by no one, springing from the communities themselves in twenty rival organizations, supported by the peoples and believed in by the people, which had "turned itself whole-souledly into a mobilization agency for the national policies" and that today "this citadel has been captured by the National Security League and by Secretary of War [Newton] Baker, whose formulas for war receive the benediction of 20,000,000 American people in the khaki tents of the Chautauqua circuits."

Some of the circuits named by Black included the Redpath circuit of New York and New England, the Swarthmore circuit of Pennsylvania and Kentucky, the Lincoln circuit of Illinois and Wisconsin, and the Keith-Vawter circuit of Iowa and Kansas. Mostly those tent circuits hit isolated areas and hamlets. That year, 1917, wrote Black, the Chautauqua circuit "is oriented to war." And, explained the journalist, "The National Security League as far back as January last shrewdly appraised the value of this social instrument for molding opinion and 'getting into the mind of America the fundamental principles for which the war ought to be fought.'" With respect to the oration people heard at the chautauquas, Black said, "It becomes tremendously important that the millions of people should understand precisely for what ideals the war is being pursued. The speakers must emphasize the cause of our participation. Chautauqua asserts its capacity for national leadership and it assumes a definite function in relation to the whole intellectual mobilization of the country."[17]

Late in August the NSL declared itself satisfied with the manner in which its efforts for an accounting of patriotism of German-Americans had been received by them. It justified the agitation which it started and clearly showed the need for the loyalty accounting requested from them. According to a journalist, in its attempts to obtain expressions of loyalty to the United States from German editors, the League "has met with even less success than its circularization of German-American organizations." While many of the German-American organizations "answered the league in replies generally abusive, most of the newspaper editors did not reply at all…."[18]

Herbert Barry, secretary of the National Security League, was the author of the "Profession of Faith" statement that the NSL called for the German-American groups and individuals to sign. Journalist Frederick F. Schrader, in speaking of that program, observed, "It is difficult to write with becoming moderation of the intermeddling policy of the National Security League which, relying on the prestige given it by the few names of eminent old men connected with it, took the lead at an early date to inflame public sentiment in behalf of its scheme to precipitate the United States into the European war and, after accomplishing its object, is now devoting itself to sowing discord among the American people." As a result of so many German editors refusing to subscribe to the loyalty pledge, the NSL declared the need for loyalty accounting to be vital.[19]

With a different target in mind for its loyalty attacks, the Philadelphia branch of the League announced plans to form a vigilante committee that would "spread a net far and wide that will enmesh every slippery slacker who has an idea that some other man ought to do his fighting for him." Apparently that proposed action from Philadelphia was in response to the substance of a report from the NSL New York City headquarters to the effect that large numbers of men gave fictitious addresses to the registration boards and that caused "grave concern" to the War Board. "The Security League, with its 280 branches throughout the country, will co-operate with Government officials in the round-up," declared the New York report. Kern Dodge, secretary of the Philadelphia branch, asserted he was ready to act as soon as he received instructions from headquarters. Less than five months later Kern Dodge, a consulting engineering firm, had an advertisement in the *Washington Times* newspaper under the title "Munitions." In the ad the firm urged all plants to get involved in the production of necessities for the war machine. Kern offered the use of itself as consultants to any plant that wished help in the production, inspection and shipment of munitions. He claimed he had British and French inspectors at his "instant disposal," to offer their assistance.[20]

Wayne M. Musgrave, representing the NSL, delivered a lecture in the City Hall at Grand Forks, North Dakota, on the evening of August 31, 1917. Because of his oratorical ability, it was reported, he was selected as the representative of the National Security League to visit the North Central states. Musgrave had already delivered speeches in many of the "important cities" of the Northwest.[21]

Governor Lynn J. Frazier of North Dakota granted permission to the People's Council of America to hold its national peace conference in that state. The NSL was unhappy about that decision. In a letter to A.M. McNair of Fargo, North Dakota, secretary of the NSL Fargo branch, the League declared, "We have an urgent appeal to aid in combating the effort of the Peace council to invade North Dakota with its treasonable utterances. Please have the National Security members in Fargo hold a meeting, urging Governor Frazier to take the same action in North Dakota as Governor Joseph Burnquist did in Minnesota." Burnquist had refused permission for such a gathering.[22]

No matter how much work the NSL did it did not seem to make much of a difference, as could be seen in the headline of a September 20, 1917, article: "Ignorance endangering country...." According to the League there was an "alarming indifference" on the part of people generally toward the war and "the imperative need of immediate steps to awaken them to the true situation." Supposedly, that was clearly shown in the letters from "prominent men" made public by the NSL. Those letters had been obtained by the organization by means of a canvass of "the leaders in its work throughout the country undertaken in connection with its campaign of patriotism through education...." Comments were then presented from many of those "prominent men," most or all of whom were NSL people, such as Charles J. Bonaparte and Lafayette Young. R.M. McClintock (managing editor of the *Wichita Eagle*) said, "There is a strong prejudice throughout this state against men who have made millions in big business. Such men in Kansas, speaking from the Wall Street point of view, would but lend point to the argument that this is Wall Street's war."²³

One of the big names recruited by the NSL was Irvin S. Cobb, a very well-known journalist who wrote for Joseph Pulitzer's paper the *New York World*. For a time he was the highest paid staff reporter in the United States. He also wrote some 60 books and 300 short stories. He produced a short, signed piece for the League that was basically a pep talk for the war effort. The byline stated, "Contributed by Irvin S. Cobb to the National Security League's campaign of Patriotism Through Education." This was another example of the public relations article generated by the League and then planted in newspapers, mostly from smaller communities, to look like, and be passed off as, real news items.²⁴

An editorial on the League's patriotism through education campaign remarked, agreeing with the NSL, that "America is not fighting today. Her government is at war but her people are not fighting. According to the editor a Middle Western Senator, not an anti-war type, told a friend recently that if a plebiscite was taken in his state on the war the people would vote four to one against it. He thought that such attitudes were fostered by the pacifists, socialists, and other agents of 'Kaiserism.'" Then the editor cited Menken as calling the people asleep in recent comments. Concluded the editor, "The National Security League and other agencies are engaging in the task of bringing a realization of these things to the people. Power to them! There is plenty of patriotism and plenty of

Irvin S. Cobb, 1916. Cobb was another very high profile person picked up by the NSL, at least for a time. Cobb was a journalist and at one time the highest paid staff reporter in America. He wrote at least one signed piece for the League's Committee of Patriotism through Education.

fighting blood in this country. But it will only be brought out by the facts! Tell them the facts! Make them mad! Then they'll fight!"[25]

During the second last week in September 1917 the National Security League conducted "Loyalty Week" in New York State under its auspices. That involved having nine teams of four speakers each, "composed of men and women of national reputation" who toured the principal cities and towns of the state, "preaching the gospel of patriotism." On the evening of September 17, seven of the teams spoke at New York City, Olean, Warsaw, Seneca Falls, Watertown, Catskill and Goshen. The other two teams were in transit that evening with one team going from Amsterdam to Oneida and the other moving from Gloversville to Wells. Loyalty Week was part of the patriotism through education campaign. Speakers included Alton B. Parker, George W. Wickersham, Charles Edward Russell, Job E. Hedges, Cleveland Moffett, Cass Gilbert, Frederick C. Walcott (an assistant to Herbert Hoover), A.R. Dugmore (from the British Army), Prof. Herbert E. Mills, Dr. Harry E. Fosdick, Henry D. Estabrook, Irvin S. Cobb, Dr. Talcott Williams, and Dr. Frank Crane. Even New York State Governor Charles Whitman was a speaker. He was slated to orate in Poughkeepsie a day or two later.

Shortly after Loyalty Week ended in New York State, the League announced that after its "highly successful" campaign the organization planned to extend the idea to Vermont, Kentucky, and Virginia. Separately, Theodore Roosevelt was to speak at Rutland, Vermont, and then in Chicago the following week "in the interest of the organization." NSL president Menken stated that 500 speakers were then listed on the organization's books, ready for oratory assignments.[26]

In his speech in Chicago, on September 26, Theodore Roosevelt denounced pacifists and unpreparedness. The meeting he addressed was held under the auspices of the NSL. After his address, described as having been "received with great enthusiasm," the organization adopted a resolution condemning U.S. Senator Robert La Follette (WI) for his recent public utterances and declared him "unworthy to represent the loyal people of America." At the end of his address Roosevelt expressed regret it was impossible to send La Follette to the German lines: "I wish we could make him a gift to the kaiser for use in his Reichstag. In the Senate he is a cause for shame to every worthy American." As well, the executive committee of the Chicago branch of the NSL appointed a subcommittee to draft resolutions to be forwarded to all members of Congress to oust La Follette from the Senate.[27]

Women were not entirely neglected in the League's loyalty and patriotism efforts. A "Woman's War Service Meeting" was held at Carnegie Hall in New York City on the night of October 17. Mrs. Thomas Preston,

Jr., presided in the chair. An advertisement encouraged mothers, wives, sisters, and daughters of sailors and soldiers to come to the meeting and "learn what is being done for your warriors and why this war is your war."[28]

Intensifying its patriotism program the League announced at the beginning of November that its "aggressive and efficient" prosecution of the war would be carried to the men who were to "follow the Stars and Stripes into the trenches." It was to be a new division of the "great campaign of Patriotism Through Education." The National Security League planned to send selected men from its list of volunteer speakers to give the men at the various training camps and who would go to the front on completion of that training "a thorough understanding and complete knowledge of why they are asked to serve their country, even at the sacrifice of their lives." Those NSL speakers were to appear under the auspices of the War Camp Community Recreation Fund. Details were still being worked out but a schedule was expected to be arranged that would include a series of meetings extending over the entire training period "at which speakers of national prominence will talk to the men at all the National Guard and National Army camps."[29]

If the women were not completely neglected in the loyalty drive then neither were younger people, the school children. When the organization announced it had finally admitted females as regular members, late in November, it also adopted a resolution urging the school authorities throughout the United States to establish courses to explain the entrance of America into the war and the necessity of victory.[30]

Also in November the NSL made public a letter sent to the heads of large American educational institutions and state education departments, asking for the donation of one professor from each institution to study "the problem of interpreting the meaning of war in school of the United States and the problem of teaching individual responsibility toward national and international questions." In its letter the NSL said, in part, that it was "impressed by the surprising lack of individual responsibility to the Government among citizens in all parts of the country." The organization claimed it came to that conclusion through its nationwide campaign, Patriotism Through Education. The NSL said it was taking steps that "it hopes will ultimately lead to the revolutionizing and vitalizing of the entire civic teaching in the schools of the United States." Carrying out the consensus of the "leading thinkers" of the country, who attended a conference of educators held under the auspices of the League, the NSL had laid before the principal educational institutions of the country a plan for the creation of a National Civic Education Faculty for the consideration of this problem.[31]

It was not just the NSL that was demanding loyalty checks, and the like. The New York City Board of Education was preparing to take action

Chapter 10. Loyalty and Education

at its next meeting, December 12, to require a pledge of allegiance from teachers entering the system. That board required teachers to hold U.S. citizenship but had not examined the loyalty of employees. In the previous spring a recommendation of Associate Superintendent William McAndrew that an oath of allegiance be required was defeated by a vote of the Board. Said McAndrew, "The issue of loyalty was in the air last spring. It did not seem necessary to the board then to guard against the possibility of misguided teaching." The NSL, in letters sent to the New York City Mayor, to State Education Commissioner Finley, and Superintendent of Schools Maxwell, requested as a part of each day's actual teaching that the children be instructed in the reasons for America's entry into the war, the menace of defeat "and the duties of citizenship in support of the Government."

The League was not confining its efforts to New York; in a statement released on November 25 it announced a national campaign to develop high patriotism in the schools. "The inauguration of this campaign was determined by the executive committee, because it realized that the best way to overcome indifference and ignorance as well as disloyalty was through a clear national understanding of the reasons for the war. It was felt that a denunciation of disloyalty was not sufficiently constructive to meet the situation, but that a broad plan of extending knowledge would be the most practical and helpful way of meeting a serious condition," explained the statement. The League was then, reportedly, sending appeals to every board of education and school commissioner in the nation to urge them to insert into their schools' daily programs instruction in war history and "national duties." A book was said to then be in preparation by the NSL to assist teachers in conducting these suggested lessons—containing matter from the National Committee on Public Information and from the NSL's own literature.[32]

One report on the success of that appeal to schools across the nation surfaced on January 1, 1918. Reportedly, the NSL had conducted a canvass of American schools to ascertain how the organization's appeal had been received—the appeal to introduce everywhere a war curriculum. In Wisconsin only 19 of 72 county school superintendents replied favorably to that NSL appeal, "Nothing approaching its failure in Wisconsin having been experienced in any other state in the Union," declared the report, although no other specific data was given.[33]

While women were rarely mentioned with respect to the NSL, labor was ignored to an even greater extent. One exception was a meeting held on the evening of January 7, 1918, under the auspices of the Committee on Public Information, the American Alliance for Labor and Democracy, and the National Security League. Supposedly, "leading labor men" told of the loyalty of the working class to the country and to its war aims. "The meeting was held to express the loyalty principles that govern labor and their determination to fight until a just and permanent peace may be obtained. Any pacifist statements to the contrary, said all the speakers, simply misrepresent a misrepresentation of the labor position...." Three speakers were named: Herman Robinson, organization director for the American Alliance for Labor and Democracy; Hugh Frayne of the American Federation of Labor; and J. Crawford Vaughan, an Australian who was for 13 years the parliamentary Labor leader of his country—that is, he was a politician.[34]

Later in January 1918, teachers, principals and superintendents of the New York City public schools met at the Waldorf Astoria Hotel and agreed to prepare a plan for the mobilization of democracy's second line of defense—the school children. "It was determined that patriotic propaganda should be started systematically in the schools to offset other influences that are at work in the country," said a report. Propaganda was to take the form "of instruction to teachers on how to instill in their pupils respect for the policies and mandates of America because it is their country, so that the problems that America must face will be met efficiently, scientifically and with patriotic devotion." Dr. Robert McNutt McElroy, chairman of the NSL Committee on Patriotism Through Education, said, "The safety of democracy depends just as much upon the training of the children in the schools as in the training of the boys in the trenches." That meeting was a gathering of the Federation of Teachers Associations. It was also reported that in this plan to develop patriotism in the schools, "The students are to be taught to obey the policies of the Government without question."[35]

Another odd reference to workers appeared when the NSL announced, on February 7, 1918, that shipyard workers were to be "impressed" with the importance of their labor in the national war plans through the organization at shipyards throughout the country of branches of the NSL "in which they will be enrolled as members it was decided today at a meeting here which the league announced was attended by representatives of the largest shipbuilding interests in the United States." Apparently the NSL had met with shipyard owners and those two had decided to enroll the workers into the organization's branches. A committee to bring that about was appointed. Reportedly, those shipyard workers "will be addressed by prominent speakers and literature will be distributed to them in which it will be made clear how vital is the shipbuilding industry to the winning of the war."[36]

Disloyalty among college and university professors was a topic taken up at an NSL executive meeting and a resolution was passed requesting the alumni associations of the various educational institutions of the country to investigate the matter. That resolution stated "That it is a duty of all educational institutions to inquire into the loyalty of the officers, professors

Chapter 10. Loyalty and Education

and instructors who are suspected of being in sympathy with the nation's enemies and to remove those found to be disloyal." One newspaper editor in favor of the idea wrote, "Nothing is more important at this time than the cooperation of all educators of the country in the work of the government for on no other class of workers devolves such responsibility to the youth of the country and the future of the republic, as upon those who are in daily contact with the boys and girls of our public schools."[37]

Another unlikely individual to become involved, again, with the National Security League was famed attorney Clarence Darrow. Reportedly there was much surprise in New York when it was announced that Darrow was one of the speakers in the League's educational and patriotic campaign, and one to whom the Board of Education required the teachers of New York City to listen. That surprise was said to have been reflected in the letters of protest that members of the NSL received in the wake of that announcement. Countering those arguments, the NSL stated that Darrow had given good evidence of "sound Americanism" since the U.S. had declared war and was one of the most vigorous foes Germany had on this side of the Atlantic. Darrow's most spectacular legal achievements had been made in connection with the defense of organized labor—he defended labor leader Eugene V. Debs, among others. Nonetheless the League defended Darrow by declaring he had scarcely missed a patriotic gathering of any kind in Chicago since the U.S. entered the war.[38]

Another account noted that Clarence Darrow was coming to New York City, from Chicago, under the auspices of the NSL to speak to the public school teachers on "Americanism," and that the notice of his coming had already stirred "considerable protest." Darrow was described as the legal defender of the McNamara brothers (in the high profile bombing of the *Los Angles Times* building) and of William D. Haywood (a leader of the radical IWW union). In answer to the objections, president Arthur C. Somers of the Board of Education and Professor Robert McElroy of the NSL declared they had "carefully gone over" Darrow's recent record and found nothing to warrant cancellation of his appearance. One of the men who objected was Calvin V. Campbell of Brooklyn, who knew Darrow in Chicago. Campbell was an NSL member and had been active in the passage of loyalty resolutions in Commercial High School, Brooklyn.

Darrow was also widely known as a speaker for organized labor. Somers claimed that as soon as he was informed who Darrow was he consulted with McElroy and obtained a report on the lawyer by wire from Chicago. Said Somers, "It appears that he was doing excellent work for the Red Cross and other organizations since the war started and I am satisfied there is no ground for refusing him the privilege of speaking here." These Americanization lectures were arranged by an exchange between the Chicago and

New York City Boards of Education for the week of March 18. Six Chicago teachers would go to New York City and six New York teachers would go to Chicago. Schools were to be closed for two hours morning and afternoon to enable the teachers to attend; "They will be instructed in methods of patriotic teaching."[39]

The idea was that when the out-of-town speakers, such as Darrow, arrived in the other city they would speak before the school teachers in that city and that those six individuals would inspire the school teachers who would, in turn, pass that inspiration of Americanization on to their pupils and that would eventually be carried by the children into the homes of New York and Chicago. Darrow, in the end, did not come and did not participate in the program. The NSL insisted the last minute change had nothing to do with the pressure and objections that had been raised about Darrow participating, declaring that it was Darrow's law practice in Chicago that precluded his appearance.[40]

Designations of university professors to carry on the educational work of the NSL in "combating German propaganda" were announced by the League in March. The academics named were each responsible to oversee programs in various sections of the nation. Assignments were as follows: Dr. Franklin H. Giddings (Columbia University) in charge of the South, Dr. W.H. Schofield (Harvard University) Northwest, Dr. C.H. Van Tyne (University of Michigan) Middle West, Dr. Walter P. Hall (Princeton University) Washington and Oregon, Dr. M.F. Libby (University of Colorado) Rocky Mountain States, and Dr. E.D. Adams (Stanford University) New England.[41]

Melanchton Fennessey Libby produced a pamphlet for the League about how to organize a state for patriotic education. It was based upon his experience in Colorado. His pamphlet was divided into three sections: (1) the need for propaganda to reach the masses who do not attend lectures; (2) how to pledge the schools to teach the justice of our cause and the duties of American citizens; (3) suggested methods of organizing a state based upon actual experiments in Colorado. His target audience in the schools was seventh and eighth graders. Said Libby, "The public school is the one great organization for a propaganda that will reach the masses of the voters in the homes.... A study of the facts in one state showed that many teachers themselves were unable to argue the American case effectively...." He believed that every state in the Union could be organized for this "propaganda." What was needed was a pledge from each county and city education superintendent to distribute suitable literature "and see that it is taught for a definite number of hours each month; also that promotion from the seventh and eighth grades requires a knowledge of this subject." The literature which the NSL had offered free "comprises a Handbook for the teacher and a small pamphlet of War Points in the form of a short catechism for the

Chapter 10. Loyalty and Education 145

pupil." According to this source the League was in receipt of dozens of letters from county boards of education in Colorado, and virtually all of them were said to be in favor of the teaching of patriotism as a required subject in the seventh and eighth grades. One example he gave was a letter addressed to him (at the University of Colorado at Boulder) from Early C. Denny, Superintendent, Baca County Schools, Springfield, Colorado. It said, "In response to your letter of recent date, I am pleased to say that I am glad to make compulsory the teaching of patriotism in my schools and I await your further instruction."

While he was doing this research Libby had been granted a temporary absence from the state university. Whether or not or how his salary was still being paid to him was not mentioned. It could have been continued by the university and thus would have constituted a donation in kind to the NSL, as compared to a straight cash donation. Part of the Libby letter that went out to all those school superintendents said, "The State Superintendent [Mary C.C. Bradford] desires me to say that she would regard it as a very patriotic move if you would work for such a change in the requirements of the schools in your district and the Governor [Julius C. Gunter] is equally anxious that this course should be adopted." Another example of the replies supposedly received by Libby in answer to his letter came from Emory E. Smiley, Superintendent of Schools, Durango, Colorado. It read, "Your communication of May 2 has come to hand. We should be pleased in the Durango schools to co-operate in the movement of which you have charge. We await your further directions."[42]

An article appeared in the newspaper on March 26, 1918, listing various opportunities for people to do volunteer war work. One listing was, "A campaign of propaganda designed to meet and combat the activities of those opposed to the war policy of the country and the prosecution of the war is being waged by the National Security League." Classes were held every Monday and Thursday evening for volunteers. "Outdoor meetings, in which the war aims of the government will be restated, are to be conducted and literature on war subjects will be distributed." Those interested in the opportunity to be a soapbox, street-corner preacher were urged to contact the secretary of the "Flying Squadron," at the NSL headquarters building in New York City at 19 West 44th Street.[43]

Robert McElroy, NSL educational director, declared that his organization "has undertaken that great spiritual drive for mental and spiritual preparedness without which physical preparedness must fail to complete success." Thus, the organization had decided the best place to focus itself was at the level of the educational institution. Giving a recap of the teacher exchange week in March between Chicago and New York City, McElroy stated that 12 "carefully chosen speakers" spoke to about 30,000 teachers in the school systems of those two cities. As well, it had more plans for the summer when it planned to establish training courses in 50 teachers' training camps. Colleges and universities throughout the United States had been asked to furnish the officers for those teachers' patriotic training camps.[44]

Yet another nationwide campaign was announced by the NSL, in April 1918. This one had as its purpose the "Americanization" of foreign-born citizens. The persistence of pro–German propaganda where the foreign-born "hold forth," NSL officials declared, and the constant efforts of "so-called radicals and obstructionists to foster discontent among aliens, have made the need for such action imperative." What the organization intended to do was to spread among the foreign-language speaking people of the United States a "clear exposition of America's aims in the war"; in addition, "There is, however, a still broader end in view—the permanent instilling of American ideals into the hearts and minds of the various faces that have taken up their lives on our shores." To that end the League had sent to its 281 branches a pamphlet setting forth what every member of the community could do "to help line up the foreign population for America, democracy and the war." Editors of foreign-language publications would be enlisted in the work and speakers would be sent out.[45]

Later in April Robert McElroy had just returned from a tour of nine states in the Midwest and said he had observed there "open pro–Germanism, apathy toward the war and ignorance of its real meanings. He blamed the educational system, saying that a great propaganda immediately was necessary to awaken the people of those states. In the three weeks he was on that trip he claimed he spoke to more than 45,000 people, chiefly school teachers: 'There are sections in the region covered in our journey which are not yet prepared to think with the mind of America. There are large regions of which are the victims of our pernicious system of nullification. We must awake to the realization that the melting pot has not melted.'" He added, "In several States which I visited a stranger can be taken into one section and told 'You are now in Russia,' into another section five minutes away and told, 'You are now in Germany,' and still again a few paces and, 'You are now in Italy.'"[46]

In one of his appearances on that trip to the Middle West, McElroy talked about a speech he gave at the University of Wisconsin to a large audience of young men. "I was telling them of America's real purposes and aims and ideals in this war. It seemed to me that from the outset the audience took strangely little interest in the things I was talking about, the cause for which I was pleading." He added, "For the most part, once they had learned that American patriotism was my theme, they sat with folded arms, staring wearily up at the ceiling. From time to time they'd turn and look at each other and smile superciliously, sort of pityingly. There was a good deal of fidgeting and shuffling of feet. Several times, generally at the most strongly patriotic portions of my talk, sounds which bore every sign of being subdued hisses could be heard." McElroy considered the whole affair to be all quite disgraceful, "especially coming from a state in which 100,000 disloyal votes were recently registered. I say that a thing like that should be investigated." He also named Oregon, North Dakota, and Michigan as states with extensive communities "that are quite undisguised in their sympathy for the foe."[47]

The "flying squadron" of the NSL went into action in the spring of 1918 for the third Liberty Loan drive. Following the conclusion of that campaign the organization planned to shift its attack to subjects of "general patriotism" and would continue its work through the summer. The squadron was composed of 400 men and women "who have been drilled throughout the winter in how to make an effective brief speech." They held forth before societies and clubs and also addressed passersby from street corners. Among those who had drilled the speakers were Job E. Hedges, former U.S. Senator Theodore E. Burton of Ohio and Dr. Robert McElroy.[48]

An announcement from NSL headquarters stated that Theodore Roosevelt would make a speaking tour through the Midwest late in May. The former president would deliver addresses in Ohio, Iowa, Michigan, and Wisconsin under the auspices of the League, as part of its patriotism through education in those states.[49]

That NSL Committee thought it was time to establish a common language in America. It believed that the way to do that was to eliminate the speaking and teaching of German in the schools, except as an elective, in colleges, and that when it was taught in the colleges, the instructors should be men of "unquestioned loyalty." The editor of one Washington, D.C., newspaper agreed with the position and even went a little further, declaring that "enemy languages" should not be taught in our schools under any circumstances during wartime. Also favored by this editor was stopping all German-language newspapers being published in the United States as "a menace to this country."[50]

In May 1918 it was reported that German was gradually being excluded from the public schools of the United States, "principally through the efforts of the National Security League, which is carrying on a crusade against the teaching of the Teutonic tongue or ideals." According to the League it was carrying on that campaign in every state through its 281 branches and the active cooperation of school authorities had effected the abolition of German instruction in many sections, together with the disbanding of German musical and literary clubs. In Philadelphia the study of German had been abolished in all high schools and in New Jersey the state Board of Education had requested all district superintendents to instruct the teachers under them to substitute Spanish for German wherever possible. In one unnamed area the number of students studying German had been reduced as much as 64 percent. Combined with its anti–German crusade, the NSL was making efforts to obtain increased teaching along patriotic education lines. That had resulted, the organization reported, in New York State, South Dakota, and Texas each passing a law making the teaching of patriotism and citizenship mandatory in the public schools.[51]

The League intensified its crusade against German-language newspapers and the teaching of German in the public schools, in June. The fight, said the group, was to be taken up by all of its 281 branches and membership of 100,000. Marshaling that army would be four educators and publishers: Charles E. Lydecker (trustee of the College of the City of New York and chair of NSL's Board of Directors); Edward H. Clark (NSL treasurer); Ernest C. Brown (editor and publisher); and Dr. Robert M. McElroy (Princeton University and educational director of the League). That committee had sent instructions to the chairmen and secretaries of every branch asking them to call meetings to express a one-language sentiment, to discourage advertising in German papers and "to procure the cooperation of newsdealers in restricting their circulation." Lydecker explained by remarking, "The duty of every citizen is to know the English tongue. To refuse to learn it is to fling defiance at the nation. To neglect to learn it is voluntarily to remain unfit for the duties of American citizenship." With respect to the foreigners in America, Lydecker added, "They must be compelled to convince themselves of the value and the justice of American ideals, and this requires a knowledge of the English language." And, he concluded, "There is no immediate need to have laws enacted to suppress the foreign language dailies. In towns where there is a strong patriotic sentiment a hostile minority should be persuaded by a clear and forceful expression of the views of the majority that ours must be, from this time forward, a one language nation."[52]

Flag Day in 1918 was on June 14 and under the supervision of the NSL the film theater patrons throughout the country would sing "The Star Spangled Banner" and at least one "patriotic war song" that night. According to the news account, "The leaders of the motion picture industry and the proprietors of movie houses, large and small, have given the league their hearty support in organizing this simple but effective celebration of Flag Day. Promises of cooperation have been received from all parts of the country...."[53]

An example of the flowery language often used by the National Security League could be seen in an announcement it released in the middle of June: "A unique departure in its great nation-wide campaign of Patriotism Through Education, designed to create a new branch of public school education in this country, has been announced...." That plan was to start with what was described as literally a "laboratory experiment in teaching," which would be conducted at Lawrence, Massachusetts, in cooperation with the Board of Education of that city and the Lowell Massachusetts Normal School. Pupils in that proposed school were to be the school teachers of the Lawrence public schools and the teachers-in-training would be students of the Lowell Normal School. The objective of the plan was "to work out a practical system of patriotic education teaching which can be standardized and adopted in all the public schools of the country." Two main items were to be covered: "Establishing school duties and obligations as well as rights and privileges" and "Making the actual teaching create a greater faith in and devotion to America and the basic principles of democracy." ["Then the time has come for you to take the last step. You must love Big Brother. It is not enough to obey him: You must love him." George Orwell, *1984*].[54]

Even cartoons and cartoonists were used by the League in its crusade for patriotism. A cartoon depicting a child torn between spending his nickel on a candy machine or buying thrift stamps to aid in and finance the war effort appeared in various newspapers in June 1918. The artist was Eugene Zimmerman, one of America's best known cartoonists of the period. The caption noted that the cartoon was contributed by him to NSL's Campaign of Patriotism Through Education. Needless to say, the child in the piece chose to spend his coin on buying the thrift stamp and financing the war. This was similar to the various drives throughout this period to buy Liberty Bonds, to finance the war. That is, the working class was expected to fight and die, but also to finance their own possible destruction. And that brought up the question; since men were conscripted to fight the war and since it was so necessary and such a noble cause, and so forth, why was capital—money—not also conscripted?[55]

An announcement from the League on July 19 was to the effect that its committee on foreign language and foreign press had obtained "definite results" in 25 states in its campaign against teaching the German language in public schools and in its fight against the publication of German newspapers in the United States. In those states the League claimed it had obtained the discontinuance of German classes in the schools of "many cities and towns," although none were specified by name. Those states were Massachusetts, Connecticut, New York, New Jersey, Pennsylvania, Maryland, Virginia, Georgia, Mississippi, Louisiana, Texas, Michigan, Indiana, Ohio, Illinois, Nebraska, Missouri, Kansas, Iowa, Arkansas, Arizona, Colorado, Montana, California, and Oregon. That committee was conducting this nationwide campaign under the motto, "Make the United States a One Language Nation."[56]

Yet another big name recruited by the NSL was that of Sarah Bernhardt,

This June 1918 cartoon showed a child torn between buying candy from a machine or buying a thrift stamp—part of the proceeds from which went to finance the war. That cartoon was contributed to the NSL's Patriotism through Education campaign by Eugene Zimmerman, then one of the nation's best known cartoonists.

regarded as one of the finest actors of her time and someone with huge celebrity status. A New York newspaper produced an image of the close of her hand-written message directed to America's "home army" from the "Divine Sarah," as she was known. It was issued by the NSL. She wrote it for Dr. William B. Otis of the College of the City of New York, who was

Chapter 10. Loyalty and Education 151

traveling through the West in the interest of the League's crusade of Patriotism Through Education. Otis received the note while staying at the Hotel Davenport in Spokane Washington. The message read, "We must fight and conquer the Socialists and the pacifists, because they are even more pro–German than the Germans themselves. And we must fight them with their own weapons."[57]

According to an NSL announcement late in July there were "several hundred thousand men and women" who were training in summer educational camps that they might better lead youth "to greater heights of knowledge" when the next school session began in the fall. Reportedly, there were then 254 such camps (out of a future total of 700) that had started to give school teachers "an intensive course in patriotism of from one to six weeks each. This course is being provided through the efforts of the National Security League. Mrs. Thomas J. Preston Jr. (formerly Mrs. Grover Cleveland) was secretary of the League's Committee on Patriotism Through Education and had spent many months in helping to set up those teachers' camps that were then in operation." Said Preston, "If we can inspire the teachers and give them a world vision they will inspire their pupils. The pupils in turn will carry the enthusiasm back to their homes thus reaching by effective propaganda many who could not be reached by public meetings or by printed arguments interpreting the meaning of America." Reportedly, the League had sent 28 tons of "war pamphlets" since June 1 to those summer schools for teachers. Preston was also the active head of the NSL's Speakers Bureau which then had "over a thousand volunteer orators making patriotic addresses in all parts of the country."[58]

Adolph Liesering, a 51-year-old waiter in New York City, born in the United States, received a sentence of six months in the workhouse on August 16 from Magistrate Koening in the Court of Domestic Relations. Liesering was accused of interfering with William Wright, an NSL speaker, by declaring that Germany was as good as the United States. Said Magistrate Koening, "We have enough to do in this country dealing with troublesome alien enemies without being bothered by native born disturbers. You are a menace to your country."[59]

A couple of days later the National Security League announced that the street corner patriotic oratory with which it had been combating German propaganda in New York City for months was to be spread over the entire county by "Street Speakers' Squadrons," which were being organized in many cities. C.A. Bill, who had organized the local squadron of 300 speakers was to be in charge of the extension of the movement.[60]

Late in August the organization announced it had held some 1,900 meetings in various parts of the United States during the previous six months at which its message of "militant patriotism" was carried to approximately 1,000,000 people, according to Dr. Thomas S. Preston, Jr., director of the League's Speakers' Bureau, in his semi-annual report. His bureau was then equipped to supply speakers in 20 languages, including Chinese. Preston had led that bureau for more than a year and then had nearly 2,000 volunteer speakers upon which to draw. He claimed that little expense was involved for the NSL because "it is our plan to have organizations desiring our speakers pay their personal expenses and transportation. Our meetings have been held in halls, schools, colleges, men's clubs, community centers, patriotic service leagues, churches, banquets, etc. We furnished commencement speakers to every high school in the City of New York, with two exceptions, for the recent commencement exercises." In the early spring his group conducted a series of 80 Americanization meetings, 16 a week for five weeks, in 12 languages, among the foreign speaking population of New York City: "Through the generosity of a group of Brooklyn friends of the League, headed by Mr. D.E. Austin, the services of the Rev. Dr. Isaac J. Lansing of Ridgewood, N. J., an orator of note, were secured for a year, beginning May 17, 1918."[61]

Mrs. Mary C.C. Bradford, superintendent of public instruction in

In this 1914 photograph Upton Sinclair (man in the white suit and black armband) is seen picketing the Rockefeller Building. Sinclair was another big-name author who wrote a signed piece for the NSL in the furtherance of its agenda. His topic was a Socialist view of a German victory in the war.

Colorado, declared in September that she had joined the NSL campaign to teach patriotism in all the public schools in America. She asserted, "The public school system in the United States can undertake no greater work at this time." At just about the same time, Miss Etta V. Leighton, who had what was described as a "national reputation" in the school world, in vocational training in New Jersey, had become the NSL Civic Secretary. Her main efforts were devoted to carrying the League's message of "militant patriotism" into the elementary schools of the country. One of the methods of promotion originated by her that had attracted particular attention was a Correspondence Course for Teachers in which she supplied teachers in the elementary grades with practical suggestions for "patriotic instruction."62

MRS. HAZEL WARNER WITH U. S. FLAG AND SERVICE FLAG

Mrs. Hazel Warner, 1918. Warner was one of the supposedly hundreds of volunteer street corner orators who preached NSL orthodoxy to the passing masses. Reportedly her husband and three brothers were overseas "fighting for democracy" and she was "doing great work as a patriotic speaker" for the League's "flying squadron."

Still another big name recruited to the cause of the National Security League, at least for a time, was renowned author Upton Sinclair. He wrote a by-lined article that appeared in the newspapers in September

1918 on a socialist view of a German victory. The byline stated, "Written by Upton Sinclair for the National Security League." Said Sinclair, in part, "the socialists of the allied countries have the best of socialist authority [August Bebel, Karl Liebknect] for supporting this war, so long as it is urged in the spirit of the declaration of our president, that we will make peace with the people of Germany, but not with their conscienceless rulers."[63]

Street-corner speakers of the League were rarely profiled. One that was mentioned briefly was Mrs. Hazel Warner. Her husband and her three brothers were overseas "fighting for democracy." But Hazel, the reader was informed, was not content to let them do it all. She was "doing great work as a patriotic speaker." She was a member of the "flying squadron" of the NSL and did her orating at street corner meetings. As well, she spoke in the drive to sell Liberty Bonds.[64]

Chapter 11

The General Campaign

On April 5, 1917, just one day before the United States formally entered the World War I conflict, the National Security League took out a full page ad as it turned to using the media somewhat more often. In this ad the focus of the League on preparedness was dropped as the organization moved on to stress loyalty and patriotism. This particular ad contained a declaration of loyalty to America which readers of the ad were urged to seek out and sign "at accessible places throughout the city [of Wheeling, West Virginia]." As an example, this ad featured the signatures of all employees of the George E. Stifel Company who were present at their place of employment on April 4, 1917, when those signatures were collected—some 159 names.[1]

Over one four-day period late in April 1917 the NSL placed three ads, on three separate days, in New York City newspapers. One ad was addressed by the League to the "Young Men of America" and urged those young male readers to contact their Senators and Representatives to urge them to immediately enact a universal military training (UMT) bill. The next day a follow-up advertisement was titled, "A Nation's Strength." It also urged readers to contact Congress to enact a UMT bill. However, the piece began with a loyalty pitch and featured ideas such as "respect for law and obedience to authority" and "Love of country and ability to serve it efficiently." The third ad in the series also touted a UMT bill.[2]

Agitating for Congress to enact a UMT bill was conducted regularly throughout this time period. The League continually contacted politicians and polled them to find out where they stood on the issue. By late in May the organization reported that 146 U.S. House Representatives and 35 U.S. Senators were in favor of such legislation. On the other hand the NSL had recorded 11 Representatives and five Senators who were definitely opposed. For some time the group had been circulating petitions to be signed by ordinary people. And late in May the League staged a photo opportunity for the media that showed people carrying petitions urging universal military training and carrying those petitions up the Capitol steps to the office

155

of the U.S. Speaker of the House, Champ Clark. Reportedly, the petition was signed by 500,000 to 1,000,000 people.[3]

Another ad from the League appeared in July 1917 demanding the United States speed up ship building. This advertisement had the dramatic title, "For God's Sake HURRY UP!" A small section at the bottom noted the League had 100,000 members and was a "non-political body." Also noted was that the NSL was conducting meetings all over the nation and distributing "vast amounts of literature" but "Our efforts are hampered by lack of funds. Do your part to aid the work by giving liberally."[4]

Also in July, it was reported that letters to the editors of 1,400 American newspapers "known to favor aggressive prosecution of the war" were sent out by the NSL asking them to appeal to their readers to write their Senators and Representatives to urge the speeding up of the war program.[5]

Early in August the NSL demonstrated, perhaps, what they meant by "militant patriotism" when it announced it had taken steps to promote the formation all over the country of "vigilance committees" to track down slackers under the draft law. To that end the group sent a letter to the heads of all of its 280 branches in America. It read, in part, "We must impress upon the house that the slacker is not only a coward and a cheat and evading national service, but that he is imperiling national honor in a war for national existence and that he is endeavoring to impose upon the men numerically below him in the draft the duty which he should perform."[6]

Methods employed by the federal government in the construction of cantonments at the various army camps, where draftees went for training before being shipped overseas, were "severely criticized" on August 25, 1917, by the NSL, which favored "industrial conscription." The League acted by coming out critically, it said, after receipt of a letter from B.S. Mason, a "prominent Lawyer" of Salinas, Kansas, in which the attorney urged the immediate adoption of industrial conscription. His views were reported to have centered around the contention there was no fairness in asking young men as soldiers to risk their lives for $30 a month, while other men were receiving from $6 to $10 a day building places for them to sleep in. As an example, a 70-year-old carpenter was cited who never was able to make more than $18 a week but was then making $52 a week: "there should be a universal and insistent demand for industrial conscription along with the conscription of soldiers." It was, of course, a logical strategy for the capitalist class to pursue. It was perfectly okay for them to make extortionate profits from war production—and they did—but it was not okay for ordinary workers to make extra income because of the real shortages in the workforce at home.

As much as the capitalist class must have loved the idea of industrial conscription, it never went anywhere, perhaps because it was just another

Chapter 11. The General Campaign 157

name for slavery. And while the capitalist class was adamant in urging human conscription to feed the battlefield and industrial conscription to feed the plants that supplied the materiel that went to the soldiers in the field, that capitalist class was still strangely mute about the notion of capital conscription. But why bother when they could convince the workers to buy Liberty Bonds and finance their own destruction. Then there was the problem with shoddy and substandard goods and services foisted off on the men in the field, all at inflated prices and profits.[7]

"Lieutenant General S.B.M. Young (retired) declared, in August, that the youth of the land had to come to the aid of their country. Simultaneously with that pronouncement came an announcement from the NSL that it would immediately undertake an 'intensive campaign for the adoption of the Chamberlain bill, which provides for universal military training.'" General Young believed the draft law was "totally inadequate to provide for the situation in which the United States finds itself." As part of its campaign to achieve universal military training, the League was preparing for a mass meeting the following month at which Senator Chamberlain of Oregon would be the main speaker. Later, James M. Beck, formerly Assistant United States Attorney General, and other orators would visit ten of the larger American cities.[8]

Near the end of August an official statement made in the British House of Commons revealed that the Allies' purchases in America reached $10 million daily and that "the banking firm of J.P. Morgan & Company had to handle a large share." An American named Edward Stettinius was described as "the biggest buyer in the world." Said Stettinius, "After careful study we decided that in placing war contracts we would have to be guided less by the nature of any concern's product than by the character of the men at its head." And, he added, "Through the knowledge and experience and ramifications of those in the Morgan firm, we had a good idea of who was who and what was what throughout the manufacturing world."[9]

According to the results of a canvass undertaken in the middle of September 1917, UMT as a permanent basis of the military system "is steadily gaining new advocates in Congress." There were then said to be 157 Representatives and 38 Senators who had already endorsed the system. League president Menken said his organization's campaign to create a demand for the passage of a UMT law was developing "entirely to his satisfaction." Since May, when the NSL first announced the results of its canvass, Carl Hayden (Republican of AZ) was the only member of Congress who had openly come out against the proposal. That made a total of 12 men in the House who had declared themselves publicly as opposed to UMT. Since the first canvass, four House members who had been noncommittal had become advocates (Representatives Rainey of Illinois, Moore of Indiana,

Booth Tarkington 1922. Tarkington was yet another very well known writer who produced at least one signed piece in support of the National Security League's agenda. He was awarded the Pulitzer Prize for fiction twice and during the time of the NSL was considered America's greatest living author.

Bruckner of New York and Johnson of South Dakota). Since that May canvass 13 new affirmative replies had been received from Representatives and three from Senators (Newland of Nevada, France of Maryland and Tillman of South Carolina).[10]

Another example of NSL press releases that were planted in newspapers and passed off as supposedly news stories could be seen in the November 22, 1917, issue of a small-town paper in Iowa. Two-thirds of the page was devoted to six different NSL stories—none with a dateline. All were clearly public relations plants of the organization as this phase of its operation was well underway. Titles of these articles were: "Many Converts for Universal Military Service"; "Security League Waging Great War Campaign"; "Sammy Parleyvoos" (about an NSL-issued phrase book to aid U.S. soldiers abroad); "School Patriotism"; "Conscript Farm Labor" (to go along with their urging of industrial conscription); and "What Victory Means." That last article was "contributed by Booth Tarkington to the National Security League's Patriotism Through Education." It was another big name that appeared on

Chapter 11. The General Campaign   159

behalf of the League. All of these "news articles" were the usual fawning and self-congratulatory puff pieces the organization regularly churned out. Fear could also be found in the League's press releases. In one NSL pamphlet, *Why We Are at War*, it was said that "Germany was planning world control and had already begun the work of dividing up the United States, a part of which she would take for herself. A few more States she would give to Mexico."[11]

Still another essay contest was announced by the NSL at the end of 1917. A $1,000 prize was offered for the best suggestion as to how to reach the German masses with the "facts." Suggestions were to be accepted by the League up to February 14, 1918. Ideas received were to be judged by NSL members James W. Gerard, Job E. Hedges and David Jayne Hill.[12]

Also at the end of 1917 the National Security League declared it then had 45 U.S. Senators and 168 Representatives definitely recorded in favor of the immediate enactment of UMT into law. The League stated that it had resumed its active advocacy of adoption of UMT as the permanent basis of the nation's defense, which it claimed it had discontinued when America entered the war, believing that the arousing of a united popular support of the war was of greater importance. The NSL declared then, at the end of 1917, that the experience of the last eight months (since entry into the conflict), particularly in the large number of young men rejected for physical defects in the draft, "gives indisputable proof" that enactment of a UMT law by Congress was a matter of immediate necessity.[13]

During this period the National Security League held very few conferences, compared to the pre-war period. The only one of note was held in Chicago from February 21 to 23, 1918, and was called the Congress of National Service. At that gathering the NSL planned to give some attention to women and declared the meeting "will be the most important gathering of American women since the start of the war. The purpose is to give special consideration to the parts that women can assume in helping to solve the war problems of the country." The females to be in charge of the women's section of the Congress were; Mrs. Thomas J. Preston, Jr., Maude Wetmore (daughter of the late U.S. Senator Wetmore), Mrs. Philip North Moore (president of the National Council of Women), Mrs. Coffin van Rensselaer (vice-chair of the National League for Women's Service), and Etta V. Leighton (civic secretary of the NSL). Other women to be present included; Virginia C. Gildersleeve (dean of Barnard College), Mrs. Richard I. Manning (wife of the South Carolina governor), Mrs. W.B. Lindsey (wife of the New Mexico governor), and Mrs. M. Carey Thomas (president of Bryn Mawr College).[14]

Writing about that upcoming Congress, a journalist said, "It will aim to arouse the morale of the American people so that hearty and loyal support may be accorded every effort to put forth to accomplish the speedy winning of the war." And, "The congress will also formulate plans to extend the great work now being done through the campaign of patriotic education inaugurated by the National Security League ... it proposes that in schools, colleges and universities the education of the present and future generations shall emphasize the duties and responsibilities of citizenship."

With regard to the women's section of the Congress the reporter remarked that more than 500 educational, commercial, patriotic and civic bodies will be represented in Chicago. Among the scheduled speakers were former presidents William Howard Taft and Theodore Roosevelt, as well as New York State Governor Whitman, Governor Frank Lowden of Illinois, and Governor Richard I. Manning of South Carolina. Two other notables slated for the Congress were Jacob M. Dickinson (former U.S. Secretary of War in the Taft Administration) and Luke E. Wright (former U.S. Secretary of War in the Roosevelt Administration). Dickinson was honorary chairman of the Chicago NSL branch and Wright was one of the League's vice-presidents.[15]

One journalist who covered the Congress declared the final session of the Congress of National Service "was in the nature of a labor loyalty rally." Among the speakers were Charles Neill, former United States Commissioner of Labor, and Victor A. Olander, secretary of the Illinois Federation of Labor, and president of the Seamen's Union. Four members of the British labor mission to the United States also took part in the speech making. At another session Charles Edward Russell, described as formerly a socialist leader, denounced the pacifists of America, declaring that the pacifists in the U.S. were "either German spies, German agents or pro–Germans." At the final meeting of the women's section Helen Taft (daughter of William Howard Taft) spoke on the topic of "Women in Farm Work," while Virginia Gildersleeve (dean of Barnard College) spoke on the subject of Americanization with reference to the foreign-born.[16]

An editor in Indiana commented favorably in his newspaper about that Chicago Congress, declaring that the NSL was "speaking in clarion tones about the necessity of patriotism and loyalty." According to the editor, "The chief value of an organization such as this one lies in educating the people that there never was a war so righteous and so ideally prosecuted as this one. The very fact that we are idealistic in this war has prevented, in some degree, the flowing of the war spirit ... if we had selfish national aims ... we might arouse the more humanly materialistic side of our people more quickly. That's why we must educate the people of the nation to the sanctity of the cause." Concluded the editor, "The time is coming when all the little centers of discontent in the country must be suppressed ... these enemies from within should be hunted down vigorously and given the short shrift of a firing squad."¹⁷

Another speaker at the Congress was Waddill Catchings, chairman of the War Revenue Committee of the United States Chamber of Commerce. He declared that' "Business men are giving their full support by deed as well as by word.... The sons of business men are at the front; the fathers seek the opportunity of also serving their country." Reportedly, he spoke before 3,000 people.¹⁸

Soon, when the war ended, the League would turn much of its attention to focus on the "dangers" presented to America [to capitalism] by the socialists and communists and Bolsheviks. One of the infrequent mentions of the Reds before the end of the conflict came at that Chicago Congress. Governor Charles H. Brough of Arkansas said, "Do you realize there is a Bolsheviki in this country just as there is in Russia? Here it is known as the I.W.W. They are dwelling in the twilight of American patriotism. There can be no twilight zone—you must be for the President or you are against the flag." At the final session of the conference resolutions were adopted urging the enactment of UMT as a permanent policy. In her address to the women's section Mrs. Preston declared the war would do away with the so-called "idle rich" women of America because, she thought, "this type of woman will have acquired the habit of working and will not be able to throw it off even after the war."¹⁹

Helen Taft (1900 to 1920), daughter of former U.S. President William Howard Taft. She was one of the speakers at the NSL's Congress of National Service in Chicago in February 1918. Her topic was "Women in Farm Work."

The National Security League's educational program was not limited to the minds of young people. A national physical training movement was started on February 16 by the organization. Motivation for the plan was said to have come from the fact that 29 percent of the nation's youth, summoned by the draft, were being rejected for service on physical grounds. Walter Camp, described as a "veteran trainer of athletes," was to be in charge of the entire campaign. The mayors of every city in the nation with a population of 5,000 or more had been asked by the League to appoint a committee to cooperate with Camp. The NSL expressed a hope that by the coming summer it would have established physical training clubs in every city, town and hamlet in the nation.

Menken, NSL president, was worried about more than just the military aspect. "There is more than the military aspect of the matter to be considered. The difficulty of supplying a full quota of labor for industries makes it imperative that the man-power of the nation be brought to a maximum measure of physical strength." Capitalists, safe away from the horrors of war, were salivating over the prospects of enormous profits from the business of war—which they indeed collected. However, they worried that their plants might be left partially empty, or stocked by physically deficient workers, and thus, their excess profits could be put at peril. It was clearly necessary to get them into better physical shape, not just those off to fight and die for capitalists but those who stayed at home, to toil and die for capitalists. The fact that many of the young men called up in the draft were physically deficient was, in no small measure, likely due to the draconian working conditions imposed on the working class by the capitalist class in the first place.[20]

Toward the end of February there was more activity on the physical

Charles H. Bough, 1915-1920. Governor Brough of Arkansas also spoke at the NSL's Congress of National Service. He mentioned a theme the League would pursue with vigor when the war was over: going after organized labor, under the guise of rooting out Communists. At the Congress Brough declared, "Do you realize there is a Bolsheviki in this country just as there is in Russia? Here it is known as the I.W.W." (a radical labor union of the time).

Chapter 11. The General Campaign 163

MR. CAMP'S EXERCISES—ILLUSTRATED

This sketch of exercises accompanied an April 1918 article about Walter Camp's program to bring good health to America. When the NSL heard of the high percentage of young men rejected for military service because of physical deficiencies, the League resolved to change all that and hired Camp to design fitness programs. The real fear for the League and the capitalist class was that, with huge profits looming for them due to the war, the remaining male workers would be unable to do the difficult physical labor in the plants owned by the capitalists from which those enormous profits would flow.

front. By then a "Committee on Physical Reserve" had been assembled by the League with Walter Camp as its chairman. Richmond Virginia Mayor George Ainslie had just received a letter from the group seeking his cooperation in the promotion of such a movement in Richmond. That letter did acknowledge that in every community there were boards of health and organizations devoting themselves to physical fitness; however, "the mass of the people are not reached by the present methods, and … it is a matter of national concern that broader measures be adopted." The letter proposed that a committee on physical reserve be appointed in every city and town in the United States to inquire into the local situation and then communicate with the Camp committee "in order that we may advise you of our plans and put into operation a simple and pleasant system of physical upbuilding which does not require any considerable time expenditure for the individual and which has proven to produce the necessary results in a remarkably short period." The letter to Ainslie continued, "Will you be good enough to designate at least three persons to constitute your local committee. When you do so, will you kindly advise us and we will forward to you at once the details of the plan. As we are anxious to produce prompt results, we would appreciate your early reply." When the letter cited the 29 percent physical failure rate of those drafted it remarked that they were "physically unfit to perform the manhood duty of citizen service."[21]

A page of book listings that appeared on March 31, 1918, contained one for "America at War," described as an "American war manual" in compact form, prepared by the National Security League and edited by NSL member Albert Bushnell Hart, with an introductory preface by James M. Beck.[22]

Beginning on April 8, members of Congress were to be deluged with 500,000 cards from the National Security League bearing this appeal: "For God's Sake, Hurry Up." In those words, said the League, Joseph Choate appealed for more vigorous prosecution of the war in his last public utterance three days before his death. Choate had been honorary president of the NSL from its beginning until his death on May 14, 1917.[23]

At a lunch meeting of the NSL at the Hotel Astor in New York City, in the middle of April 1918, Colonel Samuel McRoberts of the ordnance bureau of the U.S. War Department spoke. McRoberts was vice-president of the National City Bank, New York City. He delivered his speech to the League audience on the occasion of the United States having been in the war for one year; some 700 NSL members and guests were reportedly at that meeting. McRoberts told the meeting that American factories, formerly engaged in the production of British rifles, had switched to rifles for American troops. Contracts for 2.5 million weapons had been let, 1,050,000 had been delivered and production had reached as high as 11,250 a day. Contracts for 300,000 machine guns had been let; 75,000 had been delivered to the troops. Also, 1,350,000 automatic pistols had been contracted for; 264,000 had been delivered. Small arms ammunition orders totaled 3.5 billion rounds; 270 million rounds were produced in March. Contracts amounting to more than $500,000,000 had been let for the manufacture of various types of field and heavy artillery. More than 40,000 motor vehicles had been delivered. A total of $70 million worth of shells of all calibers had been ordered with five million shells being delivered in March. Six hundred and fifty tons of explosives were in the process of manufacture and two smokeless powder plants of a capacity of 1.3 million pounds were being built. More than $100 million had been spent

Chapter 11. The General Campaign 165

in trench warfare materiel, including hand grenades, rockets, signal lights, and so forth.²⁴

Two examples of the public relations plants of articles could be seen late in April 1918 in two different newspapers. One, in Newberry, South Carolina, had approximately one half of a page given over to five separate articles from the NSL. All identified the article as being from the League (in the subhead), and two of the articles listed an author name in that subhead. These pieces were clearly NSL verbatim press releases placed in the paper to look like regular news articles when they were, in fact, advertising. The other newspaper was based in Alexandria, Virginia, and gave two-thirds of a page over to the NSL press releases with one of the pieces called "Editorial." Nothing else was on that page; the right-side one-third of the page was devoted to actual display ads. There were eight NSL public relations items on the page, three with a listed author, the rest without. Most of the pieces mentioned the NSL in the subheads, but the "Editorial" part did not.²⁵

Also in April there were a couple of articles published in a New York City newspaper about Walter Camp's "shorthand system" of physical exercises that were, said one article, "designed to make us all fit for any duty to which our country may call us." Walter Camp was chair of the NSL's Committee on Physical Reserve. Working with him on the committee were 13 other members (named in the article). Also, it was reported that the mayors of 300 cities were cooperating with Camp and his program. His exercises required 10 minutes per day and no apparatus was needed.²⁶

Group classes were also

Walter Camp, date unknown. Camp was chairman of the NSL's Committee on Physical Reserve. Thirteen other people were on that committee to design physical programs to make everyone fit for whatever "duty" called them. Reportedly, the mayors of 300 cities were cooperating with Camp and his program.

Employees of the New York State Industrial Commission are shown in this July 1918 photograph as they go through exercises designed by Walter Camp as part of the League's Committee on Physical Reserve.

part of the Camp system. A number of male and female employees went through the physical reserve exercises on the roof of the Victoria Building at 230 Fifth Avenue in Manhattan where they were employed by the New York State Industrial Commission. The class was called typical of hundreds organized throughout the nation by the National Security League. It met three times a week at 8:45 a.m. and went through a set of exercises designed for the NSL by Walter Camp of Yale University.[27]

War, Peace and the Future by Ellen Key, the Swedish writer on economic topics, noted a journalist, "has been suppressed through the efforts of the National Security League," and the publisher G.P. Putnam (an NSL member) had withdrawn it from circulation. The League sent the following statement to all libraries in the United States: "The National Security League, with the full consent and cooperation of the publisher, wishes to call the attention of your library to the fact that *War, Peace and the Future*, by Ellen Key, contains sentiments which at present are dangerous and should be suppressed. We therefore appeal to you to withdraw from circulation this book, which the publishers have voluntarily removed from their selling list." The book was called to the attention of the NSL by Olive M. Briggs of Lakewood, New Jersey, to whom it was recommended by a public librarian as a "war book." Strangely, or perhaps not, no specific criticisms

Chapter 11. The General Campaign

This photograph from 1917 or 1918 shows the Walter Camp exercise school. Officials of the U.S. Cabinet and other government officials are pictured here in Washington, D.C.

of the book appear to have been mentioned in the League's letter to the libraries.[28]

One contest held by the NSL in which winners were announced was in late 1917; the League solicited suggestions for the best methods of getting America's war aims before the German people, with a $1,000 prize for the winner. While the deadline for entries was February 1918, the winners were not announced until June 7, 1918. Judges couldn't decide on a single winner and four men were named co-winners, entitled to $250 each.

Winners were Dr. Henry Louis Smith (president of Washington and Lee University), F.J. Neubauer (Bronxville, NY), James H. Monahan (Brookline, MA), and John C. Ralston (Spokane, WA). More than 2,000 entries had been received. Also announced was the fact the prize money had been donated by J. Clarence Davies, described as a New York real estate broker. While the names of the winners were made public the suggestions made by those men remained secret because, noted a reporter, "Secrecy of the winning methods was adopted upon the advice of judges in the contest who declared the suggestions were of such practical value their publication might frustrate their effectiveness." But then a few weeks later there was a change of heart, at least in one case.

The method of Dr. Harry (Henry earlier) Louis Smith was revealed. Smith conceived the idea of releasing thousands of small balloons with propaganda attached by six-foot threads to be carried by the winds and so timed that they would land in the interior of Germany and Austria wherever desired 'and thus defeat the ironclad censorship.'" Smith had been informed back in February, when he won, that the NSL committee of judges thought so highly of the plan that they had already forwarded it to the War College "where it is now doubtless being employed."[29]

Late in July 1918 the League announced it had developed a system of training draft registrants for military service prior to their departure for cantonments (where they really were trained), which would be carried out by the NSL's 281 branches in cooperation with local draft boards across the country. Plans involved military drills, instruction and "sanitary education." The help of retired or disabled army officers, physicians and clergymen was to be enlisted. Under the plan each local draft board, through its chairman, would select a captain who would secure an adequate training officer. That captain would also invite a local clergyman to give information, instruction and advice to the young men. A local physician would be recruited to instruct the young men in matters of health, hygiene, and so forth. All of this was to be done so that the young men, when they got to the real camp for real training, "shall present themselves with a consciousness of knowledge which will add to their strength and usefulness."[30]

A different reporter summed up the NSL's proposed military training camps by describing them as the group's "systematic preliminary course of training for the young men in the draft so that when they are called they will know something of their duties and how to take care of themselves." The League planned to be in operation in every state in the U.S. under the direction of a committee. It might have been expected that the group would set up yet another committee, this one with the long-winded and somewhat grandiose name, "Committee on Preliminary Training and Instruction of Men Registered for Draft," to be appointed later. Before acting to set up the plan, the NSL had submitted the idea to U.S. Provost Marshal General Crowder, who approved it, writing to the League, "Your proposal gives me great satisfaction. Your league can render valuable assistance in this manner." General Franklin J. Bell, commandant at Camp Upton, was called an "enthusiastic" supporter of the plan and had promised the NSL cooperation in obtaining instructors for the classes.

League president Charles Lydecker explained, "The object of our endeavor will be to make the young men understand why they are called for service to their country, what is to be expected of them, and why they should be loyal, clean, sober and intelligent soldiers." Lydecker said, of the men to be trained under the plan, "the drafted men will go to their cantonments in efficient, organized bodies, rather than as a disorganized rabble, and with a spirit of self-reliance and comradeship. All the strangeness of the new life will have been eliminated and, since the men will have been taught what lies before them, they will face duty with the confidence of solidarity."[31]

By August 19, 1918, the League declared itself ready to put its preliminary training plan into immediate action. Instructions for the origination of the system were to be transmitted that day from NSL headquarters to the 5,000 local draft boards throughout the nation. That oversight committee with the very long name had by then been named. Members were: Surgeon General Charles F. Stokes (USN, ret.), the Right Rev. Charles Sumner Burch (Suffragan Episcopal Bishop of New York), Samuel B. Potter (commission merchant of New York City), Charles A. Bill (New York City broker and NSL executive committee member), Sidney Greenfield (one of the originators of the plan), and Charles E. Lydecker (NSL president, member ex officio).[32]

Another one of the League's planting of articles could be seen in the August 22, 1918, issue of a newspaper from Bottineau, North Dakota. This was standard with half of one page given over to a series of items, mostly mentioning the NSL in the author byline. As with all such material there was no date or place; that is, no dateline at all.[33]

Still another in the NSL's seemingly endless nationwide crusades was reportedly begun late in September 1918 with the announcement of its drive against the "premature peace" suggestion of the Teutonic powers. That crusade was launched in the form of personal utterances on the subject from some of the best known writers of the country. The League said it made those utterances public "as part of a propaganda for education of the people in the necessity for a conclusive victory over Germany which will be continued indefinitely by means of material supplied by the leading writers of the United States who are members of the league's volunteer editorial corps." The NSL prefaced its anti-peace announcement by commending President Wilson for his "prompt rejection" of the Austrian peace "feeler." Writers involved in this project, who were named by the National Security League, included Gertrude Atherton, Harold MacGrath, Wallace Irwin, John A. Sleicher (who asserted, "The supreme duty upon the allies and America is to ground Germany in the dust."), Cosmo Hamilton, the Rev. Dr. Charles H. Parkhurst ("There is nothing Germany needs so much, even for her own sake, as humiliation."), Walter Camp, Albert Payson Terhune and Richard Washburn Child ("The murderer and the pirate are not exterminated by peace-making").[34]

Chapter 12

Critics and Impugners

During this time period, when the United States was officially at war, the number of challenges to the National Security League dropped considerably. Only the *Nonpartisan Leader* (Fargo ND) consistently attacked the organization for what it really was and for what it really represented. The labor press, which had occasionally commented negatively on the group in the pre-war period, was silent. Mindless loyalty to the war machine had taken almost complete control, apparently. On the other hand, calls increased from members of the United States Congress to investigate the National Security League, its activities and its individual members, compared to the pre-war period.

Thousands greeted Theodore Roosevelt on his arrival in Chicago on April 28, 1917, where he was scheduled to give a speech under the auspices of the National Security League. According to the account Roosevelt was backed by "big business concerns" led by the Chicago packers and coal trust heads. Some of his backers were named: Arthur Meeker and J. Ogden Armour (stockyards, packers), Samuel Insull (public utility boss with Morgan and Rockefeller associations), and R.R. (Bertie) McCormick (editor of the *Chicago Tribune*). Roosevelt was then touting a bizarre notion of leading a private army to France and then his backers would run him for president, again, if he made good; this group was then referred to as "Teddy's Scouts." Said a journalist, "Teddy's Scouts have a press agent division, too, known as the National Security League." The head of the Chicago NSL branch was Harry Merrick (who drew his pay as a department head for Armour & Company, packers). Second in command to Merrick was Frank Rock (another department head at Armour). Another official of that Chicago branch was B.E. Sunny (head of the Chicago branch of the Bell Telephone Company).[1]

"The National Security League, a so-called 'patriotic organization' convicts itself of being something entirely different in a recent statement. It gives ground for the belief that, instead of being a patriotic organization it is a political organization of a sinister nature, existing for the purpose

Chapter 12. Critics and Impugners

of discrediting people's candidates for office especially candidates who indorse reform measures that are disapproved by the Big Interests and their servants among the politicians and newspapers," began a February 11, 1918, editorial in the *Nonpartisan Leader*. The message received by this editor was that the League was warning "voters to 'shy clear' of any candidates for congress put up this year by the organized farmers, because such candidates will be 'disloyal' and 'pro-German.'" Cited by the editor was the statement about the Nonpartisan League and Governor Frazier of North Dakota who were scored because delegates of the People's Council were welcomed to meet in that state. Frazier sanctioned such a meeting on the grounds of free speech and free assembly. That stance was attacked by the League and, in attempting to use the charge of "disloyalty" against the organized farmers and their candidates, the NSL was "attempting to place honest and patriotic citizens with whom it differs politically under suspicion. In addition it is being made the tool of the sinister interests which would halt all progress and reform on the ground that progress and reform are seditious."[2]

Later in 1918 the editor of the above newspaper began an editorial on the League by remarking that, "When, early in the war, the *Nonpartisan Leader* branded the National Security League as a cheap attempt to use patriotism to discredit democracy and liberalism in America we were called 'pro-German.' It was said we attacked a 'patriotic activity.'" Now, in September 1918, the editor declared the NSL "is now frankly in the field as a political organization." He went on to mention the rating of politicians done by the League and its nationwide effort to return to Congress "men of eminent ability and undoubted loyalty." Referring to a letter from the NSL to businessmen asking for money to help it in its "patriotic" work, the editor quoted, "The advantages to the business interests of the country of such representation in congress are self-evident." The editorial continued, "Alton B. Parker, reactionary Democrat and one-time big business candidate for president, is an officer of the Security League. Elihu Root is president. Root is an eminent gentleman who has devoted a lifetime to fighting democracy in America and trying to head off all liberal tendencies of the people.... The Security League is a stupid camouflage for big business. It is one of the sinister organizations trying to use the war to lay low progressive men and measures."[3]

A month later the same newspaper returned with an editorial about the NSL's campaign of patriotism through education. In one of its bulletins the League had said it wanted to "lay the foundations for a permanent system of patriotic education in the public schools." It also claimed it wanted to carry "a message of militant patriotism into every nook and corner of the land," through the schools. And that it wanted "to create a more responsive American citizenship through the medium of better methods of permanent patriotic instruction in the public schools." Said the editor, "Reads well, doesn't it. But do you know what the NSL means by 'a permanent system of patriotic education and by 'militant patriotism?' You don't know unless you know what the NSL is." Explained the editor: "It is the foremost society in America promoting militarism. It means by these high-sounding terms nothing less than compulsory military training in the schools." As far as the campaign for patriotism through education it "is damnable and anti–American and should be immediately suppressed by official government action. Lacking that, it can be headed off by educators with backbone, if there are any such left."

The editor then cited an editorial from a different newspaper (*Capital Times*, Madison WI) with respect to the patriotism through education crusade: "We don't want that sort of thing in this country. We are not satisfied that the activities of the National Security League are actuated alone by consideration of patriotism. The league is the foremost exponent of military preparedness and compulsory military service in this country." And, continued that editorial, "There are too many men identified with the Security League who are interested in financial emoluments arising out of preparedness and compulsory service to make us view with anything but suspicion this campaign of 'patriotism' that the league is undertaking. The danger of the present plan lies in the arrogance of the Security league and the timidity of educators."[4]

Another voice raised against the League came from the editor of the *South Bend News-Times* (Indiana) who wrote, on November 2, 1918, that it had recently received a communication from the NSL that was critical of

This editorial cartoon appeared in the *Nonpartisan Leader* newspaper in October 1918 and poked fun at the National Security League's determination to force "patriotism" onto elementary education pupils as part of their standard curriculum.

Chapter 12. Critics and Impugners

some of the newspaper's positions. Said the editor, referring to the League, "Its disguise of monopolists of American patriotism and infalliblists as to what constitutes legislative wisdom, having had something of a hole kicked into it, it is beginning to threaten." And, he continued, "We are frightened, terribly frightened. We know they are great lawyers, these counsel for the arms and munitions manufacturers, whose only seeming idea of wise patriotism is arms and munitions making, and big congressional appropriations to fatten the makers, but we guess we have a right to print facts from the *Congressional Record*, and are not so very particular about their roar." Concluded the editor, "The test of loyalty is anti-surrender to Germany—not surrender to the American army supply profiteers—or their special political pleaders."[5]

Investigation by the Judiciary Committee into the activities of the National Security League was asked of the United States House of Representatives on September 23, 1918, by Representative James A. Frear (WI). He had been attacked by the NSL during the recent primary campaign in which he was renominated for the election. He described the letter sent to members of the House as "insolent" and he specifically criticized NSL officials Root and Parker. In calling for an investigation Frear said, "This is no time for recrimination, but the days are too critical for a selfish war-profiteering league to denounce as disloyal practically 90 per cent of the membership of this House...." He characterized Root and Parker as "Wall Street patriots." He was criticized by the League for, among other things, voting against the declaration of war by the United States, in April 1917. That fact is mentioned to this very day in his Wikipedia page. However, he survived, electorally, the League criticism. Frear served in the U.S. House continuously from 1913 to 1935.[6]

The resolution Frear intro-

James A. Frear, ca. 1915–1920. Frear was a Republican Representative from Wisconsin who was one of many politicians attacked by the NSL for views that did not align with its own views. He was one of the first politicians to stand up and attack the League, demanding that Congress launch a full investigation into the activities and financing of the League.

duced into the House charged that the NSL was "composed of and financed by war profiteers living in New York and elsewhere." He introduced his resolution after delivering a "scathing arraignment of the methods adopted by the league to constitute itself a judge as to the patriotism and loyalty of members of Congress and pass upon their fitness for re-election." Frear claimed the League had expended upwards of $1 million in carrying on its propaganda, such expenditures being denounced in the resolution as contrary to the Corrupt Practices Act. In his House speech, Frear declared that "An insolent letter received by Representatives in Congress from the National Security League, of New York, with an impudent questionnaire, comes from an organization that has prostituted the name of Americanism to defeat Congressmen. The letter carries the name of Elihu Root and Alton B. Parker to give it character. I will not discuss undenied reports that one of its sponsors hired a substitute during the Civil War. Another sponsor for the libelous league was snowed under in a popular election a few years ago by over 2,500,000 votes because of his alleged subservience to Wall Street." The resolution introduced by Frear was referred to the House Rules Committee.[7]

When another newspaper tackled the subject two weeks later, it referred to the League in a subhead as "Self-assured know-it-all of American patriotism in danger of scorching." It reported that because it had been aroused by the "unscrupulous attacks" made upon its patriotism and Americanism in the broadsides of the NSL, the House of Representatives was taking steps for an investigation of that organization, its personnel, its political and big business affiliations and the source of its funds. In the meantime, Representative Ferris, chair of the Democratic Congressional Committee, had started a little investigation of his own. He had been informed by members that the NSL had made plans to "horn in" on the Liberty Loan drive with people of its own who, in addition to boosting the Liberty Loan program, would adroitly sandwich in arguments for universal military training (UMT). During the third Liberty Loan drive, the NSL, it was reported, did precisely that on at least one occasion when one League official mixed up the two items to suggest they were fundamentally if not officially related. Frear's resolution was still under consideration but, "It is a matter of lively interest to almost everyone in the country who has been flooded with material from the league. There is scarcely a weekly paper which has not repeatedly been offered by the league free 'plate matter' on the benefits of a conscript training system after the war. According to a recent private bulletin of the league this 'plate matter' has been paid for by one Ridley Watts. *Who's Who* contains no mention of Mr. Watts but the *Directory of Directors* puts him down as one of the directors of the Chemical National Bank of New York City." (Chemical formed the core of today's J.P. Morgan Chase

Chapter 12. Critics and Impugners

banking firm.) This article speculated that perhaps a Congressional probe into the activities of the NSL "will explain still further where their funds come from and something about the motives behind their attacks upon the patriotism of everybody who does not agree with them."[8]

Another member of Congress who spoke out about the NSL report cards was J. Hampton Moore, a Representative from Pennsylvania. "This aggregation has been setting up opposition to many members because of their votes before the war and on the war issue and has stirred up a good deal of resentment," he asserted. "If speeches made by McLemore, of Texas, Democrat; McCullough, of Ohio, Republican, and Hilliard, of Colorado, Democrat, may be accepted as criterion, the National Security League is 'a bunch of Wall Street profiteers.'"[9]

An Indiana newspaper published an editorial about the NSL that was originally published in a different Indiana paper. With respect to the NSL report card, "The league, in our judgment, despite the patriotic purpose of its founders, is in a fair way to become an unqualified public nuisance. We have been of the opinion that many of its methods were operating directly to prevent the maintenance of the unity so essential to national security." And, continued the editorial, "It is time for the thoughtful people of the country to call sharply to account any man or organization that hurls about loose charges of disloyalty and pro-Germanism. Do the patriotic and distinguished men who are lending their names to the Security league desire longer to promote the campaign of abuse, disunity and terrorism that it is carrying on?"[10]

Part III

*Americanization,
1918 (November 11)–1922*

Chapter 13

The Organization

In the period from its formation up until the official entry of America into World War I the National Security League devoted itself mostly to proselytizing for the war machine under the banner of "preparedness." From the date of entry until the official end of that conflict the League devoted itself mostly to proselytizing for the war machine under the banner of "loyalty." From the date of the armistice and onward, until the group faded away, the League devoted itself most to proselytizing for the war machine under the banner of "Americanization."

One day after the armistice Mrs. Thomas J. Preston was made director of the National Security League's Speakers' Bureau. At that time the bureau reportedly had nearly 2,000 volunteer "patriotic" speakers enrolled. Said Preston, "The bureau is considered one of the most important features of the league's work." Several days later, Joseph T. Cashman, NSL organizer, arrived in South Bend, Indiana, with the intention of organizing a branch in that community. Explaining the purpose of the League, Cashman stated, "It is a bi-partisan organization, which has been fighting the re-election of congressmen and senators who have voted wrong on war measures, and which now is taking up the work of reconstruction, etc." A somewhat different mission statement came from NSL headquarters in New York City, still in November 1918. Since peace had arrived the League announced that it would carry on a "vigorous campaign to educate Americans in the 'meaning of Americanism.'"[1]

Late in December, NSL president Charles Lydecker was asked why Menken had resigned the presidency of the League back in June of that year. Lydecker explained that after Menken had referred to "reprobate William Randolph Hearst for opposing certain national preparedness measures" both Menken and members of the League's executive committee had decided it would be better for him to resign. Hearst complained it was not fair for the NSL to abuse him after he had rendered such aid to the League in the early days of its life. In an interview Menken had given earlier, the former head of the League agreed that Hearst's newspapers had given aid to his group and added that the public's "opposition toward Hearst was due more to the way they looked at his articles than to the facts the articles contained." Lydecker added, "That statement burned its way into the minds of the people, as Hearst was being seriously criticized at that time for his attitude toward the war, and as any one who stood by him came under the most severe condemnation of the National Security League, it was believed a new league president should be chosen."[2]

When H. M. Byllesby became head of the Chicago branch of the NSL, in April 1919, it drew a response from J. L. Pelton of Erie, Pennsylvania, who, in a letter to the editor, declared Byllesby was "absolutely owned and controlled by the Morgan-General Electric copper interests, and it is safe to say that all candidates having the league's support will be sworn enemies of municipal and government ownership, and those not indorsed by the league will be Bolsheviki, disloyal, etc."[3]

The League held its fifth annual meeting on May 7, 1919, in New York City. A number of resolutions were passed with one urging the necessity of universal military training, a priority for the group in peacetime as well as in wartime. Its Americanization program applied to everyone in the United States, it was reiterated at the gathering, "whether native born or foreign-born." And the organization also declared, "Insistence upon the duty of every American to fit himself for the work of national defense as an indispensable element in citizenship." The League reviewed its own record and then "ridiculed" the Congressional investigation into its activities that had recently concluded and, speaking to the NSL's critics in and out of Congress, stated, "To those people and to their press the National Security League bids defiance." Officers were elected for 1919–1920; they were honorary president Elihu Root, honorary vice-president Alton Parker, vice-presidents Stanwood Menken, Robert Bacon, Myron T. Herrick, George Wharton Pepper, Willet H. Spooner and Luke Wright. Alexander J. Hemphill was elected treasurer and Charles D. Orth, secretary. The men placed on the board of directors were Herbert Barry, Charles A. Bill, Franklin Q. Brown, Thomas W. Churchill, Hayden B. Harris, Frank Presbrey, Charles F. Rand, Lloyd Taylor and Augustus Thomas.[4]

More changes in the organization's structure took place in late 1919 and early 1920. Dr. David Jayne Hill was named to the NSL' executive committee and Ole Hanson had added his name to its roster. The organization had underway a campaign to raise membership from 100,000 to one million members. That was a very grandiose idea in light of the fact that the National Security League was in the process of fading away. Charles D. Orth was elected NSL president to succeed Charles Lydecker, who was retiring in ill health. Orth had been League secretary for the previous year. Lloyd Taylor was elected secretary to replace Orth.[5]

The NSL held its sixth annual meeting in New York City on May 5, 1920. Lindley M. Garrison (former United States Secretary of War) was elected honorary president with Alton Parker re-elected honorary vice-president. Orth was re-elected president of the organization. Other elected vice-presidents were Stanwood Menken, Myron Herrick (Ohio), Theodore Roosevelt (NY), Willett M. Spooner (WI), Michael J. Friedsam (NY) and Luke E. Wright (TN). Alexander J. Hemphill was elected treasurer while Lloyd Taylor was re-elected secretary. The following directors were also chosen: Herbert Barry, Charles Alfred Bill, Franklin Brown, Thomas W. Churchill, Mrs. Oliver Harriman, Adolph Lewisohn, Frederick J. Lisman, Charles F. Rand and Louis W. Stotesbury.[6]

Alexander J. Hemphill died at the end of 1920, aged 64. He was chairman of the Board of Directors at Guaranty Trust Company and he was, noted a journalist, "for many years one of the foremost financiers of America." He had been treasurer of the NSL and chair of the League's finance committee. Also, Hemphill was on the boards of about 26 other firms that were involved in banking, insurance, railroads, public utilities, and so forth. He was also involved in the J.P. Morgan banking firm.[7]

Further evidence of the decline of the National Security League came late in 1921 when the organization announced it had called upon its founder, S. Stanwood Menken, to again head the group, despite the fact he had been essentially fired fairly recently. Menken, the first president, was succeeded by Robert Bacon and when Bacon resigned to take a post on General Pershing's staff, Menken again was chosen as president. Orth followed (under circumstances not explained herein) and then Orth resigned, opening the position up, once again for Menken. A couple of days later it was reported that NSL membership stood at 25,000. The group announced a plan to advance the study of "foreign and domestic economic problems," under the slogan "Economic Preparedness," but provided no details.[8]

More dissension from the League was reported in January 1926 when Professor William Bradley Otis of the College of the City of New York resigned as director of the NSL at the request of the group's president, Robert Bullard, who opposed the view of Otis against compulsory military training in colleges. The vote by the board of directors to expel Otis was unanimous, although chairman of the board Menken argued for free speech. Otis explained that he favored military training in colleges—but that it should be voluntary.[9]

At the NSL's 14th annual meeting in June 1928 Franklin Q. Brown, president of the Army and Navy Club of America, was unanimously elected honorary president of the League; he was described as one of seven founders of the group. Mrs. Mary B. Pollard of St. Louis was elected to the board of directors, the first woman to be so selected "in several years." Bullard

Chapter 13. The Organization

was re-elected president, Menken chairman of the board and T. Hubbard as vice-president. Also George Chamberlain (former U.S. Senator from Washington) and Myron T. Herrick (former U.S. Ambassador to France) were both elected as honorary vice-presidents. Percy H. Johnston was chosen as treasurer.[10]

Mrs. Thomas J. Preston (Frances Folsom Cleveland Preston) was born on July 21, 1864, and died on October 29, 1947, at the age of 83. She became the wife of President Grover Cleveland (age 49) in a White House ceremony at the age of 22, on June 2, 1886. Cleveland died July 24, 1908, and on February 10, 1913, she married Professor Thomas Preston, Jr., who had taught at Wells College. In 1918 she succeeded Mr. Preston as director of the National Security League's Speakers' Bureau. It was reported that she had inherited about $250,000 from her father (a wealthy lawyer) and a "comfortable fortune" from Grover Cleveland. As the widow of a U.S. president, under legislation passed in 1940 she received a pension of $5,000 annually.[11]

Robert Lee Bullard, 86, died on September 11, 1947. He retired from the United States military upon reaching the army age limit of 64 years on June 15, 1925, and one obituary said, "Thereafter he devoted himself to

Mrs. Thomas J. Preston, ca. 1915–1920. Preston was atypical for an NSL member only from the perspective of her gender. In all other ways she was very typical. She inherited a fortune when her father (a wealthy lawyer) died and then another fortune when her first husband died (former U.S. President Grover Cleveland).

spreading the ideas of military preparedness, adherence to the Constitution of the United States and similar patriotic efforts. Most of this work was done as president of the National Security League, to which position he was elected in 1925."[12]

General Robert Lee Bullard, 1919. He came to the League late and was elected president of the organization in 1925. However, by then, the NSL was a forgotten force.

CHAPTER 14

The Reds

The main focus of the League's Americanization activities was said to be against the Bolsheviks, the Socialists and any other ideology that was remotely contrary to the American capitalist system. It was, in fact, directed at suppressing dissent in America. While on the surface Americanization was directed at the foreign-born it was also directed at those born in the United States. Peace officially arrived on November 11, 1918. Two days later New York City Police Inspector Daley declared that Socialists could obtain permits for parades whenever they asked for them. The NSL and the American Defense Society took steps on that same day to prevent what they termed the "flaunting" of the Bolshevist emblem (a red flag). The American Defense Society appointed an anti-anarchist committee while the NSL urged a legal prohibition against the use of the red flag in any public assembly or parade.[1]

Some two weeks later a furious Charles Lydecker of the National Security League wrote a letter to a New York City newspaper to complain about the city's unwillingness to ban the red flag, to bar Socialist parades, and so forth. Apparently this newspaper had published an editorial on that subject on November 23. Grumbled Lydecker, "But to rally crowds about the red flag is to invite revolt and rebellion against constituted authority, and the duty rests upon the agents of government to prevent the act when threatened and to stop it when it occurs." In Lydecker's view a law was needed. "Why should Mayor [John] Hylan wait for the Board of Aldermen or the state Legislature if demagogues brazenly defy his executive authority and threaten the orderly administration of the law." With respect to the protesters themselves, thundered Lydecker, "These people are encouraged to formulate and state their views under the Stars and Stripes, but not under the symbol of rapine, murder, lawlessness and hate of all conservatism."[2]

To combat Bolshevism the National Security League launched, late in November, another in its seemingly endless series of "nationwide campaigns." This one proposed to counteract "un–American propaganda. It proposes to inculcate, especially in the foreign born element of the country's population, an understanding of the ideals of American citizenship and of the constitution of the United States." And "It is also urged that the utmost efforts be exerted to combat the tendency toward socialism by explaining to the people that socialism is an unsafe foundation upon which to rest and that its leaders are not men who can be trusted to conduct the government." After reviewing the above, an editor with a Texas newspaper remarked, "But the best way of all to combat Bolshevism is to provide plenty of work and good wages. The more money workers get in the bank the less inclined they are toward visionary government schemes of a revolutionary nature."[3]

Pressure brought to bear on New York Mayor Hylan led to a summary order to New York City Police Commissioner Richard Enright to prevent the display of the red flag in the streets and at public meetings in New York City. Coupled with that announcement, declared a journalist, "is the warning that the league's new activities must not be understood to be directed against social or economic free thinking, but only against the various disturbing elements that masquerade in the guise of socialism." The NSL also announced that a series of meetings for the instruction of speakers to spread the anti–Bolshevist propaganda would be held urging the coming winter. The first such meeting was held at the rooms of the New York City Bar Association on December 2, 1918, and was addressed by Martin W. Littleton.[4]

Soon thereafter the NSL outlined its reasons for combating the "un-American" Socialists and Bolsheviki. The points on which Socialism or Bolshevism were to be attacked were specified as follows. Point number one was the "consistent attitude" of many Socialists before and during the war that was "seditious, anti–American and distinctly and definitely pro–German in purpose and effect. Since the armistice was signed the outgivings of many Socialist leaders have been aimed at helping Germany to escape retribution and punishment." Point number two was that the NSL characterized as un–American and would combat as such the principles of any group that forbade its members to enter the army or the navy "and required every member to vote only for certain candidates under penalty of expulsion."

Point number three was that "Heretofore, the un–American Socialists assumed the attitude of putting the defenders of government on the defensive. Americans had a tangible government to defend, while they had only untried theories. They and their brothers in Russia now have a record of achievement, a record of murder and atrocity." Point number four was: "The published constitution of the Soviet government and the doctrines of Lenin show that the Bolshevist program includes ideas on labor control which are absolutely contrary to the ideals of American labor."

During this latest nationwide campaign against the Reds, the NSL's "patriotic propaganda" on the subject was aimed to reach two classes of people: "first, patriotic Americans who do not realize the malevolence and the seditious attitude of the un–American wing of the parties of demoralization; second, the rank and file of Socialists who are unaware of the autocratic ideas of many of their leaders."[5]

Troubles for the Socialists in finding places to hold meetings were aired in a January 1919 letter signed by the New York City Socialist Aldermen and sent to Police Commissioner Richard Enright asking him to use his influence with the owners of auditoriums in obtaining the freer use of meeting halls. The charge was made that city policemen had advised hall owners not to rent their venues for Socialist meetings. Algernon Lee, one of the New York City Socialist aldermen, accused the NSL of backing this alleged move. Lee said, in part, "members of the National Security League are boasting that they helped to defeat the Socialist members for Congress in New York City, and that it is even impossible for the Socialist party to hold a meeting in a hall." And, added Lee, the "Constitution means little to a body like the National Security League. We are certain that the citizens of New York City, regardless of party affiliations, will resent

Algernon Lee, ca. 1915–1920. New York City Socialist Alderman Lee accused the New York Police Department of advising owners of halls and other venues not to rent their premises for Socialist meetings. Lee believed the NSL was behind that impetus.

any effort to deny the Socialist party the same rights that the Democrats and Republicans enjoy."[6]

Widespread approval, in April 1919, of New York City Mayor Hylan's steps "to wipe out Bolshevism and anarchy in the city" manifested itself when the NSL and the American Defense Society each adopted resolutions pledging their support. The League resolution, from the executive committee, "expresses its appreciation of the position taken by Mayor Hylan in his letter to the President of the Board of Aldermen of New York City suggesting the adoption of an ordinance that will operate to prevent the holding of meetings in this city whose proceedings are conducted in a foreign language for the abuse of our government or by or under the auspices of any person or persons who are not citizens of the United States, and pledges the support of the National Security League in carrying this suggestion into effect."[7]

Still in April, the NSL outlined "A comprehensive plan for combating the menace of Bolshevism in this country through a new medium, the youth of the land in the high schools...." Reportedly, this particular plan was based on the idea that "Bolshevism is purely a question of education." Through Miss Etta V. Leighton, a "well-known" teacher of civics who for some time had been the NSL Civic Secretary and who conducted the League's "Correspondence Course in Patriotism" for teachers during the war, thousands of high-school teachers were already enrolled in NSL work "and have immediately joined in the new effort." Reportedly, Leighton had obtained the cooperation in this "good citizenship teaching" of nearly 100 parochial schools, in 23 states—with many of those states having been participants in that earlier program.

Leighton wrote: "The ultra-radical forces have long known that any doctrine of seeming humanity appeals to the hearts of young high-school people aflame with a desire to quickly correct all the evils of the body politic and to reform the world over-night." The NSL, it was reported, "believes that the only antidote needed for the poison gas of sedition is a clear knowledge of the fundamental ideals of our government." Once those pupils reached that point, explained Leighton, "These young high-school students will strip the anti–American doctrine of all camouflage; they will show the difference between full-blooded democracy and the rattling skeleton of 'the dictatorship of the proletariat....'"

The appeal from the League to high school students to engage in that work read as follows: "I.W.W. and Bolshevist doctrines are rampant in the land.... They menace the formulations of the Republic and can only be met and conquered by continued and earnest preaching of American doctrine which exposes their fallacies and proves that dictatorship of the proletariat, as by any other single group, brings tyranny, not freedom." High school teachers were urged to prepare "simple talks explaining how the radical reactionary doctrines, which are at present making so much progress, are opposed to our American institutions…" A further statement on the topic by the National Security League asserted, "Besides being thoroughly familiar with all that America stands for, by taking up this work in the high schools, these young crusaders will go forth and explain to others the fallacies of class doctrine and the failure of Bolshevist rule."[8]

E. L. Harvey, National Security League director of publicity, explained the anti–Bolshevik campaign by declaring, "By Bolshevism we mean anarchy, communism and every other kind of seditious agitation. Reports from our correspondents all over the country have convinced us that a campaign is called for." Harvey added, "We feel that suppressing such activities is not enough. If a man's mind is filled with that kind of idea you must not only drive it out but give him something to take the place of it. Our campaign will supply him with the idea of loyal Americanism, show him what the United States is and means." To facilitate this campaign the League was recruiting for its flying squadron of stump speakers and literature was being prepared.[9]

According to an NSL report of early May, more than one million American women pledged themselves to assist in an educational campaign to combat Bolshevism. All women's clubs were urged to enroll in the movement, which was said to be largely the work of Etta Leighton. One women involved was Mrs. Reginald De Koven, wife of the "well-known" composer, who had enlisted in the League's nationwide crusade against "the menace of Bolshevism" in America. Another aspect that was envisioned in the effort was the prospective formation of a national high school clearing house to disseminate through the high schools of the land standard forms for patriotic and civic study. A preliminary basis of the plan was a report based on the current methods of such instruction in certain schools in New York City. That report was said to have been made by De Koven, who had been investigating them.[10]

The League of Nations was attacked on May 7, 1919, as standing for internationalism, which the Bolsheviks also favored, by Miles Poindexter (U.S. Senator, WA) in his address before the 5th annual meeting of the National Security League in New York City. At that meeting League President Charles Lydecker also declared war on Bolshevism: "It is a seditious and treacherous movement of the worst autocratic form. Its aims are the overthrow of religion and the home." Upon those sentiments the audience of a reported 2,500 gave cheers to Lydecker. He continued, "Patriotism at this moment calls for open, strong and intelligent exposition of the insidious teachings of the International Socialists … who are assiduously disseminated through the most revolutionary doctrines and polluting all the springs of knowledge." One of the resolutions adopted at that meeting stated, "We, therefore, pledge ourselves to oppose in every lawful manner that reactionary movement called Bolshevism, falsely claiming to be progressive which to-day is menacing the civilization which free peoples hold in trust for all humanity."[11]

As part of its nationwide educational crusade of Americanization to counteract the growing influence of "the doctrine of disorganization and destruction," the National Security League announced on June 19 that it had enlisted the heads of all teachers' Normal Schools in 22 states for active work against Bolshevism. That effort was based on the idea that the school teachers of the nation, "while intensely patriotic, are largely unqualified to answer the insidious arguments of present day radicals. The League has found this contention supported by many of the leading educators of the country and is exerting every effort to overcome this condition." All the cooperating Normal Schools, it was said, "have promised to create special courses for the instruction of their teachers in sound pro–American arguments against Bolshevism." It was the League's intention to expand that program to all states.[12]

Later in June the League announced it had completed plans for the anti–Bolshevik drive in every state of the union. The campaign was to be carried on with each state as a unit by various patriotic organizations which had become associated with the National Security League in the project. That campaign was directed by the NSL organization committee of which Dr. David Jayne Hill was chairman. An auxiliary committee was reported to include the governors of 19 states and within each state the drive was led by a director. September 17, 1919, was the day slated for mass meetings in every city, town and hamlet in the country, to which 28 chambers of commerce and 17 bar associations had promised to furnish speakers. Other organizations involved in the campaign ranged far and wide, from the American Defense Society to the Boy Scouts of America.[13]

Mrs. William L. Black was described as a "star member" of the National Security League's New York City "Flying Squadron" of "anti–Bolshevist soapbox orators." That group of street corner speakers had existed within the NSL for some years but in the period after the armistice they were "now concentrating on shattering the arguments of radical disturbers." Mrs. Black had just returned to New York City from Minneapolis where she assisted in the organization of a similar squadron in that city. In her speeches Black based her attack on the "internationalist's menace of the home." She worried that "if there exists no private property relation, the family as we understand it, will disappear."[14]

Warning the public generally to wake up before it was too late to the real meaning of the "radical agitation" throughout the United States, the NSL executive committee issued the following statement, on October 19, 1919, on the industrial situation: "It is social revolution downward—nothing else. The radical agitation which is menacing the foundations of our industrial life is not based upon specific grievances, but is aimed at the overthrow of American institutions and ideals just as surely as if a Bolshevik army was marching on Washington. The American people are confronted with all the destructive forces of minority rule which have made a waste of Russia."

The statement urged Americans to promote "the protection of personal liberty and the right of property.... Loyalty, patriotism, love of country are, in the final analysis, a willingness to abide by the laws of the land which give to all their rights, and demand from all the rights of each." Focusing on destroying labor, the statement asserted, "The true American spirit has been splendidly illustrated in recent times by the prompt action of Mayor Ole Hanson in dealing with the I.W.W. revolutionary element in Seattle, and equally so by Governor [Calvin] Coolidge in punishing the deserters among the police force in Boston" who went on strike. "Property rights must be declared inviolable to protect every man in the community in his rights and ambitions, and those who would try to break down that law should be reasoned with gently, if that will suffice, firmly, in any and every case, and without mercy if persisted in."[15]

Another famous name recruited by the National Security League was author Mary Roberts Rinehart. The byline of the piece said, "Written by Mary Roberts Rinehart for National Security League." That article was the usual League rant against "radicalism" and perhaps wasn't

Mary Roberts Rinehart, 1914. Author Rinehart was yet another famous name recruited by the League. She produced at least one signed piece for the NSL. It was a mirror image of the usual League rant against "radicalism."

written by Rinehart herself, but penned by the organization with Rinehart allowing her name to be used as author. One part of the piece declared, "Radicalism in its present form is simply the attempt to impose the will of a militant minority on an unsuspecting majority."[16]

When Eugene V. Debs was nominated for U.S. President in 1920 by the Socialist Party the NSL leader Orth declared that move to be a refutation of any idea that the Socialist Party had abandoned radicalism.[17]

During the summer of 1922 the NSL was sending around a form asking for the universal condemnation of the activities of the Women's Peace Society and other similar bodies with their "No More Wars" campaign being conducted throughout America as "part of a plan by parlor socialists and bolshevists to decry patriotism as the greatest of vices."[18]

By the early 1920s the League had become almost irrelevant and often a subject of scorn as its tirades and rants became increasingly silly. Countess Karolyi, wife of Michael Karolyi, the President of Hungary, visited America in late 1924. Her visit was well publicized and warmly noted. Described as an "aristocrat of aristocrats," she was welcomed by a committee of prominent American women and members of the social elite, including Margaret Woodrow Wilson and Mrs. Franklin D. Roosevelt, and so forth. Menken, of the NSL, called her "Red Catherine" and demanded that she be deported as she was a menace to American institutions. With respect to Menken's charges against Karolyi, one newspaper said that the NSL "is nothing if not amusing in its latter activities." Other papers treated the topic with much "ridicule heaped upon Mr. Menken." Any idea that she would tear down American institutions was jeered at as ludicrous.[19]

Continual warfare on the "secret enemies" of our country was urged by General Robert Lee Bullard (ret.) in an address in Little Rock, Arkansas, on April 29, 1925, before the annual convention of the Arkansas Bankers' Association. Bullard, who went on to head the NSL, declared the same conditions existed then in the United States as during World War I when "aliens, radicals and Communists were working secretly." He added, "It is the duty of American citizens to guard against these undesirables. That is what I'm trying to teach in my National Security League work."[20]

In a surprise move, in September 1930, Menken declared he and the National Security League now favored the recognition of Russia—i.e., the Union of Soviet Socialist Republics. They had always vehemently opposed the idea that the United States would officially recognize the Soviet Union. Menken did add that he remained as much opposed to communism as ever. Two months later Menken, the originator and president of the NSL, announced that he had resigned as chairman of the board as the result of a vote by 11 members of that board against American recognition of Communist Russia. Trying to explain his rash decision to favor recognition,

Menken explained that he favored recognition only on the condition the Soviet government paid its debts and agreed not to conduct Communist propaganda in the United States. However, it did not save him from being voted out by the board.[21]

In the spring of 1933 a mass meeting was held, under the auspices of the American Legion, to protest against American recognition of the USSR. Eight or nine speakers were listed for that event, but none of them were from the NSL. Other organizations that had agreed to participate in the meeting were listed; a total of 22 groups were involved, the NSL was listed in 17th place. It had faded away and no longer existed in any meaningful form. The United States officially recognized the Soviet Union in 1933; it was the last major power to do so.[22]

CHAPTER 15

The General Campaign

A letter to the editor of a New York newspapers about 10 days after the November 1918 elections noted that the defeat of all six Socialist party candidates in New York City did not mean the danger was over: "An important work in this connection is being done by the National Security League's 'propaganda regiment' of open-air soapbox orators, known as the 'flying squadron.' ... The speakers never attacked socialism per se, but always made it clear to their street audiences that their objection was purely to Socialists who denounced the objects of America in the war." The letter writer added, "I am glad to see that to-day we are not ashamed to preach a good healthy, red-blooded Americanism and love of country on the highway and byway."[1]

A little later that month the NSL announced that its Congressional Committee was to be continued as a permanent bureau, for the advocacy of Congressional reform—supposedly still on a nonpartisan basis. Charles Orth, chairman of the committee, said, "It would be well for the people of the country to awaken immediately to the probability that a battle is going to be waged in the United States Senate for its practical control by the three Senators whose records during the period of the country's crisis were the most disgraceful. They are Senators [George] Norris [NE], [Robert] La Follette [WI], [Asle] Gronna [ND]." While Orth argued his committee would continue because, for one thing, reforms in the system were needed, he was vague about what those reforms were. He declared that in the 65th Congress there was only one anti-war Socialist in the House of Representatives, Meyer London, who was defeated, but the 66th Congress would still have one anti-war Socialist in the person of Victor Berger of Milwaukee. "Notwithstanding this excellent showing, twenty-four men who voted against the declaration of war were reelected to the Sixty-Sixth Congress," said Orth. "The National Security League believes the partisan issue should not have been made predominant in the election and that if it had not been the natural sentiment of the country would have defeated every man who voted against the declaration of war, or who otherwise failed in the 'acid test' of true loyalty and genuine Americanism."²

On the same day the League appealed to the 500,000 American women "who are cooperating in the organization's propaganda to 'be on the alert against sympathetic sentimentality for the defeated enemy and to stand firm for a peace of justice.'" The appeal was made in the form of a warning sent out by Etta V. Leighton, secretary of the NSL's education department, to women's civic and patriotic organizations throughout the United States. Said the warning, "Be on guard ... against the apparently concerted movement to start a wave of sympathy for the enemy and to work for leniency in the armistice and final peace terms." Already in the works were plans for a "proposed boycott of German-made goods by various groups and organizations, including the National Security League."³

Asle Gronna, 1911. After the November 1918 congressional elections, Senator Gronna of North Dakota was described by the NSL as one of three U.S. Senators whose records during the nation's previous war crisis had been "disgraceful." The others were George Norris of Nebraska and Robert La Follette of Wisconsin.

At the end of November the League announced it had chosen a committee on organized education that would handle all questions pertaining to Americanization and the work that was to be done in schools, colleges, and other educational institutions. Dr. Robert M. McElroy was the chair; Mrs. Thomas J. Preston, Jr., was secretary; and Dr. Henry D. Thompson was educational secretary. Other members of the committee were Dr. Albert Bushnell Hart, Dr. Talcott Williams, George Haven Putnam, Thomas W. Churchill, Charles E. Lydecker, Calvin W. Rice and Arthur Wolfson. As well, an advisory board was named for the committee—Dr. Philander P. Claxton, Jacob H. Schiff, Henry J. Allen, Dr. Thomas F. Moran, among others.⁴

At the beginning of December the NSL claimed that 50,000 school teachers in the United States had finished their post-war courses in "good citizenship" conducted by the organization in some 954 locations. This program of peace time "propaganda," which was expected to reach more than one million young school children (by way of those trained teachers) was projected as a part of the organization's new "War for Peace" movement.[5]

The NSL further explained its educational efforts in the middle of December 1918. They had begun, the group said, a nationwide campaign for the equalization of educational opportunity throughout the nation "without attempting to centralize control of methods...." A start had been made in the previous summer when the League "induced scores of the most eminent educators to visit summer normal schools." But now the end of the war opened up new vistas and the NSL "will vigorously prosecute the work by much the same methods that won the support of patriotic and philanthropically inclined persons in the last year and a half." Robert McElroy did, in fact, go on to outline a system of centralized education but was vague on the content: "The child trained to think locally will be not an asset but a liability as we face our new world problems." That previous summer the National Security League sent to "considerably" more than 100,000 teachers the *Handbook of the War* with "suggestions for the use of this material in classes."[6]

As late as January 1919 the NSL still wielded a fair amount of influence. A full page ad appeared in a New Jersey newspaper on behalf of Tom Scully, in advance of the governor's race that coming fall. That ad featured an endorsement of Scully from President Woodrow Wilson. Also prominently featured in the middle of the advertisement was a box with an endorsement from the NSL—Scully was one of those who made that organization's "Roll of Honor" because he had voted "right" 100 percent of the time, in the report card issued by the League prior to the November 1918 election. Scully never became governor of New Jersey.[7]

Charles Lydecker produced a lengthy signed article on the military training for young men. According to Lydecker after the U.S. entered World War I the education of the people had been so complete that the necessity for creating an army made the solution of universal service by selective conscription "the plain, logical and righteous method of putting our combatants on the firing line. To those who had contributed to that result, and to no body of workers, can credit be given more fully than to the National Security League, to which the country owes a debt of gratitude." Before the entry of America into the war "the subject of universal military training was very generally urged and discussed. Few appear to understand that universal military training was applicable only to a condition of war and that service was not devised in time of peace or compatible with our national life." Lydecker felt a majority of people would not favor universal

Chapter 15. The General Campaign

military training but many different methods of UMT existed, thus there was no unanimity there. He remarked that some thought "in making a soldier it is a prime necessity to cover the field of the psychology of the soldier and that the greatest work is accomplished when a man has been trained to comprehend that a soldier is a man who obeys implicitly, comprehends duty, is above fear and is loyal, generous and strong." Lydecker was still touting a National Guard under federal control. The title of Lydecker's piece was "Your boy, and the right military training for him." That may have implied a number of options; however, no military training was not among them.[8]

Woodrow Wilson on Tom Scully

In the Campaign of 1912, Woodrow Wilson, Then Governor of New Jersey, Spoke About Representative Thomas J. Scully As Follows in the Lyceum at Red Bank:

"I call him 'Tom' because it is apparent we can't manifest our love for a man unless we call him a nickname.

"The willingness to serve, the unselfishness of the man, the public spiritedness of his work inspires all.

"Mr. Scully is a straight man, a public spirited man, and what is rarer than that, a disinterested and unselfish man. I HAVE HAD REASON TO ASCERTAIN THAT AGAIN AND AGAIN.

"He is willing to take a chance against public popularity to do the thing he knows is right rather than to drift along with the tide. If a man would not risk a licking for the sake of his conscience, he is not worth licking or electing.

"When I come into contact with Scully I feel that I come into contact with the fibre of a man."

The National Security League to TOM SCULLY

"WE HAVE PUBLISHED A CHART OF THE VOTES OF THE MEMBERS OF THE HOUSE OF REPRESENTATIVES ON PREPAREDNESS AND WAR.

"YOU WILL FIND YOUR NAME ON WHAT WE HAVE CALLED 'THE ROLL OF HONOR.' WE CONGRATULATE YOU ON YOUR RECORD.

"TO PREVENT ANY MISAPPREHENSION, PLEASE NOTE THAT OUR WORK IN THIS MATTER IS STRICTLY NON PARTISAN. THIS LETTER IS BEING SENT TO EVERY NAME ON 'THE ROLL OF HONOR,' WITHOUT REGARD TO PARTY."

100 PER CENT. RIGHT

TOM SCULLY'S RECORD HAS SPOKEN.
OUR COUNTRY'S PRESIDENT HAS SPOKEN.
THE GREAT PATRIOTIC LEAGUE HAS SPOKEN.
THE PEOPLE OF NEW JERSEY WILL SPEAK NEXT.
THEY ELECT A GOVERNOR IN THE FALL

This ad from Tom Scully was placed in January 1919. Even then, as the League was being discredited, Scully was still trying to trade on his good rating from the NSL in preparation for an upcoming election for governor.

Even as the United States Congress was investigating the NSL the organization claimed that such activities would not dissuade it from its proposed educational campaign "looking toward the Americanization of the people of the United States." Not only was the League going to teach the people "love of country," it was also going to teach them to exercise more care in the selection of their national elected representatives. Said an NSL announcement, "The league will continue its nation-wide educational teaching for insistence by the people upon the nomination at the primaries of candidates for Congress who shall be representative men, and, in so doing, will publish without hesitation the records of members of Congress." It raised a caution that, although the war was over, national security remained a paramount issue. Before the war preparedness was the outstanding feature of security.

During the conflict "win the war" was the watchword. "In the future national security consists in meeting correctly the problems of readjustment and reconstruction. Now that the world has been made safe for democracy, democracy must be made safe for the world." And, the announcement continued, "The best way in which the powerful organization which the National Security League has become can be utilized for the general good at the present time is in helping to teach Americanization. This means the fighting of Bolshevism and other un–American tendencies...." There were, argued the NSL, two phases to the problem. One was Americanization as applied to those receiving instruction in the school system. The other was Americanization as applied to those beyond school age. One strategy was, for the first phase, to teach the teachers. Another strategy to produce more "patriotic citizens" was to ensure that "The propaganda against the spirit of Bolshevism must be met by a stronger propaganda by American Americans."[9]

Governors of eight states and the mayors of 72 "important" American cities reportedly accepted membership in the honorary committee that would assist the NSL and "associated patriotic bodies" in the promotion of a great nationwide celebration of the birth of the American Constitution on September 17, 1919. These other groups would also assist the NSL's Dr. David Jayne Hill "in the preliminary educational propaganda of constitutional popularization and interpretation...." More and more as time went by in 1919 and beyond, the League was simply part of a larger grouping of organizations engaged in some activity, as opposed to earlier times when it was important enough that it could also act alone, or be the dominant group in the few cases where other organizations were involved.[10]

In an analysis of race riots in the U.S. in August 1919, Dr. Robert M. McElroy, NSL educational director, declared the existing tension between whites and blacks throughout America "is due principally to disregard of law, incitement of negroes by agitators, not only of radical organizations like the I.W.W., but by their own race...." McElroy's analysis was based on reports from NSL agents in various sections of the country, principally on those of L.B. Moore of Howard University, who was in charge of the League's educational campaign in the South. Throughout the South, Moore said, he "found evidences of extremely dangerous sensitiveness among Negroes, due to the activities of I.W.W. agitators." And "He also noted a tendency among the negro soldiers to question the justice of a country which in many sections denied them the right to vote but compelled them to take up arms in its defense." Commenting on those reports, McElroy said the problems of the races were not likely to diminish "and the supply of evil propagandists always will be equal to the opportunities furnished by the existence of an ignorant population of 11,000,000 with an official adult illiteracy of 30 per cent and with an actual illiteracy vastly higher."[11]

According to the NSL, as of late July 1919, an "Americanization Advisory Service," initiated by the group to supply information and suggestions to teachers, women's clubs, civic societies, and others for use in combating un-American radical doctrines had been extended to "every state in the union." It was all under the direction of Etta V. Leighton, who was then conducting an advanced course in Americanization methods at the Rhode Island State Normal School at Providence. Also noted was that the various central organizations of women's clubs published NSL literature in their club magazines.[12]

Two weeks later, despite the above claim of all states being involved in the campaign, this latter report stated the NSL campaign against all un-American radical doctrine was then active in 38 states and in each of them "an influential citizen has accepted the appointment of state director for the immediate supervision of the campaign in his state. Additionally, two notable national committees were announced by the League as having been formed. One was the Constitutional Celebration Organization Committee, which included representatives from the NSL and associated bodies. It was headed by NSL executive Dr. David Jayne Hill. The other grouping was the Constitutional Celebration Honorary Committee, which included the governors of 22 states and mayors of 100-plus large cities."[13]

An ad that appeared in the New York City newspapers of September 16, 1919, outlined the "Constitution Day" meeting slated for the next day in New York City. The three men listed as speakers were all long-time NSL members and executives. That session was billed as "Americanism vs. Radicalism." One of the speakers was Elihu Root. He commented on the Boston police strike, then ongoing. Root argued that the Boston police, by going on strike, had challenged the Constitution of the United States. What did it mean? He said they "are refusing to perform that solemn duty unless they are permitted to ally themselves with and become members of a great organization which contains perhaps three per cent of the people [the police wanted union recognition and the right to affiliate with a larger group, the American Federation of Labor]. Now, if that is done, that is the end, except for a resolution. Government cannot be maintained unless it has the power to use force."

On September 17 at about 6 p.m., a 21-year-old woman by the name of Mollie Steiner was arrested by the police as she was flinging out circulars that denounced the NSL's "Constitution Day" meeting. She was charged with disorderly conduct in connection with that distribution of what was described as "anarchistic literature." At the time she was out on bail pending an appeal from her conviction for violation of the Espionage Act. On September 18 she was arraigned in the Tombs Court before Magistrate Ten Eyck. Steiner was described in the article as a "Russian radical" in the text of the article and as a "Red leader" in the headline, although no evidence was introduced to verify such claims.[14]

Under the slogan "A square deal for the public, for labor, and for employers," the National Security League made public a "comprehensive program of direct activity against social and industrial unrest, which it will prosecute in all parts of the country" in a campaign to enroll one million new members in the organization. It claimed then to still have 100,000 members. The League characterized the current situation in America as "industrial and social revolution" and declared immediate action was necessary by the "loyal American majority" if disaster was to be prevented. For the NSL the solution to the problem came in four broad lines of activity: (1) reformation of the deportation process, (2) changes in immigration and naturalization laws, (3) universal military training, and (4) revision of citizenship training in the schools.[15]

A special showing for Boy Scouts of an "Americanization film" took place on the afternoon of December 20, 1919, in Richmond, Virginia. The film was Richard Harding Davis' *Soldiers of Fortune* (1919). According to the article, "It marks a new precedent in the method of circulating Americanization films." While it had been shown before to adult audiences, that screening marked the first time it had been pitched to children. "The National Security League, whose ideals of preparedness author Davis preached, is responsible for this innovation," declared a journalist. Several short talks preceded the film.[16]

Despite opposition in the U.S. House of Representatives to universal military training, the National Security League announced that it would redouble its efforts to create a public demand for that legislation. Herbert Barry was chair of the NSL Committee on Universal Military Instruction and Training and the League had UMT "as one of its basic tenets since its organization." According to NSL President Orth, "The American people must not forget the lessons and tragedy of our unpreparedness. We must construct and have ready the 'big stick' which Theodore Roosevelt had in mind when he said: 'Speak softly and carry a big stick.'"[17]

Still another of the organization's nationwide crusades was announced in February 1920. It would campaign to aid in the Americanization of foreign-born adults and make certain that applicants for American citizenship were "qualified" before naturalization was granted. That work was to be accomplished by a committee of citizens cooperating with the 2,500 naturalization courts throughout the nation. Members of that committee included William Howard Taft, Alton Parker and Stanwood Menken. They said they had written to the judges of the naturalization courts asking them to take up with local civic and patriotic organizations the creation of appropriate committees. It was to be the duty of each of these local committees to investigate the qualifications of all local applicants for citizenship by interviewing each applicant personally and making recommendations to the judge in each individual case.

Menken, chair of the League's Americanization Committee pointed out that federal and state authorities had been trying to do the work with inadequate forces. For example, he explained, the New York office had only three people to investigate applicants in its area, which numbered around 50,000 annually. Other members of that committee were George Sutherland (former U.S. Senator from Utah), William D. Guthrie (New York City), Judge Peter W. Meldrim (Savannah GA), George Wharton Pepper (Philadelphia), Walter George Smith (Philadelphia), Guy Murchie (Boston) and Morefield Storey (Boston).[18]

The League went so far as to try and counter May Day, generally around the world a day to celebrate workers, ordinary people. In February 1920 the NSL announced plans for a nationwide demonstration by parades and municipal celebrations on May 1, to make the day "American Day ... in opposition to the usual 'Mayday' demonstrations of radical organizations." Those parades were to be similar to the "Preparedness Parades" the League staged in 1916. Governors of states, mayors of "large cities" and other officials had, reportedly, given their approval to the project and affirmed that it had their support—such politicians as Governor Alfred E. Smith (CT), Governor Frank Lowden (IL) and Governor Henry Allen (KS). Lowden said, "Let us by all means make it clear to the world that there is not a single day of the year in which American citizens, devoted to their own institutions and their own flag, do not overwhelmingly preponderate over all the destructive forces within our midst." The NSL envisioned each one of these planned parades as having several sections: for example, a section of American Legion members (to be called "The Defenders of America"), one for school children ("Young America"), and one made up of teachers ("The Makers of America"). Those parades would be top heavy as well with members from the United States Army, the United States Navy, National Guard, veterans' organizations, and so on.[19]

An editorial from a Montana newspaper in March 1920 concerned the upcoming American Day celebration. The piece began with the report of a letter from William B. Dwight, director of the NSL's Speakers' Bureau, to Mayor William T. Stodden of Butte Montana about May 1 and the reply from Stodden that he would cooperate with the League in its American Day program. Said the paper, "The National Security League is an organization of capitalists and capitalist henchmen with headquarters in New York. Their work is the organization of a spy system in the United States and they have encouraged and furthered the terroristic campaign against all working-class organizations that has not yet subsided." And, the editor added, "Last May, when various organizations of the workers, attempted to celebrate the First of May, International Labor Day, they were shot, beaten and clubbed, jailed and tortured by the agents of just such organizations as the National Security League."[20]

An ad appeared in a Texas newspaper on April 30 that told readers about the American Day celebration to take place the next day in El Paso. It was a day for Americans to "show their colors." That advertisement took up almost a full page in the newspaper. Listed in the body of the ad were the names of eight contributors, presumably those who paid for the insertion of the ad. All were business concerns, including the El Paso Stock Exchange.[21]

In a letter in March 1920 to Anning S. Prall, president of the New York City Board of Education, New York City Mayor Hylan declared the movement of the NSL for better schools was "purely camouflage." He said that it was the "old Rockefeller Foundation crowd" that was again endeavoring to get control of the schools. Prall had asked Hylan about the NSL plan with respect to schools. Hylan said, "The National Security League with a few exceptions is made up of the old educational clique that favored the Gary school and wanted the children of the city trained for the shop and factory, instead of for higher professions. Their so-called movement for better schools is purely camouflage. You do not hear them advocating more schoolhouses or a better fundamental education for the children. Their motive is to get control of the schools of our city and state."[22]

In the spring of 1920 the NSL expressed worry over the Congressional elections coming in November of that year. Orth said he feared the Socialists would elect four Congressmen from New York City, and possibly eight, unless the Democrats and Republicans chose the path of selecting a fusion candidate. Fusion was urged by the League in other areas as well, not just in New York City, to insure no Socialists were elected. According to the League their fusion idea had been endorsed by the governors of many states, by mayors of cities and by "other prominent Americans."

Among those identified as in support of fusion were Governor Cornwell (WV, identified herein as on the NSL's executive committee), Governor Russell of Mississippi, Governor Boyle of Nevada, and Governor McKelvie of Nebraska. Other "prominent New Yorkers" behind the plan were Henry A. Wise (former United States District Attorney), Henry Stoddard (editor of *The Evening Mail*), Alexander J. Hemphill (chairman of the board of directors of the Guaranty Trust Company) and ex-judge W.M.K. Olcott.

Chapter 15. The General Campaign

Hemphill was also a member of the League but not identified herein as such.

Most worrying to the NSL with respect to the upcoming Congressional elections were New York City's 12th, 13th, 14th, and 20th Districts. Socialists nominated for those districts were, respectively, Meyer London, Charles W. Ervin (editor of *New York Call*), Algernon Lee and Morris Hillquit. The other four constituencies were the 18th, 22nd, 23rd and 24th Districts but nobody else expected Socialist victories in any of them. Socialists lost all four of those districts in 2018 by large margins, although none of those districts had a fusion candidate. On the other hand the other four all had a fusion candidate in 1918 but the Socialists still lost by small margins.[23]

The League held another one of its contests in the spring of 1921. This one was a competition for grammar school pupils to come up with ideas for the dramatization of the United States Constitution. Reportedly that contest had been endorsed by state and city school superintendents and was being participated in by pupils in the public schools of 35 states and the parochial schools of 12 states.[24]

To "consecrate and sanctify American citizenship," the "National American Council," composed of representatives of the main civic welfare and educational associations of the nation, came into existence in March 1921. An attempt was to be to coordinate existing agencies into a belief that a unified program of education for patriotism and good citizenship could be effectively waged. Dr. David Jayne Hill of the NSL presided at the NAC organizational meeting. Dozens of groups were said to have been involved. Some of them were, besides the National Security League, the National Guard Association, the American Legion, Sons of the American Revolution, the Council of Churches of America and the United States Department of Labor. Two months later very little had happened. One action was to rename the umbrella organization the "American National Council." Hill was named president of the group with Charles Orth selected as a vice-president. A total of 25 directors were listed, four of which were women. U.S. President Warren Harding was named honorary president of the group and U.S. Vice President Calvin Coolidge was selected as honorary vice-president.[25] The proposed umbrella organization, under either name, existed in name only; it held no meetings and did no business.

An editorial that appeared in June 1922 discussed the size of the United States military, with respect to the fact that the NSL continued to agitate for a larger military. In 1914, the editor explained, the authorized strength of the U.S. Army was 100,000 men while the actual strength was 86,000. For the U.S. Navy the maximum enlisted strength allowed by law was 51,500 men. "A widespread popular demand for limitation of armament is coupled with a general recognition of competitive armament as a breeder of war," wrote the editor. "How much intelligent public opinion supports the view that we have pressing need for an army more than 50 per cent larger than in 1914, or a navy 65 per cent. larger on a basis that the Security League considers inadequate?"[26]

Around that same time the NSL argued that an English translation should accompany every foreign language poster or advertisement that appeared in public spaces such as in the subway, elevated and surface cars, on in the transportation stations. The League announced that it had taken up with New York City Mayor Hylan, Murray Hulbert, president of the Board of Aldermen, and with George McAneny, chairman of the Transit Commission, the advisability of adopting a city ordinance to that effect. Having been keeping their eyes on such posters the NSL had complained of the "revolutionary character" of one of those ads. After that complaint was lodged, the contract the advertiser had with the Transit Commission was "annulled promptly." It was all part of the NSL push for one language and one only in America.[27]

"A law requiring definite courses of instruction on the Constitution of the United States in all public schools, will be placed on the statute books of all the states when the work of the Committee on Constitutional Instruction recently appointed by the National Security League, is completed," declared the League in September 1922, pointing to a special campaign to that end was in the works. Lloyd Taylor of the League was named chairman of the committee. Reportedly that committee had a membership of 200 that included the presidents of "practically all the leading colleges and universities of the country, the State Commissions of Education or Superintendents of Public Instruction of nearly all the States." Of the seven members of the committee named, three were long standing NSL members. Five states were said to then have such laws on their books—Illinois, Iowa, Michigan, Vermont, and Rhode Island. According to this account, "The National Security League secured the passage of this law in Rhode Island last spring." Supposedly, this need for courses in the United States Constitution came about because of the NSL contest for school children to dramatize the Constitution: "School children in only fourteen states competed and the discovery was made that the Constitution was most inadequately taught."[28]

In August 1924 a nationwide canvass of candidates for the U.S. Senate and House of Representatives to determine their views on preparedness was contemplated by the National Security League, which announced that a committee was being formed under the direction of president Menken to be called the National Preparedness Committee. Plans as announced included having a representative of the League visit each candidate individually to seek a "definite expression" of his views on preparedness. The

Chapter 15. The General Campaign 203

statements collected from the candidates were to be broadcast to the electorate along with a report of evasive or non-committee attitudes. Some of the other members of that committee who would serve with Menken were B.L. Winchell (president of the Remington Typewriter Company), Percy H. Johnston (president of Chemical National Bank—now part of the Morgan banking system) and Mrs. Douglas Robinson (sister of the late Theodore Roosevelt).[29]

Eighteen organizations sponsoring further Americanization of aliens met on March 5, 1929, at the headquarters of the Sons of the American Revolution to discuss aliens and general education work. The National Security League was listed as one of those groups. In the summer of that year in the listings of radio programs there was a small mention of the League. Broadcasting from 422.3 WOR Newark New Jersey the League had a 15-minute slot at 7:15 p.m. on Saturday August 31. It was listed simply as "National Security League talk."[30]

According to the Wikipedia page for the National Security League it went bankrupt in 1939, although it survived on paper until 1942, at which point Bullard closed the National Security League.[31]

CHAPTER 16

Critics and Impugners

Articles in opposition to the National Security League were limited to only a couple in this period, two in 1918 and one in the following year. Partly that was due to the increasing irrelevance of the group, a spent force by 1920. Mostly, though, it was due to the Congressional investigation of the League, which ran into early 1919 and effectively neutered them after airing out their considerable collection of dirty laundry. The League never acknowledged that the Congressional investigation dealt them a death blow but, rather, tried to continue as if nothing happened, all the while growing a little crazier and crazier as time passed with, ultimately, Menken being openly and publicly ridiculed.

One newspaper that consistently attacking the NSL, besides certain of the labor press, was the *South Bend News-Times* (IN). It began one scathing editorial with a suggestion to the effect that a name change was in order for the group to "Remington and Savage Arms, and Dupont Powder Security League," along with others who hoped to "fasten upon the land." Commenting on the various test measures they devised to grade congressmen and prepare their report cards, the editor said, "P. T. Barnum once said the 'American people like to be humbugged,' and evidently the National Security League fully believes in it. Quite evidently, too, with about sixty per cent of the press of the country—the capitalist press—at their command, they hope to be able to put their humbug over.... They have a great system, calculating to brow-beat, bullyrag and coerce into subjection, in case their humbuggery doesn't work." The editorial added, "If it isn't militarism, that and nothing more, why is it that the league in its schedules of 'war measures,' says nothing about espionage laws, nothing about war revenue measures, nothing about the building of the merchant marine? Is it because its little darlings in the Senate and House voted so far in the majority against these things, even to including the declaration of war itself?" The conclusion was, "Our guess is that the National Security League is nothing more or less than a 'big business' propaganda league; particularly of the 'big business' that hopes to profit by so-called

Chapter 16. Critics and Impugners

'preparedness' measures. It is all that it thinks about; all that it talks about."[1]

One day later the same newspaper returned with another attack on the League. This time it began by talking about League executive Elihu Root and rumors that he was being pushed to be appointed as some sort of peace commissioner in the Woodrow Wilson Administration. Before such consideration, Wilson should "investigate the undenied public report that Mr. Root, of military age at the time, hired a substitute to do his fighting for him during the latter days of the civil war—when he was drafted." With regard to Alton Brooke Parker, an executive in the League and the losing Democratic candidate for U.S. President in the 1904 election and a man "constantly hyping preparedness": "[he] was defeated by 2,500,000 votes because of his Wall St. connections," while running on a dishonest platform demanding "a reduction of the army" (to fool the voters); the army numbered only 25,000 men at the time. Added the editor, "The league is super-partisan at that; super-partisan in the bi-partisan sense—designed for 'invisible government' activities, grasping for a capitalistic hold and employing every false pretense on the political calendar to gain it." And, "Certainly the so-called National Security League would rather have Democrats in Congress who would serve its Wall St. interests, than Republicans who wouldn't and it would rather have Republicans there to serve them than Democrats who wouldn't."[2]

With respect to their preparedness programs, the editor wrote about "their quite exclusive program: preparedness measures that would fill the pockets of the arms and munitions makers—clients of Attys. Root and Parker—there to be supplemented now by a reconstruction program that runs quite as exclusively to universal military training and more profits for the munitions and arms manufacturers, displays their gold-plated patriotism quite distinctively." Witness, he continued, "that the League is always interested in legislation that has to do with markets for arms and munitions, and they don't calculate to stand for anything that interferes with it, or that doesn't promote such a market.... Is it possible that the League doesn't regard the war revenue measures as war measures, merely because Wall St. and particularly its arms and munitions makers, don't like the excess profits tax?" Attorneys Parker and Root, "while giving 'patriotic character' to the league, appear to be serving their arms and munitions clients very nicely and now what they want is for you to blindly put up your money, to help put their propaganda over." In conclusion the editor noted, "Remington Arms, Savage Arms, and Aetna and Dupont Powder. Isn't the National Security League program, indeed, more suggestive of being their humble servant than of being yours—or America's?"[3]

In the summer of 1919 another editorial appeared that attacked the

League. This one was presented in the form of a fable, a sarcastic one. It was the story of the pickpockets with the brass band. The NSL was working the fleecing game: "The league was a patriotic organization to protect corporations in the patriotic business of frisking the general public. The league provided the martial music, the profiteers did the rest. Every man or woman who told Big Biz to keep his hands out of the blindman's cup was called a traitor, or a menace to our fighting efficiency or a red agitator by the National Security league. The program of the league was to use the war situation to have everybody locked up in jail who opposed the reign of King Loot and Queen Larceny." Then the editor took note of the Congressional investigation into the organization, which by then had ended. "Well, we see by the progress of a few days ago that the league is still on deck and beginning to operate along the old lines, despite the fact that it was mugged and measured and thumbprinted by Congress."[4]

Calls in the United States Congress for an investigation into the activities and personalities involved in the National Security League, which had begun sporadically much earlier, began in earnest in this period, intensified, and finally led to an official probe into the organization. U.S. Representative James A. Frear (Rep., WI) addressed the House on the subject, again, on December 4, 1918, and demanded an investigation of the NSL, denouncing the League as having been organized "to serve as a convenient cloak for libelous attacks on public men," and "for its attempts to defeat 300 members of Congress whom it had blacklisted as disloyal." Frear declared, "Tons of literature were circulated throughout the country by the league, branding certain members of the House as disloyal and votes of members contrary to the wishes of the league were misinterpreted." His resolution for an investigation was referred to the House Rules Committee.[5]

In his statement Frear also charged that "the records of the league would show that it received contributions for its support from business interests, known as war profiteers." He also asserted, "The league is a powerful, irresponsible New York corporation, arrogant and un–American in its methods, a slanderous libel on the patriotism of our public officials and of our citizenship, inimical to the best interests of the country and has done more to create public discord and unwarranted suspicion and division among a patriotic people than any other single agency." Republican James Mann asked if the League had filed a campaign expense account and Frear replied that he understood it had not filed such an account. Said Mann, if Frear was correct in his charges, "I should think that the Department of Justice might well investigate not only the corporation, but the officers of the corporation. An anonymous body, created by itself, certainly ought to be compelled to live up to the law." If an organization had spent money in an election campaign then a statement of such expenditures was required, by law, to be filed.[6]

Pressure for an investigation increased on December 7 as Frear was joined by Representative Roscoe C. McCullough (OH) in calling for a sweeping investigation of the League's political activities. When the House Rules Committee met that day it was then, reportedly, that members of that committee decided that such an investigation should be made. Frear testified before that committee that the NSL had admitted to having "handled" $1.2 million in waging a nationwide campaign against members of the House and Senate that it had charged with disloyalty. "The league has slandered Congress. It has misrepresented Congress. There is and can be no objection to honest criticism but when false accusations of disloyalty remained either openly or by innuendo a deadly poison is being used— and those responsible for its use shall be held responsible," said Frear. McCullough read into the record correspondence he had received from Charles Orth, chairman of the NSL's Congressional Committee, a letter signed by Root, Lydecker, Parker and Henry L. West (executive secretary of the group). He declared that letter contained a "veiled threat" against him as a member of Congress. Representative Pat Harrison (Dem., MS) read some correspondence he had in connection with an attack on him by the NSL that he described as "manifestly unfair and unjust."[7]

On December 10, 1918, the U.S. House of Representatives adopted a resolution authorizing the appointment of a special House committee of seven men for that purpose. They were U.S. Representatives Ben Johnson (KY), Pat Harrison (MS), Edward Saunders (VA), Thaddeus Caraway (AR), Horace Towner (IA), C. Frank Reavis (NE) and Joseph Walsh (MA). The idea that the investigation might be more about the politicians vindicating themselves—as being patriotic, loyal, and so forth—than about condemning the NSL could be seen in the two-hour debate that preceded the authorizing of the special committee, during which, wrote a journalist, "both sides of the House paid tribute to the patriotic zeal with which the House as a body supported the Administration in the war." Speakers in the debate, generally, criticized misrepresentations made by the NSL in seeking the defeat of members of Congress.

The League was charged by speakers on the floor with questioning the loyalty, patriotism, character and congressional record of candidates for nomination and election in the last congressional campaign. Said one, "No committee, however organized or of whatever political proclivity, has ever indulged in the slimy politics that was indulged in by this organization." Before the hearings began Towner disappeared from the committee and was replaced by Edward E. Browne (WI). That formal House resolution declared the purpose of the special committee was "To investigate and make report as to the officers, membership, financial support, expenditures, general character, activities and purposes of the National Security League."[8]

And so the formal investigation of the NSL by the House Special Committee—it did not have any other name—was begun, on December 19, 1918, with Representative Ben Johnson as head of that body. Officers of the League appeared for excoriation, bringing with them many of the group's papers and records. In that delegation were Charles E. Lydecker (president), Dr. Robert M. McElroy (educational director), Henry L. West (executive secretary), Charles D. Orth (chairman of the NSL's Congressional Committee), Lloyd Taylor (chairman of the Universal Military Training Committee), E.L. Harvey (publicity director) and P.D. Calhoun (cashier). Johnson asked Lydecker whether the organization had taken a partisan or political stand or interfered in any way with the election of any officials. Replied Lydecker, "The aim of the league since its organization, and its only aim has been to win the war. I can say with all sincerity that there has never been any digression from this aim. The league has made every effort to keep entirely out of politics. Its hands are clean." Salaries received by officers were given by Lydecker: McElroy ($10,000 a year), West ($8,400), E.L. Harvey ($4,160), Etta V. Leighton ($2,400—director of the American naturalization bureau) and Calhoun ($2,080).[9]

When the Special Committee resumed the next day for the second session of hearings, Lydecker was asked about the post-war activities of his organization. He cited the NSL committees on world peace and organized education; he also mentioned demobilization activities, naturalization and citizenship issues as well as constitutional and national integrity. He also cited concerns his group had over unity of language and universal military training and said that committees had been appointed in all of those areas and were then beginning work. He mentioned nothing about the NSL's anti–Red crusade. Lydecker told the committee that expenses of the NSL for the period September 1, 1917, to August 31, 1918, amounted to $226,018 while receipts totaled $284,358 in the same period. During the Congressional election campaign leading up to the November 1918 voting day he stated the NSL had spent a total of $5,995.68 for postage, salaries, printing, furniture and other expenses. Receipts for that campaign amounted to $8,752.85[10]

One article on the Lydecker testimony began by pointing out that instead of the million or more dollars alleged to have been spent by the NSL in trying to defeat candidates for Congress "it was shown today that less than $6,000 was so disbursed." This article also noted that all but one member of the seven-man Special Committee had failed to reach the "100 per cent Americanism" standard set by the NSL when it rated politicians prior to the 1918 election. Johnson was "wrong" on six of eight measures; Harrison and Caraway each were wrong on four measures; Saunders and Reavis each scored five wrong votes; Browne was wrong on seven measures.

Chapter 16. Critics and Impugners

Representative Walsh was graded as "right" on all eight measures.

Reavis asked Lydecker on whose authority the eight measures were decided. He replied that former U.S. Secretary of War Stimson and former U.S. Secretary of the Navy Meyer were involved, among others. The Special Committee wanted to know where large contributions to the NSL came from. Lydecker said that the Carnegie Corporation gave $150,000 and John D. Rockefeller contributed $50,000. Also, Lydecker repeated the idea that the origination of the League came from suggestions by Stanwood Menken and Representative Augustus Gardner of Massachusetts. When Lydecker was asked what political influence the NSL intended to have, or

This composite photograph appeared in December 1918 and showed four of the people due to become part of the just announced investigation of the NSL. Top left is Representative Ben Johnson, chair of the investigating committee. The other three were all League executives: Charles Lydecker, top right; Alton Parker, bottom left; and Elihu Root.

desired, he replied, "I don't care to mention any names, but the National Security League would have been sorely disappointed if certain members of the House had been returned. Our efforts were used to defeat men who we thought by their speeches were pro–German, and in many cases they were defeated by means of fusion. Many men spoke words on the floor which were not acceptable to the American spirit."[11]

Lydecker told the committee that the NSL's total expenses from

December 14, 1914, when formed, until September 30, 1918, were $521,678. Total receipts for the same period were given as $619,165. That latter number included membership fees and contributions. Presenting to the committee records showing NSL's expenses since it was formed, Lydecker stated that the largest disbursement had been $471,153.47 for "general expenses" and that $13,198.06 had been used for publications, and $37,376.57 had been placed in six special accounts for conducting campaigns, paying speakers, purchasing French books for soldiers, and so forth. No accounting system would ever accept a concern claiming that 90 percent of its total expenses went to something called "general expenses."[12]

After two days of hearings the Special Committee adjourned until after the Christmas and New Year holiday period. That break was enough time for some editorials to appear. "Congressmen are beginning to find out that the National Security League is another Standard Oil, Steel, Copper, Grain Trust, excuse for mob violence and terrorism," wrote one disgusted editor. "Couldn't find out during the war and denounce it, of course. Some one might have called them pro–German, and that would have lost votes. Ugh! what a thing the professional politician is!"[13]

"In the course of the investigation of the National 'Security' League it is admitted that the league was very busy sending out literature in an attempt to poison the minds of the people against Pres't Wilson; admitting that it was more concerned in damning men who in days of peace were not in favor of war, than in condemning men who in days of war failed to respond to the appeals of the commander-in-chief of the army," said an editor from an Indiana newspaper, that was reprinted in another paper from that state. "All of which explains why Mr. Carnegie and Mr. Rockefeller were the heaviest contributors to the $1,200,000 fund. Enough has been developed to make it clear that the American people are menaced by organizations of this character, which have all the earmarks of having been created for commercial and not for patriotic purposes. And it makes quite clear the meaning of an old English statement that 'patriotism is the last refuge of a scoundrel.'"[14]

Representative Frear renewed his attack on the NSL in the House on January 2, 1919. He was so moved by an "erroneous statement" concerning himself that appeared in the *New York Herald*'s account of the NSL probe. A published statement declared Frear had charged that the League had spent more than $1 million to defeat members of Congress. Frear clarified the situation by declaring he never said that League pamphlets turned over to the Special Committee contained a claim that the group's annual expenses reached $1.2 million. Frear did mention that $200,000 in total contributions had come from Carnegie and Rockefeller and that U.S. Steel (formed in 1901 from Carnegie Steel, by Morgan banking interests) had profited by

Chapter 16. Critics and Impugners 211

hundreds of millions of dollars from the war. He added that Rockefeller's contribution to the National Security League probably represented less than one-quarter of one percent of war profits "wrung from the American people through boosting the price of gasoline alone. That is a source of poisoned gas and easy money used to defeat blacklisted congressmen in 1918."[15]

That Special Committee probing the NSL had been authorized $25,000 to spend by the House of Representatives. Lydecker was asked to explain to the committee the importance of the following plank in the League program: "Creating a greater regard for representative government as distinguished from mass administration; protecting our national legislature from dangerous proletarians." Explained Lydecker, "We are doing everything in our power to educate the people by our public speakers and our literature, that a republic of a hundred million can be governed wisely through wise representatives and not by mass rule or mob, and we believe that our people should be taught to have the greatest respect for their representatives." Caraway asked Lydecker, "What do you understand a proletarian is?" The reply was, "Well, I don't know exactly what a proletarian is, but a dangerous proletarian is an ignorant demagogue." Lydecker did observe, though, that his League was not opposed to "the class that needs help and uplifting education—the poor class." When Lydecker told Caraway the organization was then bringing that about, the questioner asked how the group was doing that. "We are doing everything in our power to educate the people by our public speakers and by our own literature," replied Lydecker, largely to elect "wise reps." and "not by mass rule or mob" and "to create a greater regard for representative government as distinguished from mass administration, which appears at present to be the curse of Russia."[16]

Hearings resumed after the Christmas break with the first hearing in the New Year being held on January 6, 1919. At that session, it was reported, NSL president Charles Lydecker "was sharply reprimanded for evasiveness and unwillingness to answer questions" put to him by the committee. That reprimand was delivered by Representative Ben Johnson, chair of the Special Committee. On that day Lydecker admitted in his testimony that he approved the chart (report card) accusing members of Congress of disloyalty without knowledge as to whether the information it was based on was correct or properly prepared. He had not even read the McLemore resolution—one of the items the NSL declared to be part of the eight measures that the League considered to be its "acid test." Additionally, it was developed that the NSL's books showed nothing about the money spent by the branches of the League in political campaigns. When asked what results the NSL had obtained from its campaign to target politicians for removal, Lydecker declared that as far as he knew the only result of the League's political effort was the defeat of four Socialist candidates for Congress. But he admitted the League had made no effort to enlighten the voters of the district that elected Victor Berger—a Socialist.[17]

Looking at the League and the investigation until that point from a critical perspective was another Middle West paper. "This organization got along fairly well in bulldozing school teachers and others who might have some lively conceptions of democracy, but it went too far. In the past election it sent out misleading and lying reports abut the patriotism of many of our Congressmen. According to the Security league all standpat reactionaries were 100 per cent American and all the progressives, even the mild progressives, had some flaw which made them unfit for congress." Lydecker explained that the $150,000 donation from the Carnegie Corporation was made in March 1918 and of that total $100,000 had been paid in—in two separate payments of $50,000 each. In answer to a question Lydecker stated that Stanwood Menken and Dr. McElroy had solicited that donation (McElroy was then drawing a salary of $10,000 per year as the NSL educational director). According to a journalist, "it is learned that the trustees of the eminently respectable Carnegie Foundation voted the $150,000 to Root's league through the Carnegie Corporation in order to carry on a campaign of so-called Americanization, which was to consist first of all in agitation for universal compulsory military service, or training, and in agitation for the establishment of a state constabulary system throughout the country." That is, a federalized National Guard type of organization.[18]

Lydecker became NSL president on June 26, 1918. His view of the objective was: "The league is established to promote patriotic education and national sentiment among the people of the United States, and to promote recognition of the fact that the obligation of universal military service requires universal military training..." He admitted that he had no office at the NSL New York City headquarters and that he did not go to the League office every day. When he did he visited the office of the executive secretary at headquarters, something he did maybe three or four times a month. There were 40 or so employees at headquarters, with E.L. Harvey paid $80 a week; Etta Leighton paid $200 a month and P.D. Calhoun receiving $40 a week as the bookkeeper.

According to Lydecker neither he nor Menken ever received any salary for their NSL work. He stated he owned stock in one railroad and bonds of certain railroads but that he could not recall the names of those railroads. Much of his legal work, he explained, involved representing estates but he said he could not name any of the estates he managed as that was privileged information. Finally, he did acknowledge that there were U.S. Steel bonds in various estates (but only, he said, "small amounts") and that railroad securities were held in some of those estates, but also, "not large amounts." Vagueness was a characteristic of Lydecker's testimony. When Walsh asked

Chapter 16. Critics and Impugners

him how many members were in the League Lydecker stated, "I can't tell you." Walsh then asked if a record of the membership was kept. Replied Lydecker, "There is a record thought to be kept throughout the country, but I can not say that that record is very accurately kept or that anybody could at any moment tell precisely; but we estimate that there are somewhere around 80,000 enrolled, or 85,000." Walsh then asked how many states did the NSL have branches in. To which Lydecker replied, "That I can't tell you."

After more prodding from the committee members he produced a list of 24 states—two of which were Hawaii (a "territory") and Cuba. Changing subjects, Walsh asked Lydecker if the NSL sent out what was known as "boiler plate" matter to newspaper. Admitting such was the case, Lydecker said no money was paid to or received from the recipient newspapers and the material was distributed through the Western Newspaper Union. Caraway pointed out to Lydecker that the 47 Representatives who had made the League's honor roll by getting "right" answers on eight of eight NSL measures made up almost 10 percent of the total House membership but they formed 40 percent of those who voted against the income tax, to fund the war effort.[19]

When Caraway asked the League official about universal military training, Lydecker asserted, "every man who reaches the age of 18, every boy who reaches the age of 18, has imposed upon him by law the obligation to be a defender of his country and may be called on to carry a gun, and he has that duty three years before he gets the right to vote, at 21." The budget for the Patriotism Through Education campaign was set at $1.2 million per year. Receipts for the League for the six months from March to August 1918 totaled $144,496.76 in donations: $1,100 from founders; $2,750 from life memberships; $1,654 from contributing members; $4,974 from annual memberships; $346 from "war service"; $1,237.08 received from branches; $1,457 from sales; $2,486 from the congressional campaign; $2,801 from executive committee assessments; $18,260 from educational work; $5,614.25 from miscellaneous, $12,023.10 from renewals; $1,525 from proceeds from a special luncheon—making total receipts of $198,203.55 for the period.

With respect to donations Browne asked Lydecker if anyone made any contribution other than cash to the organization. He replied by mentioning specifically contributions of literature by well known writers of the day such as Gertrude Atherton and George Ade but other than that, "I do not know of anything." When Reavis asked the executive for clarification about point six in the platform, the supposed danger from proletarians, Lydecker stated, "I mean that any particular community or part of the great democracy of the United States which is so tinged with false ideas—either derived from the Lenin philosophy or the philosophy of those who believe that all property should be annihilated, that law should be the subject of abolition—that we should not have those representatives in our National Legislature who would continue the propagation of what I regard as in the nature of disease."

When Reavis asked where such conditions might emerge, Lydecker suggested New York City and San Francisco. The latter city, explained Lydecker, "had its sand-lot orators and its Coxey crowd [referring to a protest march by unemployed workers in 1894, led by Jacob Coxey]. And there are from time to time groups that create—I can't say where germs may grow best." Saunders pushed him for a definition of the term proletarian, prompting Lydecker to declare, "That member of society who is devoid of thrift, industry, or any accumulation of reason thereof. The proletarian are a very inconsiderable part of any American constituency, but our imported people are, unfortunately, some of them from that class."[20]

It was reported in January that the Carnegie Corporation of New York City had complete control over $25 million set aside by Andrew Carnegie in 1911 "to be used to promote the advancement and diffusion of knowledge." Andrew Carnegie was president of that concern with Elihu Root and Henry S. Pritchard being vice-presidents.[21]

Charles D. Orth, chairman of the NSL's Congressional Committee, began his testimony on January 17, declaring that although six "wrong" votes were recorded against Representative Claude Kitchin of North Carolina on the League's chart, no campaign was made against the Democratic House leader in the fall of 1918 because his district was regarded as "hopeless." According to his testimony the League's educational campaign was only conducted "on an intensive scale" in the 47 congressional districts where the vote was expected to be close. Orth added that congressmen who voted against important war measures, although they thus recorded the sentiment of their districts, were "disloyal" to their country.

During his testimony Orth acknowledged that Elihu Root, as a lawyer, had been retained by railroad corporations to represent them in their efforts to be turned back to private ownership, after a brief period of nationalization in 1917 as an emergency war measure—they went back to private hands early in 1920. Orth admitted his firm (Hanson & Orth—Charles A. Hanson) held some $75,000 in railroad stocks as well as $250,000 in Liberty Bonds. When Orth was asked by the committee to give the value of his firm's assets on any January 1 date since 1914, Orth claimed he could not do so, except for January 1, 1918, when he said his firm's assets were $600,000. Reavis asked Orth about the labor strife and agitation then pervasive in the United States, especially with regard to the I.W.W. (Industrial Workers of the World, better known as the Wobblies), and if Orth

Chapter 16. Critics and Impugners 215

feared an "unusual unrest" as a result. To which Orth replied, "And I have that fear now."[22]

While he was testifying Orth was warned by Ben Johnson, chairman of the Special Committee, that his attitude had been exasperating and that if it continued he would recommend Orth be taken before the bar of the House for contempt. Orth's answers to hypothetical questions about the report card rating system of politicians were called, by Reavis, "evasive." Said Johnson, in his warning, "If such answers as Mr. Orth has made were given in any court of the land he would have been in jail long ago. They have been unmistakably evasive. I will not attempt to say what his motive is, but will say the committee has stood for them long enough."[23]

On January 21 Henry L. West, NSL executive secretary testified. He denied that any of the large donations made to the League, previously mentioned in the hearings, were used in the 1918 congressional election. West claimed those donations were made for and used in the general educational and patriotic campaigns of the organization. He cited the "less than $6,000" figure that had earlier been used. West was a former Commissioner of the District of Columbia and admitted that he had been employed once by 60 men in Washington at a salary of $100 a week "to work in behalf of the half-and-half principle of financing the National Capital."[24]

In explaining his work as a paid lobbyist West admitted he was employed in 1913 by those 60 Washington men to work for the retention of the "half-and-half" taxation plan for DC. Those men contributed $25 each at stated intervals. He held that job, he said, until Congress adjourned in March 1915. Chairman Johnson explained that the expenses of conducting the DC government were met from taxes on property within the District of Columbia; the other half came from the U.S. Treasury, collected from the States and Territories of the Union. A partial list of the names of the men who employed him, which West gave the committee, embraced wealthy Washingtonians who were heavily invested in DC property. Abolition of the half-and-half plan, as had been voted for by the House several times, would result in the material increase in the taxes of those wealthy property owners who would have to finance 100 percent of the cost of DC government, instead of 50 percent of the expenses.

Under pressure West named some of those men who paid his salary. One was William Moses, the head of the firm of William B. Moses and Son, furniture dealers on F Street. Others included Harry Wardman (real estate) Julius Garfinkle, Samuel W. Woodward, John Jay Edson (president of Washington Loan and Trust) and J. Maury Dove (owner of the Shoreham Hotel, appraised for tax purposes at $1 million). During an exchange between Browne and West the former suggested the NSL auditing firm was Marwick, Mitchell, Peat & Company, and that the man who did the audit was a member of the League. West denied that allegation but did admit that two auditors, after performing an audit for the NSL, did voluntarily join the NSL, but only after they had completed their auditing work. He also denied that any auditing firm had donated $2,000 to the organization. West also admitted that of all money donations of over $100 that had been made to the League, 95 percent had come from people who were listed in the annual publication *Directory of Directors*.[25]

For the first time since the inquiry had begun, the NSL was placed on the record as flatly having engaged in political activities during the 1918 Congressional election campaign. Refusing to follow the lead of Lydecker and Orth, all of whom claimed the League was not engaged in politics, West admitted to that charge. Henry Ford was one of the candidates selected for defeat. The NSL executive committee adopted a resolution directing that a committee of 50 Michigan citizens be formed for the purpose of opposing Ford's candidacy for the United States Senate. On July 25, 1918, West wrote a letter to Lydecker, stating, "Committee composed of citizens of Michigan had that day been appointed by league to inquire into the Ford situation and determine what is the most effective way to work against him and what assistance league can give its branches in Michigan if desired."

Representative Browne read into the record a "long list" of contributions of $100 or more made during the summer of 1918. "Nearly every one of these contributors was connected with the 'big business' interests of New York City." That occurred in the summer of 1918 when the NSL issued a "hurry up" call for money. After some denials West admitted that, at that time, "a very earnest effort" was made to get money. However, West denied any of that money was used in the Congressional campaign but admitted that a large portion of Ridley Watts' donation was expended for "boilerplate" matter furnished to county newspapers and that part of that was devoted to the Congressional campaign. Browne called attention to an NSL *Bulletin* in which it was stated that labor and agriculture had been recognized by the League in the form of appointments of representatives from those sectors on the executive on the group. When West was asked what the NSL had done for labor, West admitted the answer was "nothing" for labor as a class. For agriculture an effort had been made to speed up deliveries of fertilizer.[26]

With respect to the candidacy of Henry Ford, Dr. Hobbs wrote to Dr. McElroy on September 23, 1918, that he felt sure "Ford is not dead till after the election, if then, and I hope you will turn loose your guns." McElroy replied that he was glad "to have your opinion on his death" and that he was "sorry it had been postponed." On September 25 Dr. Hobbs urged, "By all means turn loose on Ford. He is not dead yet." Then the NSL issued a pamphlet containing a summary of Dr. Hobbs' article setting out Ford's alleged record. One of the paragraphs in that "record" declared Ford had openly opposed the U.S. loan to the Allies in 1915. When confronted with the fact that this government made no loans to the Allies until after war was declared by America in 1917, E.L. Harvey, League press agent, through whose department the pamphlet was sent out, confessed that he attempted to convey the false impression that Ford had set himself up in opposition to the government.[27]

At the same time the hearings into the League were underway, Representative Barnhart (IN) openly criticized the League. He declared it to be an "organization fathered by the capitalists of the country to defeat Congressmen who refused to bow to their wishes and to give clean records to those who had put money into their pockets for the declaration of war and who sought to protect them by voting against the income tax."[28]

One road trip taken by the Special Committee was to Chicago at the end of January 1919 where it planned to take the testimony of wealthy Chicago residents who were connected with the Chicago branch of the NSL. Before that Chicago hearing started, H.H. Merrick, head of the Chicago NSL branch, denied that his organization was connected to the NSL that was headquartered in New York City. Witnesses who appeared there included Willet M. Spooner (secretary of the Milwaukee branch of the League), August H. Vogel (president of the Milwaukee branch), Peter S. Lambros (a member of the Chicago branch committee that investigated the qualifications of certain congressional candidates in the 1918 election) and Edgar A. Bancroft (chair of the Chicago branch executive committee). The Milwaukee men testified that their league adopted a resolution in 1916 binding it to stay absolutely clear of politics and that it "adhered scrupulously to it."[29]

That the NSL's Chicago branch was willing to subvert the avowed purpose for which it was organized if by doing so it could secure the adoption of a city ordinance granting franchise rights desired by traction (streetcar) corporations, was a charge made to the Special Committee by Representative William E. Mason of Illinois. Mason and Representative Fred A. Britten (Illinois) also told the Special Committee that the political activities of the Chicago branch during the 1918 election campaign stamped it as "an auxiliary of the Brundage faction of the Republican party in Chicago." Mason stated that the NSL supported in the primaries all the candidates of the Brundage faction and that the insincerity of their supposed desire to elect patriotic men to Congress was conclusively shown by the fact that when they failed at the primaries they made no further effort to defeat "disloyal" men in the elections.

Representative Reavis added that the NSL campaign against Britten was discontinued after his nomination, in spite of the fact that they had sent out a letter saying he would be a "menace in the halls of Congress." Said Reavis, "Mr. Britten said his chief opposition from the Chicago branch of the league came from men born in England, who wanted the United States to enter the war on the side of the allies long before it did so, and from men connected with the corporations making enormous profits out of the production and sale of war materials. Mr. Britten voted against the declaration of war." Britten said, "The principal effort of the league against me was directed by Samuel Insull, Britisher. He was referred to in a London newspaper as the most prominent Britisher in America." He added that Insull's heart was in England and the heartstrings of the other league officials fighting him "were in war profits."[30]

In testifying in Washington on February 6, 1919, Elihu Root (honorary president of the NSL) defended the work of the League during the Congressional elections of 1918. He insisted the sole purpose of NSL activities then had been to educate the voters of America regarding the records made by their Congress. The reason why the NSL opposed Henry Ford, said Root, was because "Mr. Ford was a pacifist. He was against the war and he made public utterances which in my opinion made it of great importance for the successful prosecution of the war that he be defeated." Representative Browne then asked Root if it was not true that after war was declared Ford did everything possible to aid the country to defeat Germany. "Well, I'm not so sure about that," replied Root. "President Wilson thought so, didn't he?" countered Browne. "I disagree with the President in that matter," said Root. Browne then asked, "You can't classify Ford as disloyal can you?" Replied Root, "I think he came to the very, very verge of being disloyal, if he didn't go over."

Browne asked if the League had not "meddled in politics" in opposing the nomination of Chicago Mayor William Hale Thompson as senator? Later Root stated that he resented the imputation that the NSL had been organized in the interests of munitions makers and others who would benefit by the war. Said Root, "I cannot find strong enough terms to deny the imputation." Chairman Johnson then said, "Do you consider impossible that the league had ulterior motives when the chairman of its congressional committee [Orth] was a broker interested in increasing the price of hemp, and his chief assistant was a well known lobbyist?" Said Root, "Yes, impossible. The policies of the league were determined by all the members and the men you mention only carried them out." Root also remarked that the League had opposed Miss Jeannette Rankin as a candidate for Senator from Montana because she had voted against the declaration of war, as a U.S. Representative.[31]

Commenting further on the targeting of Chicago Mayor Thompson, Root observed, "It was the broadest kind of patriotism to awaken the people of Chicago to the danger which lay in his nomination.... In a broad sense the league sought to defeat men whom it did not consider patriotic, and in that sense it was engaged in politics." Representative Johnson asked Root if the NSL was supported by wealthy profiteers. Root replied, "The members of the league were actuated solely by patriotic motives and I deny that there were selfish motives behind the movement. You cannot get an organization together without having wealthy men in it, those interested in big affairs. If you need money you must go to the people who have it." As an additional comment on Rankin, Root declared, "She should not have been reelected and was not qualified to sit in Congress."[32]

An article appeared on February 7, 1919, with a headline that proclaimed the investigation of the NSL by the U.S. Congress as "silly." According to the report, "Prominent newspapers in a part of the country give editorial support to the patriotic body. In the first paragraph the terms 'silly,' 'absurd' and 'ridiculous' were said to be used by many of the important newspapers in all parts of the nation to describe the investigation of the National Security League." The article then listed brief excerpts from eight different newspapers: the Bristol (VA) *Courier*; Paducah (KY) *Sun*; Macon (GE) *News*; New Orleans (LA) *States*; San Antonio (TX) *Light*; Davenport (IA) *Democrat*; Kansas City (MO) *Times*; and St. Joseph (MO) *Press*.[33]

Another member of Congress stepped forward to brand the NSL as "a tool of Wall Street and its interests." Congressman Roscoe C. McCulloch (OH) told the Special Committee that officers of the League "responsible for the libel of Congress" should be brought before the bar of the House of Representatives for "punishment commensurate with the great wrong they have done." McCulloch was one of those politicians selected for intensive opposition from the NSL—he was "wrong" on seven of the League's eight measures. To show the falsity of NSL claims, McCulloch read into the record a summary of his votes on all of the war and preparedness measures. This showed that of the 126 measures of that matter which passed the House he voted for 111 of them and was absent on 15 votes. On final passage the Congressional Record showed he did not vote against a single war or preparedness bill, he testified. The major motive behind the League's attack on him, McCulloch said, "was that he had been in favor of placing the financial burdens of this war upon the shoulders of those who can best afford to meet them."

Attacks by the NSL amounted to a libel of Congress, said McCulloch and "it is the duty of the Congress not only to bring to account those responsible for the libel, but to expose the underlying purposes that actuated men to spend hundreds of thousands of dollars in an effort to destroy representatives of the people in order that they might advance their own personal interests." Raymond C. Schroeder, secretary to Congressman

Edward John King of Illinois, corroborated King's testimony that during the "inquisition to which Mr. King was subjected by the Chicago branch of the league, loyalty was merely an incidental proposition The league representatives were more concerned with securing the returns of railroads to their private owners, he said, than with the loyalty of Mr. King."[34]

Another member of Congress who testified against the League before the Special Committee was Brigadier General Isaac Sherwood, a Representative from Ohio. Sherwood stated that the NSL had furthered the interest of those who would benefit by the declaration of war and had descended to "underhanded means to get men in Congress who would bow to its wishes." The NSL attacks on him, said Sherwood, were "absolutely unjustified." Representative Frear, after reviewing the testimony given by the officials of the organization at the hearing, declared that "it proved conclusively that the league had ulterior motives." Sherman was 83 years old and one of the first men in Ohio to volunteer for service in the Civil War when it broke out. He took part in 42 engagements and rose to the rank of brigadier general. Yet the NSL branded him as disloyal and unpatriotic.[35]

As the hearing moved along in February, Representative James A. Frear urged that the Special Committee recommend to the House that NSL officials be brought before it "and the severest penalty within the power of the House be imposed." Chairman Ben Johnson and other committee members seemed in accord with those sentiments, with Johnson stating that criminal as well as civil action for libel could be instituted. A journalist predicted that NSL officers would not escape punishment for its attacks on the loyalties of Congressmen because it "loomed up with a greater degree of certainly" after the above comments from Frear and Johnson.[36]

Testifying on February 12 was Judge Alton B. Parker, of the NSL. He apologized for the work of the League, rather than defending it. While declaring he believed NSL officials were not animated by partisan politics in their part in the 1918 election campaign, he admitted their activities were susceptible to that interpretation. "If the chart and the other literature sent out by the league had been brought to my attention before they were put in circulation I should have objected to them going out." Asked for his opinion regarding the propriety of bringing into question the loyalty of members of Congress, Parker said, "I will say that such a statement ought not to have been put in the papers issued in connection with the chart."[37]

Representative Browne looked into the situation of excess profits in the mining sector, mainly copper, as part of the Special Committee investigation. He found that Arthur Curtis James (vice-president of Phelps-Dodge mining company) had given the NSL $29,750 during the previous three years. James was the director of 28 different companies, many in the mining sector. Charles Hayden (New York City) was a director in Nevada

Chapter 16. Critics and Impugners 221

Consolidated Copper Company, and 25 other corporations. He gave $2,500 to the NSL. The brothers Simon, Daniel and Murray Guggenheim gave a total of $3,700 to the League and Cleveland H. Dodge (of Phelps-Dodge) also donated to the NSL. Dodge was a director in 30 companies, most of them in mining, fuel or railroads.[38]

One of the best summaries of the investigation as it neared its end came from the Fargo, North Dakota, newspaper *Nonpartisan Leader*. It ran a long recap piece on February 24, 1919. In a set-off box in the middle of the piece was text that discussed the fact that "very rapidly the special privilege interests are building up in our country.... They have organizations such as the one described on this page [NSL], the primary object of which is to fight the battle of privilege with any weapons available. The orderly processes of democracy have not yet been able to bring them to justice and they are becoming stronger in the use of the tools of autocracy all the time." One of the politicians blackballed by the League was Henry A. Barnhart of Indiana—a conservative. He exchanged a number of letters with the NSL over their allegations of his disloyalty. On October 19, 1918, he wrote Orth of the League's Congressional Committee, "You say my inquiry as to your league being interested in militarism for the benefit of a class is wicked and dishonest, not at all, but your false inference that I am disloyal to our administration and to our country, when I have given my all for the prosecution of this war, and that I dodged votes when I was at the bedside of my dying wife, are damnable ... characteristic of sneaking curs.... I am as honest, loyal, patriotic and brave as you or any of the Wall street war-profiteering hyenas and character assassins in your organization. The code of gentlemanly ethics does not permit me to speak frankly and fully." When questioning Barnhart, Reavis remarked, "I wonder whether or not you know that the 47 men who are declared by this league to be loyal and patriotic men are the only men who voted for these pre-war measures that would have gone to a certain section of the country necessarily?" He was referring to revenue bills to pay for the war, bills such as increasing taxes, a luxury tax measure, and so forth. "And that likewise 40 percent of these men voted against the increase of the income tax that would have taken the money out of the same section...." Barnhart replied yes and "I charged it in speeches and I have charged, furthermore, that those big interests there interested in manufacturing implements of death in war were all speculating in war bonds, etc., had been preaching the doctrine of preparedness, etc."[39]

Special Committee member Reavis then said "That the 47 men declared loyal by this league are the men who voted for measures of preparedness that would have created large expenditures on the part of the government with the steel companies, in which are interested Morgan, Rockefeller, Frick and Carnegie, and that 40 per cent of those men voted against an increase of the income tax that would have taken money out of the pockets of Rockefeller, Morgan, Frick and Carnegie, and that an organization is formed to support those 47 men, financed by the men who would financially profit." Representative Browne looked into the report of the Federal Trade Commission on war profiteers and into the Directory of Directors "and discovered that virtually every war profiteering concern in the country was either represented on the board of the Security League or upon its list of heavy contributors."

Reavis noted that total contributions to the NSL were said to be about $600,000. J.P. Morgan gave $2,300 and was on the board of directors of seven large corporations; Nicholas F. Brady gave $4,500 and was a director of 50 large concerns; Henry Frick gave $3,500 and was a director on railroads and banks. Browne showed that 94 percent of the money collected in sums of $100 or more was raised in the stronghold of the war profiteers—the downtown section of New York City. Arthur Curtis James donated his $29,750 between March 19, 1915, and November 20, 1918. He was a director in 42 companies. Pre-war profits of Phelps were $7,444,399; war profits were $21,974,263, leaving excess profits over normal profits of more than $14,500,000 in one year.[40]

In a report submitted by the Special Committee on March 3, 1919, to the House, it was stated that the failure of the NSL to file an itemized statement of expenses made during the Congressional election campaign of November 1918 was a direct violation of the Corrupt Practices Act. That report was signed by six of the seven committee members. Representative Walsh filed a minority report. It was charged in the majority report that the National Security League was supported by the large interests of the country, which made "enormous profits" as the result of American entrance into World War I and that its plea of doing patriotic work was only a mask behind which it could secure the big interests and protect them in the reconstruction period.[41]

Walsh, in the minority report, commended the League for having done patriotic work, but he criticized its officials for having been evasive while testifying before the Special Committee and he also agreed the NSL had probably violated the Corrupt Practices Act. That act provided that any political organization that endeavored to influence a Congressional election in two or more states must file expense accounts with the Clerk of the House of Representatives. The Special Committee determined the League had taken part in the campaign in nearly every state. The real purpose of the NSL, said the majority report, "was to elect to Congress a majority which would entertain its view of reconstruction which follows the war," and the fight made by the League upon the loyalty of men of the "highest patriotism was so glaringly unjust and so patently false that it failed its purpose...."

Chapter 16. Critics and Impugners

Coincident with forming the league began the thought of financing it "and of coupling it with names of persons in which the people would have confidence." Joseph H. Choate of New York was made honorary president and upon his death Elihu Root was selected to take his place. Alton B. Parker was selected as honorary vice-president. Those people were selected for two reasons. One was to give the NSL an appearance of being nonpartisan, Root being a Republican and Parker a Democrat. The second reason was the league's desire to trade on their names for the purpose of raising money for NSL activities.[42]

The majority report of the Special Committee noted that the principal officers of the NSL were described as "a lawyer with a private clientele, a professional lobbyist, a sisal importer directly interested in the price of binder twine and a young newspaper man without a job." Upon entering the office of the League in New York City "one would see only Mr. West, the lobbyist; Mr. Orth, the sisal importer, and Mr. Harvey, an everyday newspaper man" said the report. "But if the curtains were only pulled back the hand of Rockefeller, of Vanderbilt, of Morgan, of Remington, of Du Pont, and of Guggenheim would be seen, suggesting steel, oil, moneybags, Russian bonds, rifles, powder and railroads." With respect to the eight measures that many Congressmen were graded on, the Special Committee called them "unfair, misleading and unjust" and drawn up by a man "utterly unqualified for such work."

The League cared not about a candidate's political affiliation but "how the candidate's attitude would affect certain interests that would be subjects of legislation by Congress during the reconstruction period. When the NSL began its campaign activities a fund separate from the general fund was collected for that particular purpose; $95.40 of every $100 was collected in New York City. Summing up its report the committee said the NSL had done the greatest injustice to loyal, patriotic men and this injustice was done 'by men seeking partisan ends and undertaking to hide their self-interest beneath the cloak of public service and national good.' It declared that the National Security League and similar organizations constituted a 'serious menace to representative government.'"[43]

Edward J. King was described as an "ordinary" Republican Congressman, from Galesburg, Illinois, who got into trouble during the 1918 election campaign with the "Chicago gentlemen who were doing their bit of war profiteering and who had chosen as their camouflage for this crime the National Security League." The Chicago NSL branch selected a committee of 12 men to conduct the "acid test" of the records and opinions of candidates for Congress, in the Chicago area. Then the daily press announced, day by day for two weeks, that King would be called before this group to answer to charges about his loyalty. As the primary was then on it had the effect of finding him guilty of some mysterious crime.

Emil C. Wetter (head of the Chicago branch) was the chair of that Chicago committee, with other members including H.H. Merrick, Cyrus McCormick, John F. Smulski, Edgar Bancroft, James A. Patten and Joseph W. Moses. Patten, the wheat king, was the man who just prior to the declaration of war bought up millions and millions of bushels of wheat for the National Biscuit Company and had it stored away from the common masses. McCormick was in the International Harvester Company (known as the harvester trust); the price of farm implements went up close to 300 percent during the war. Edgar Bancroft was a lawyer and front man of the harvester trust—he was chief counsel for the International Harvester Company. He went after any legislative bills designed to offer protection to injured workers. Merrick, president of the Chicago Association of Commerce, showed his patriotism by asking King, "How do you feel on government ownership of railroads?" Reportedly, the questioning of King by the Chicago committee was brief with respect to loyalty but more extensive and detailed regarding King's attitude to J.P. Morgan, giving labor unions a more extensive voice in politics, the governing of industry, and so forth.[44]

A brief editorial noting the NSL had been found guilty by the Special Committee said, "The noisy National Security League organized, we were told, to promote loyalty and '100-per-cent' Americanism, has been found guilty of being a mere political organization, financed by munition makers, war profiteers and millionaire reactionaries to furnish a patriotic camouflage for activities against liberal and progressive men and organizations."[45]

Another newspaper commented that the NSL had been funded with the announced purpose of securing "100 per cent Americanism"—but was

This cartoon appeared in March 1919 and spoofed the League and its questioning of politicians and their attitudes in the run-up to the election. The League pretended it cared only for preparedness, an increased military, and so forth. In reality politicians were often questioned more about their views of John D. Rockefeller, the role of government in industry, and the place of labor unions in society.

first planned in a foreign country, according to findings of the Special Committee. And "It sent out 'boiler plate' and other publicity to between 1700 and 1800 newspapers throughout the country. It was notable that the candidates opposed by the National Security League were nearly all men who had been prominent in the progressive politics of the county.... The league was supported by the big financial interests in throttling liberal thought."

Among the contributors to the NSL named in this account were Carnegie Corporation, John D. Rockefeller, J.P. Morgan, Guggenheim Brothers, T. Coleman Dupont (multi-millionaire munitions manufacturer), Charles Deering (International Harvester Company), Henry Frick, (United States Steel Corporation), George W. Perkins, W.H. Vanderbilt, F.W. Vanderbilt, Bernard M. Baruch, and others.

Menken first conceived of the idea for the organization during a visit he made to London, England, and the UK Parliament in August 1914, long before the U.S. entered World War I. The first man Menken consulted regarding the organization of the League was Frederic C. Coudert, a corporation lawyer who represented the British Ambassador to the U.S. as well as the British, French, Russian and Italian governments. That was long before Germany began to "interfere" with U.S. commerce (one of the pretexts, ultimately, to justify U.S. entry into the conflict). "The munition makers, at this period were the only ones that wanted the United States to go to war, because at this time no reason for our entering the world conflict existed." As a result of a conference of Menken, Coudert and others, the NSL was organized with another early player being Charles D. Orth. Orth was a member of the London and New York firm which virtually controlled the sisal market, as manager. The so-called sisal trust. It was said that northwestern U.S. farmers would remember that trust as "responsible for their paying about four time the former price for their binder twine."[46]

Early in May 1919 the prosecution of NSL officials for violating the Corrupt Practices Act was recommended by the Special Committee. Some of those committee members visited U.S. Attorney General Palmer and urged him to give prompt consideration to their recommendation. The penalty for violating that act was a $1,000 fine or one year imprisonment, or both. More reports of contributors to the League emerged at this time. Ridley Watts (New York City) gave $15,000 while Eversley Childs and William Hamelin Childs (both of New York City) of the U.S. Letter Company and other foreign letter companies, whose excess profits in the previous year were $12,016,397, donated $7,500. T. Coleman Dupont (powder interests) gave $9,000; Charles Hayden (director in 26 large corporations whose war profits were $12,527,948) contributed $2,500. R.B. Price (U.S. Rubber Corporation, $700), George W. Perkins (International Harvester Company, $750), W.W.K. Vanderbilt (railroads), Clarence H. Mackay (telegraph and cable companies), and Bernard M. Baruch (stockbroker) also all contributed to the League. Menken, in his testimony before the Special Committee, said he was a member of the law firm of Beckman, Menken and Griscom and also involved in corporations in New Orleans, Knoxville, Houston, Buffalo, Lockport (New York), Bloomington (Illinois), and elsewhere. His law firm acted as counsel for a corporation known as "The American Cities." That company, explained Menken, was employed "in controlling railway and public utility corporations."[47]

During the questioning of Menken, the founder of the League admitted he was a director of half a dozen firms, mostly real estate concerns. His law firm were the attorneys for "a considerable number" of corporations, he admitted, one of which was United Gas and Electric Company. According to his testimony before the Special Committee he conceived of the League as he sat in the UK House of Commons around August 5, 1915, when he heard speakers such as H.H. Asquith, Bonar Law, Gilbert Parsons and others explain their support for an appropriation of $100 million for the war effort and offer warning of that nation's unpreparedness. When he returned to America he had his attention drawn to the utterances of Augustus P. Gardner, especially on October 18, 1915, about American unpreparedness.

He recalled that the invitation to attend that initial meeting on December 1, 1915, was sent to a list of 300 names although he said he no longer had that list nor could he recall the names that were on the list. He did name a few of the men he spoke to early in his efforts to form the organization. One was Herbert Barry, a corporation lawyer with the firm of Wallace, Barry and Wainwright. Frederic R. Coudert was a lawyer with "a great many foreign interests" who represented the nations of Great Britain, France and Russia in international matters. Luke E. Wright was a lawyer and one of his clients was the Memphis Street Railway. Another man consulted early was John Purroy Mitchel (a lawyer in Menken's firm prior to the NSL forming, and later the Mayor of New York City). Another spoken to was G. Creighton Webb, who practiced law at one time but "he has always been a man of means." William Frederick Dix (secretary of the Mutual Life Insurance Company) was described as "very interested" in the idea. Frederick H. Allen was a lawyer with Allen and Cammann but "he is a man of independent means." Another man consulted early was David H. Miller, a lawyer with Miller and Auchincloss who practiced largely in the cotton trade. After hearing all these names from Menken, chairman Ben Johnson said to him, snidely, "we have confined ourselves, Mr. Menken, almost altogether to the legal fraternity in looking after the welfare of the Nation."[48]

Menken acknowledged that, as a corporation lawyer, he formed the Carnegie Foundation and he admitted that while the Rockefeller Foundation gave to money to his organization, John D. Rockefeller gave a total of

$35,000. During his testimony Menken insisted the League never received any money or donations from firms engaged in the sale or manufacture of war munitions. Johnson asked Menken about three donations made by "anonymous" or "a friend." The details were October 20, 1915, $1,000, January 29, 1916, $1,000, March 2, 1916, $500. According to Menken the donor on all three occasions was Joseph Choate. Yet other donations made by Choate were listed under his own name. When Johnson asked why sometimes Choate was listed by name and other times listed as "anonymous" Menken had no answer except to say Choate "preferred to give anonymously...."

The same explanation was offered for Eversly Childs, who gave money many times under his own name but also many times anonymously. Johnson named T. DeWitt Tyler, who had appeared in Washington before a Senate hearing in favor of railroads; Menken admitted Tyler had donated $2,500 to the NSL Philadelphia branch. The Guggenheim brothers (Simon, Murray and Daniel) gave a total of $3,750 and had interests in railroads, mining concerns, smelters and copper mines. Nicholas C. Brady had traction and corporate interests in New York City and gave $4,500 in total from three separate donations in his name, plus another $1,000 carried on the NSL books as from "anonymous." Henry Frick gave $3,500 while J.P. Morgan donated $2,500. Arthur Curtis James (a member of the firm Phelps, Dodge and Company—a large owner of smelting and railroad properties) donated $35,000 or $40,000. Mortimer L. Schiff and Jacob Schiff (father and son brokers in New York City) donated a total of $3,250.

Menken called financier Bernard Baruch—an old friend and classmate and an active promoter of the NSL from the beginning—although Baruch refused to accept any office in the League. Baruch donated $6,500. Another member of the League was George Wharton Pepper (Philadelphia) who was a trustee of the Carnegie Institute. Franklin Q. Brown was on the board of directors of a dozen or more concerns. Robert Bacon was president of the NSL from around January 1916 until about August 1917. He was a director of U.S. Steel and donated $15,000 to the NSL. He resigned the presidency when he did because he was running for public office.

While he was on the stand Walsh asked Menken what Bolshevism meant to him. The reply was: "the opponents of orderly, constitutional government; of radical social tendencies." At another point in his testimony Menken declared, "I would not coddle the workingman in any sense whatsoever." He didn't mind the idea of a health care fund for employees, but only if the employee contributed part of his wages to the fund; that is, the employer or the state would not also contribute—it would be solely employee financed. Caraway asked him if he believed in a mothers' pension fund (for women with children to raise who were left destitute by the death of their husbands). He replied, "I don't think I do." He was asked what good could be taken from Germany that could be applied to the United States. Said Menken, "The respect of the individual for the duty, the sense of service that they have to the state, and the willingness to observe wise laws." With respect to the "boiler plate" material the League had sent out at no charge to mostly small newspaper in smaller communities, Menken estimated the NSL sent such material to around 1,000 newspapers around the country and that the NSL had spent $15,000 to $20,000 in doing so.[49]

After that recommendation to prosecute the League was delivered that was the end of it. No prosecution of any kind was launched, nor were there any ramifications of a legal kind leveled against the National Security League. But, of course, none had really been intended. Congressmen were incensed by the League because it had impugned their loyalty, their patriotism, their Americanism, and so forth. The investigation had vindicated them in that regard. The darker side of manipulation and control of the state by outside groups of wealthy elites engaged in concerted action to rig elections and the entrenching of the deep state through lobbying and revolving door procedures were brushed aside, after the personal vindication. In the end the Special Committee's concern lay with themselves (members of Congress) and with themselves alone; it was not about control of the system by the elite capitalist class. However, the National Security League soon faded from sight. It tried to continue as it had in the past but what the League offered was no longer being bought, at least not from them. It even thumbed its nose at Congress again, for perhaps the last time. In November 1922, through Menken, the League filed a statement with the Clerk of the House of Representatives, in supposed compliance with the Corrupt Practices Act, which claimed to show expenditures by the League of a whopping $176 in the recent Congressional election campaign of November 1922.[50]

But by then the League was irrelevant and fading away. It had been somewhat successful in achieving a large increase in the American war machine. In other ways it was less successful. However, other organizations pursued the same goals and so, over time, the dreams of the NSL were achieved. Over time labor unions were effectively smashed or neutralized. Any idea of a socialist/communist ideology spreading in America, never mind prevailing, also went nowhere over time, remaining little more than a paranoid spot in a capitalist's brain. Methods by succeeding groups never changed; the capitalist class was never creative. In the wake of World War I the increased agitation by blacks for a better society were blamed on external sources; as such agitation was in the 1960s; as such agitation was in the 2010s. Russia was a scapegoat from its very moment of birth. Russia was trying to destroy American democracy from that day forward. Never mind that it made no sense in 1919 or in 2019, or anytime in between. Although its successes were limited, the National Security League was a pioneer in establishing and refining organizations that were financed (in hidden fashion) by the ruling capitalist class but presented and pitched to the average citizen as something of a grass roots organization that was expressing the prevailing mood while fighting for the little guy.

Chapter Notes

Chapter 1

1. "National Security League organized." *Missoulian* (Missoula MT), Dec 2, 1914.
2. "Business men in defense league." *New York Tribune*, Dec 2, 1914.
3. *Ibid*.
4. "Would recruit and train 5000 men as U.S. officers." *El Paso Herald* (TX), Dec 2, 1914.
5. "Why should we not defend ourselves?" *New York Tribune*, Dec 3, 1914.
6. "Congress will decide great army and navy problem." *Bridgeport Evening Farmer* (CT), Dec 3, 1914.
7. "The National Security League." *Sun* (NY), Dec 3, 1914.
8. "Major Putnam explains the purpose of the National Security League." *Sun* (NY), Dec 5, 1914.
9. "Menken names board." *New York Tribune*, Dec 7, 1914.
10. "Nation's demand heard by Congress." *New York Tribune*, Dec 8, 1914.
11. "Defense inquiry aims of security league defined." *Sun* (NY), Dec 9, 1914.
12. "Songs and saws." *Richmond Times-Dispatch* (VA), Dec 12, 1914.
13. "U.S. assembles powerful armada." *Grand Forks Herald* (ND), Dec14, 1914.
14. "How United States field artillery compares with that of other nations." *Grand Forks Herald* (ND), Dec 14, 1914; Leonard Wood, wikipedia page, accessed May 9, 2019.
15. "1,500 business men cheer pleas for U.S. defenses." *Sun* (NY), Dec 16, 1914.
16. "Target practice is urged." *Princeton Union* (MN), Dec 24, 1914.
17. "Predicts Security League will win." *New York Tribune*, Dec 27, 1914.
18. Charles J. Bonaparte. "Increase size of our army and navy, PDQ, says Charles J. Bonaparte." *Sun* (NY), Dec 27, 1914.
19. S. Stanwood Menken. "End haphazard control of the nation's defenses." *Sun* (NY), Dec 27, 1914.
20. "Movement for adequate defense meeting nation-wide response." *Sun* (NY), May 23, 1915.
21. Gardner and Putnam profiles from individual Wikipedia pages, accessed March 20, 2019; "Charles E. Lydecker, lawyer, dies at 68." *New York Times*, May 7, 1920.
22. "S. Stanwood Menken, who believes in being prepared." *New York Tribune*, Feb 24, 1918; "S. Stanwood Menken." *Richmond Palladium* (IN), Dec 2, 1921.
23. "Trio bind man, get $150,000 gems." *Evening Star* (Washington), Jun 17, 1931.
24. "Menken league styled as tool." *Sun* (NY), Mar 4, 1919.
25. "Timeline of United States military operations." Wikipedia, accessed June 21, 2019; "Rumor U.S. is to quit Haiti and San Domingo." *Evening Star* (Washington), Jan 25, 1917.
26. "National Defense Act of 1916." Wikipedia, accessed Jun 21, 2019.
27. "Making war profitable." *Washington Socialist* (Everett WA), Aug 27, 1914.
28. "Fight on war profits at cost of U.S. buyers." *Sun* (NY), Aug 22, 1914.
29. "Congress can shake off grip of war trust." *Day Book* (Chicago), Oct 20, 1915; "War orders will make J. P. Morgan the richest man in the world." *Mitchell Capital* (ND), Sep 16, 1915.
30. "Morgan firm's war contracts now $500,000,000." *New York Tribune*, July 5, 1915.

31. "Here's how Morgan makes war pay." *Tacoma Times* (WA), Sep 20, 1915.
32. "Allies spend ten million daily in America." *Harrisburg Telegraph* (PA), Aug 28, 1917.
33. "Lusitania was carrying first world war explosives from New York when sunk in May 1915, British files reveal." Centenarynews.com May 2014, accessed June 20, 2019.
34. "Inquiry planned to sift strikes." *Washington Herald*, Jan 6, 1914.
35. "Unions attacked." *Labor Journal* (Everett WA), Apr 3, 1914; "Military officers making arrests." *Fergus County Democrat* (Lewistown MT), Sep 3, 1914; "Socialism in Huntington." *Socialist and Labor Star* (Huntington WV), Oct 16, 1914.
36. "Peace." *Day Book* (Chicago), May 31, 1916; "Ripley—labor would have all." *Evening Times-Republican* (Marshalltown IA), Sep 13, 1916; "The drama, the stage and the actors." *Labor World* (Duluth MN), Nov 25, 1916; "Few sales on local market." *Washington Herald*, Aug 8, 1916.
37. "Mr. Gompers' dinner." *Bridgeport Evening Farmer* (CT), Jan 30, 1917.
38. "Columbus ships deported I.W.W. back." *Arizona Star* (Tucson), Jul 13, 1917.
39. "The gray ghost of socialism." *New Ulm Post* (MN), Jul 30, 1917.
40. "A revolution approaching." *Northwest Worker* (Everett WA), Apr 5, 1917.
41. "Must crush Bolshevism, says Gompers." *New York Tribune*, Feb 23, 1918.
42. "Revolution?" *Nonpartisan Leader* (Fargo ND), Jan 13, 1919.
43. "Queen of Reds on Soviet Ark, predicts ruin." *Washington Herald*, Dec 22, 1919.
44. "Aim revolution in America." *County Record* (Kingstree SC), Nov 6, 1919; "Red Russians plan anarchy." *Watchman and Southron* (Sumter SC), Jul 2, 1919.
45. "The election case of Truman H. Newberry of Michigan (1922)." www.senate.gov/artandhistory/history/common/contested_elections. Accessed June 20, 2019.
46. Ibid.
47. "Washington men in list of nation's defenders." *Evening Star* (Washington), Jul 30, 1917.

Chapter 2

1. "To investigate defenses." *Sun* (NY), Jan 15, 1915.
2. "Henry L. Stimson heads advocates of bigger American Army." *Evening Times-Republican* (Marshalltown IA), Jan 22, 1915.
3. "To argue for national defense." *Evening Star* (Washington), Feb 15, 1915.
4. "Security League to form branch here." *Washington Herald*, Feb 15, 1915.
5. "Peace folk arm against armament." *New York Tribune*, Feb 16, 1915.
6. "Defense league is enlisting aid." *Washington Herald*, April 8, 1915; "Overpreparedness made war, he says." *Ordway New Era* (CO), Apr 23, 1915; George von L. Meyer, wikipedia page, accessed May 10, 1919.
7. "Organize branch of security league." *Gate City* (Keokuk IA), May 30, 1915; "Security league's new chairman tells what it will do here." *Evening Public Ledger* (Philadelphia), Aug 3, 1915.
8. "Defense plan at Mill City." *Bemidji Pioneer* (MN), Aug 14, 1915; "Organize league tomorrow night." *Gate City* (Keokuk IA), Aug 18, 1915.
9. "All for defense." *Topeka State Journal* (KS), Sep 10, 1915.
10. "Conference is held on national defense." *Richmond Times-Dispatch* (VA), Sep 17, 1915.
11. "10 governors for league." *South Bend News-Times* (IN), Oct 7, 1915.
12. "Pledge personal service." *Richmond Times-Dispatch* (VA), Oct 29, 1915.
13. "Would help in case of war or disaster." *Evening Star* (Washington), Jan 21, 1916.
14. "Women will raise funds to help train 5,000 aviators for national defense." *Sun* (NY), Feb 11, 1916.
15. "Watchful waiting's end sure Nov. 2, says Choate." *Sun* (NY), Feb 17, 1916.
16. "Security league want 500 members in city Pensacola." *Pensacola Journal* (FL), Feb 24, 1916.
17. "Mayor shows nation's weariness in defense." *Sun* (NY), Apr 19, 1916.
18. "Annual Report." *Our Country*, May 1916.
19. "To form security league branch." *Evening Star* (Washington), Apr 24, 1916; "Security league wants members." *Gate City* (Keokuk IA), Jul 22, 1916.

20. Ad. *New York Tribune*, Jan 2, 1917.
21. "Band together to urge nation's preparedness." *Evening Star* (Washington), Jan 16, 1917.

Chapter 3

1. "Security league to form branch here." *Washington Herald*, Feb 15, 1915.
2. "Join in fight to build army." *Washington Herald*, Feb 26, 1915.
3. "Defense league is enlisting aid." *Washington Herald*, Apr 8, 1915.
4. "Florida to get branch of Nat'l Security League." *Lakeland Evening Telegram* (FL), Oct 1, 1915.
5. "Wants committee appointed on national defense." *Lakeland Evening Telegram* (FL), Oct 14, 1915.
6. "Champ Clark and O'Gorman declare in favor of preparedness." *Washington Herald*, Oct 11, 1915.
7. "Congressmen strongly favor adequate defense." *Grand Forks Herald* (ND), Oct 20, 1915.
8. "Twelve governors cooperating in move for preparedness." *Sun* (NY), Oct 24, 1915.
9. "Whitman pledges preparedness aid." *Sun* (NY), Nov 4, 1915.
10. "Mayor's defense plan acclaimed." *New York Tribune*, Nov 18, 1915.
11. "Mayor leads 800 in defense demand." *Sun* (NY), Dec 17, 1915.
12. E. B. Johns. "The Herald's army and navy department." *Washington Herald*, Dec 23, 1915.
13. "Elihu Root hold out for a monster federal army." *Harrisburg Telegraph* (PA), January 7, 1916.
14. "Gardner says conscription is only safe plan." *Honolulu Star-Bulletin*, Jan 11, 1916; "Gardner thinks city forts can't stop foe. *Sun* (NY), Jan 11 1916.
15. "Watchful waiting's end sure Nov. 2, says Choate." *Sun* (NY), Feb 17, 1916.
16. "Security." *Democratic Banner* (Mt. Vernon OH), Mar 3, 1916; "American mayors meet in St. Louis." *Evening Star* (Wash), Mar 3, 1916.
17. "Robert Bacon, Senate candidate." *Sun* (NY), Aug 18, 1916; Robert Bacon wikipedia page, accessed Mar 24, 2019.
18. "Defense petitions out." *Evening Public Ledger* (Philadelphia), Feb 17, 1917.
19. "Seek public views on bills." *Evening Star* (Washington), Mar 9, 1917.
20. "Jersey urged to prepare." *New York Tribune*, Mar 11, 1917.

Chapter 4

1. "Peace conference here June 14–15." *Evening World* (NY), June 3, 1915.
2. "Peace convention now labor's plan." *Sun* (NY), Jun 10, 1915.
3. "Former Secretary of Navy will talk of preparedness." *Bridgeport Evening Farmer* (CT), Jun 10, 1915.
4. "Modern war engines shown at exhibition." *Evening Star* (Washington), Jun 12, 1915; Ad. *Sun* (NY), Jun 14, 1915; "War men to talk peace." *New York Tribune*, Jun 12, 1915.
5. "Roosevelt tells league pacifists are undesirable." *Evening World* (NY), Jun 14, 1915.
6. "Press reports untrue." *Evening Star* (Washington), Jun 15, 1915.
7. "Peace; prepare." *Topeka State Journal* (KS), Jun 14, 1915.
8. "United States Army not able to conduct war of magnitude." *Albuquerque Morning Journal* (NM), Jun 15, 1915.
9. "The duty of preparedness." *Sun* (NY), Jun 15, 1915.
10. "George von L. Meyer, once Secretary of the Navy is sure it is now going to pot." *Evening Herald* (Albuquerque NM), Jun 15, 1915; "Bares inferiority of American navy." *Evening Star* (Washington), Jun 15, 1915.
11. "Wilson urged to move for defense." *Evening Times-Republican* (Marshalltown IA), Jun 16 1915.
12. "Armament agitation." *Grand Forks Herald* (ND), Jun 21, 1915.
13. "Preparations for peace." *Capital Journal* (Salem OR), Jun 24, 1915.
14. "Like a bright red flag before a herd of bulls." *Gate City* (Keokuk IA), Nov 28, 1915.
15. "Great defense move launched." *Washington Herald,* Nov 28, 1915.
16. "Urges navy bigger than Wilson plans." *Washington Times*, Nov 28, 1915.
17. "Security congress to meet January 20." *Evening Star* (Washington), Jan 2, 1916.
18. "To show the need of defense is aim." *Evening Star* (Washington), Jan 12, 1916;

"National security congress will discuss America's vital needs." *Pensacola Journal* (FL), Jan 13, 1916.

19. "Mayor Mitchel heads delegation." *Evening Star* (Washington), Jan 16, 1916.

20. "Our country." *Washington Times*, Jan 20, 1916.

21. "National Security League voices cry for preparedness." *Evening Star* (Washington), Jan 20, 1916; John B. Stanchfield. Wikipedia page, accessed March 12, 2019.

22. "T. R. would force all into military service." *Sun* (NY), Jan 21, 1916; "Claim Japan is menace to U.S." *El Paso Herald* (TX), Jan 22, 1916.

23. "Plan for a union of all increased armament bodies." *Evening Star* (Washington), Jan 22 1916.

24. "Down with the extremists." *West Virginian* (Fairmont), Jan 21, 1916.

25. "Mayors of 75 cities in league for defense." *Sun* (NY), Jan 23, 1916.

26. Paul V. Collins. "President may roar like lion for preparedness." *Perth Amboy Evening News* (NJ), Jan 26, 1916.

27. "Security league sessions wind up with banquet." *Evening Star* (Washington), Jan 23, 1916.

28. "Dr. Bell for preparedness." *Evening Star* (Washington), Apr 24, 1916; "Preparedness sessions in Charleston end." *Evening Star* (Washington), Apr 29, 1916.

29. "Patriotic congress to meet in Washington." *Richmond Times-Dispatch* (VA), Nov 27, 1916; "Constructive patriotism for America." *Grand Forks Herald* (ND), Dec 4, 1916.

30. "Preparedness educator named." *Bryan Eagle and Pilot* (TX), Jan 9, 1917.

31. "Reserve of 20,000,000 men planned for U.S." *Evening Star* (Washington), Jan 21, 1917.

32. "Women prominent in civic and social service work." *Grand Forks Herald* (ND), Jan 24, 1917.

33. Ad. *Washington Times*, Jan 24, 1917.

34. "U.S. preparedness." *Evening Star* (Washington), Jan 25, 1917.

35. "Rumor U.S. is to quit Haiti and San Domingo." *Evening Star* (Washington), Jan 25, 1917.

36. "League of women for war service." *Evening Star* (Washington), Jan 27, 1917.

37. "Washington, or any other American city near coast, could be destroyed by enemy airmen, Peary says." *Albuquerque Morning Journal* (NM), Jan 28, 1917.

38. "Senator warns of peril to U.S." *Evening Star* (Washington), Jan 28, 1917.

39. "Anti-military pastor assailed." *New York Tribune*, Jan 30, 1917.

Chapter 5

1. "New York open to foe, expert says." *Washington Times*, March 19, 1915.

2. "Get ready now for war, urged." *El Paso Herald* (TX), May 10, 1915; "Declare nation in sad state." *Evening Herald* (Albuquerque NM), May 10, 1915.

3. "Million defenders sought by league." *Sun* (NY), May 11, 1915.

4. "We are weak as a military power." *Ogden Standard* (UT), May 13, 1915.

5. "Daniels attacks many detractors." *Tulsa World* (OK), May 16, 1915.

6. "Ships and men ready, Daniels and Dewey say." *New York Tribune*, May 16, 1915; "A first army of defense." *Richmond Palladium* (IND), May 18, 1915.

7. "Purchase of Belgium urged by Wanamaker." *Evening Star* (Washington), Jul 23, 1915.

8. "Wanamaker wants U.S. to buy Belgium." *Sun* (NY), Jul 23, 1915.

9. "John Wanamaker quits chairmanship of security league." *Evening Public Ledger* (Philadelphia), Jul 28, 1915.

10. "Company formed to buy Belgium." *Washington Times*, Jul 28, 1915.

11. "Armored car on way west." *Harrisburg Telegraph* (PA), May 27, 1916.

Chapter 6

1. "Safety first, League's cry." *Washington Herald*, March 7, 1915.

2. "Country not prepared for war." *Evening Public Ledger* (Philadelphia), March 12, 1915.

3. "Over-preparedness made war, he says." *Ordway New Era* (CO), April 23, 1915.

4. "Security league wants 'war navy.'" *Sun* (NY), May 4, 1915.

5. "Standing by the president." *New York Tribune*, May 21, 1915.

6. "Movement for adequate defense meeting nation-wide response." *Sun* (NY), May 23, 1915.

7. "Famous men say United States must

Notes—Chapter 6

get ready." *Guthrie Leader* (OK), May 24, 1915.

8. "Ralston on record favoring Wilson policies on war." *South Bend News-Times* (IN), May 27, 1915.

9. [No title] *Commoner* (Lincoln NE), July 1, 1915; "Spiritual drill in nation urged." *New York Tribune*, July 3, 1915; Ad. *New York Tribune*, Jul 5, 1915.

10. "Employers urged to help militia." *Sun* (NY), Jul 7, 1915.

11. "Urges development of National Guard." *Evening Star* (Washington), Jul 14, 1915.

12. "Citizen soldiers." *Topeka State Journal* (KS), Jul 14, 1915.

13. "Security league calls U.S. defense lacking." *Evening Star* (Washington), Jul 26, 1915; "Says vast army can invade U.S." *Washington Herald*, Jul 26, 1915.

14. "National Security League fever has reached Florida." *Lakeland Evening Telegram* (FL), Jul 29, 1915.

15. "Security league wants dynamite." *New York Tribune*, Jul 29, 1915.

16. "Civilian leaders under army officers." *Evening Star* (Washington), August 9, 1915.

17. "500 leave city to learn war's ways at camp." *New York Tribune*, Aug 10, 1915.

18. "The cost of defense." *East Oregonian* (Pendleton), Aug 16, 1915.

19. "Nation-wide campaign for adequate defense." *Richmond Times-Dispatch* (VA), August 22, 1915.

20. "Security league says nation cries out for better defenses." *Bridgeton Pioneer* (NJ), Aug 26, 1915.

21. Ad. *Evening World* (NY), Sep 11, 1915.

22. "To spread preparedness." *Sun* (NY), Sep 17, 1915.

23. "Five hundred dollar prize for good story." *Logan Republican* (UT), Oct 5, 1915.

24. "Working for real preparedness." *Richmond Times-Dispatch* (VA), Oct 14, 1915.

25. "Make nation look silly." *Little Falls Herald* (MN), October 15, 1915.

26. "Wilson estimates national defense cost $400,000,000." *Little Falls Herald* (MN), Oct 15, 1915; "Congressmen for national defense." *Perth Amboy Evening News* (NJ), Oct 18, 1915.

27. Henry Litchfield West. "Criminal neglect of national defenses." *Richmond Times-Dispatch* (VA), Oct 24, 1915.

28. [No title] *Commoner* (Lincoln NE), Nov 1, 1915.

29. "Claude Kitchin's statement on the nation's preparedness—he gives facts." *Commoner* (Lincoln NE), December 1 1915.

30. "Woman heckles ex-Senator Young." *New York Tribune*, Dec 15, 1915.

31. "Offer prize for the best essay on security." *Perth Amboy Evening News* (NJ), Dec 16, 1915.

32. "Society day at the Automobile Show." *Sun* (NY), January 5, 1916.

33. "Gunboat hat joins in national propaganda for preparedness." *Evening Public Ledger* (Philadelphia), February 11, 1916.

34. Ad. *Topeka State Journal*, February 11, 1916.

35. Hudson Maxim. "Why the government should not make its war supplies." *Richmond Times-Dispatch* (VA), Feb 13, 1916.

36. "Veterans at eighty urge U.S. defense." *Washington Times*, Feb 18, 1916.

37. "Squadron of orators to urge U.S. defense." *Evening Public Ledger* (Philadelphia), Mar 2, 1916.

38. "149 speakers to give preparedness talks." *Evening Public Ledger* (Philadelphia), Mar 15, 1916.

39. "Baseball players' frat is in favor of national defense." *Albuquerque Morning Journal* (NM), Mar 19, 1916.

40. "Defense, marchers' slogan." *Evening Star* (Washington), Apr 2, 1916.

41. "Industrial preparedness." *Bisbee Review* (AZ), Apr 19, 1916.

42. "Women urged to serve country." *Washington Herald*, May 13, 1916.

43. Ad. *Harrisburg Telegraph* (PA), May 17, 1916.

44. "Marching with the legions of Preparedness." *New York Tribune*, May 21, 1916.

45. Ibid.

46. "Now for the preparedness parade!" *Richmond Times-Dispatch* (VA), May 21, 1916.

47. "Nation aroused to sense of need of preparedness." *Sunday Telegram* (Clarksburg WV), May 28, 1916.

48. "Throngs in Kansas City wildly cheer Roosevelt." *Sun* (NY), May 31, 1916.

49. "The National Security League and its purpose." *Sun* (NY), Jun 18, 1916.

50. "Military training straw vote." *Ardmoreite* (Ardmore OK), Aug 28, 1916.
51. "Try to extend military service." *Labor World* (Duluth MN), Jan 6, 1917.
52. Frederic L. Huidekoper. "The Argentine system of military training." *Wheeling Intelligencer* (WV), Jan 29, 1917.
53. Frederic L. Huidekoper. "Making Americans." *Wheeling Intelligencer* (WV), Mar 6, 1917.
54. Ad. *Sun* (NY), Mar 2, 1917.
55. Louise Bryant. "A day with lady militarists." *New York Tribune*, Mar 11, 1917.
56. "Wide interest in defense." *Evening Star* (Washington), Mar 13, 1917.
57. S. Stanwood Menken. "Patriotism to nation what soul is to man—without it come decay and death." *Mexico Missouri Message*, Mar 15, 1917.
58. "Favored by most editors." *Evening Star* (Washington), Mar 22, 1917.
59. Ad. *Sun* (NY), Mar 22, 1917.
60. "Womanhood, the Glory of the Nation, displays feminine patriotism." *Evening World* (NY), Mar 29, 1917.
61. Ad. *Washington Times*, Mar 29, 1917.
62. "Give him a chance." *Richmond Palladium* (IN), Mar 30, 1917.
63. "Military census urged for capital." *Evening Star* (Washington), April 3, 1917.

Chapter 7

1. "Peace folk arm against armament." *New York Tribune*, Feb 16, 1915.
2. [No title] *Capital Journal* (Salem OR), Mar 17, 1915.
3. "Against American militarism." *Twin Falls Herald* (ID), Mar 23, 1915.
4. "Security league should put the punch in its platform." *Tacoma Times* (WA), May 24, 1915.
5. "Morgan firm's war contract now $500,000,000." *New York Tribune*, Jul 5, 1915.
6. "Hate war but fight says Jane Addams." *Sun* (NY), Jul 10, 1915.
7. "Another insidious lobby." *Commoner* (Lincoln NE), Sep 1, 1915.
8. Ibid.
9. "Are we prepared." *Evening Public Ledger* (Philadelphia), October 30, 1915.
10. William J. Bryan. Investigate. *Commoner* (Lincoln NE), Nov 1, 1915.
11. "Bryan accused of falsifying." *Harrisburg Telegraph* (PA), Nov 5, 1915.
12. "Menken denies Bryan's charges." *New York Times*, Nov 16, 1915.
13. Charles A. Collman. "Why the money trust wants war." *New Ulm Post* (MN), Nov 5, 1915.
14. Ibid.
15. "Capital press and munitions makers get a panning at C. F. of L. meeting." *Day Book* (Chicago), Nov 22, 1915.
16. "The interest back of preparedness." *Commoner* (Lincoln NE), Dec 1, 1915.
17. "Hudson Maxim's interest in preparedness." *Commoner* (Lincoln NE), January 1, 1916.
18. "Fools and their war talk." *Tribune* (Cape Girardeau MO), Dec 17, 1915.
19. [No title] *Hattiesburg News* (MS), Dec 22, 1915.
20. "What happened to Capper?" *Sun* (NY), Feb 7, 1916.
21. "Patriotism at so much per." *Labor Advocate* (Cincinnati), Apr 1, 1916.
22. "Duck the Natural Security League." *Labor Advocate* (Cincinnati), Apr 8, 1916.
23. Henry Ford. "Humanity—and sanity." *Rock Island Argus* (IL), Apr 13, 1916.
24. "Security league dodges socialism." *Northwest Worker* (Everett WA), Apr 27, 1916.
25. Thomas Levish. "Influences." *Day Book* (Chicago), Jun 7, 1916.
26. "Military training in public schools." *Commoner* (Lincoln NE), Jul 1, 1916.
27. "Most vigorous arraignment of militaristic tendencies." *Labor Journal* (Everett WA), Mar 23, 1917.
28. "Gardner makes inquiry into pacifist and propagandist." *Evening Public Ledger* (Philadelphia), Dec 6, 1915.
29. "Opens Mex fight." *Topeka State Journal* (KS), Jan 6, 1916.
30. "Ask to be investigated." *Barre Times* (VT), January 20, 1916.

Chapter 8

1. "Pershing in security league." *Perth Amboy Evening News* (NJ), May 18, 1917.
2. "Steps taken to remove Mayor Thompson of Chicago." *Norwich Bulletin* (CT), Aug 16, 1917.
3. "Security league to oust Thompson." *East Oregonian* (Pendleton), Aug 22, 1917.
4. "Chicago's mayor ignored." *Evening Star* (Washington), August 29, 1917.

5. "Must be either for or against the government." *Arizona Republican* (Phoenix), Sep 4, 1917.
6. "Hang him in effigy." *Topeka State Journal* (KS), Sep 5, 1917.
7. "Times and persons." *Evening World* (NY), Sep 6, 1917.
8. "Darrow picked for security league." *Free Trader-Journal* (Ottawa IL), Sept 11, 1917.
9. "Root defines treason to America in the war." *Richmond Times-Dispatch* (VA), Sep 15, 1917; "Root heads security league." *New York Tribune*, Sep 16, 1917.
10. "Women in National Security League." *Tulsa World* (OK), Nov 20, 1917.
11. "Security league calls a congress." *Sun* (NY), Nov 12, 1917.
12. "The National Security League." *New York Tribune*, Nov 25, 1917.
13. "News in brief." *New York Tribune*, Jan 1, 1918.
14. "Society in Washington." *Washington Herald*, Feb 3, 1918; "Late president's widow at her desk working for patriotism." *Albuquerque Morning Journal* (NM), Feb 4, 1918; "Society news." *Chicago Eagle*, Feb 9, 1918.
15. "Elect loyal men to congress, plea of Elihu Root." *New York Tribune*, May 9, 1918.
16. "National Security League selects new president." *Albuquerque Morning Journal* (NM), Jul 17, 1918.
17. "He helped make the National Security League." *Tombstone Epitaph* (AZ), Sep 22, 1918.
18. "Will investigate National Security League." *Newark Post* (DE), Oct 9, 1918.
19. "Will direct speakers." *Tulsa World* (OK), Nov 3, 1918.

Chapter 9

1. "Drive to keep pacifists out of Congress to be started." *Grand Forks Herald* (ND), Jan 1, 1918.
2. Ibid.
3. "Security league praises solons." *Missoulian* (Missoula MT), Jan 20, 1918.
4. [No title] *Capital Journal* (Salem OR), Jan 21, 1918.
5. [No title] *Capital Journal* (Salem OR), Jan 29, 1918.
6. "Country is aroused over Creel's unprepared speech." *New York Tribune*, Apr 21, 1918.
7. "Security league in congress fight." *Sun* (NY), May 6, 1918.
8. "Big campaign to elect loyal war congress." *Alexandria Gazette* (VA), Jun 22, 1918.
9. "League bares war record of Hearst guests." *New York Times*, Jul 6, 1918.
10. "Election of loyal congressmen urged." *New York Tribune*, Jul 8, 1918.
11. "Old party leaders shy at fusion offer." *New York Tribune*, Jul 10, 1918.
12. "Fusion call issued by security league to beat Socialists." *New York Tribune*, Jul 15, 1918.
13. "Socialists predict 300,000 votes as a result of fusion." *New York Tribune*, Aug 1, 1918.
14. "47 of 347 members of Congress called 100 per cent loyal." *New York Tribune*, Aug 5, 1918; "List of United States Representatives from [name of state]," wikipedia, viewed, Apr 2, 2019.
15. "47 of 347 members of Congress called 100 per cent loyal." *New York Tribune*, Aug 5, 1918.
16. "Questionnaire on war views sent to all candidates." *Evening Capital and Maryland Gazette* (Annapolis), Aug 12, 1918.
17. Ibid.
18. "Roosevelt urges a loyal Congress." *Sun* (NY), August 20, 1918.
19. "Republicans lead in war support." *Abilene Reflector* (KS), Aug 29, 1918.
20. "Dent strikes at security league." *Pensacola Journal* (FL), Sep 7, 1918.
21. Ad. *Perth Amboy Evening News* (NJ), Sept 12, 1918.
22. "The draft and the war." *South Bend News-Times* (IN), Sep 16, 1918.
23. "Loyalists only in congress." *New York Tribune*, October 21, 1918.
24. Ad. *Shepherdstown Register* (WV), Oct 24, 1918.
25. Ad. *Richmond Palladium* (IN), Oct 29, 1918.
26. "Security league puts 17 senators on its honor roll." *New York Tribune*, Oct 30, 1918.
27. Ad. *Perth Amboy Evening News* (NJ), Oct 30, 1918.
28. "Rep. Barnhart exposes lies of security league." *South Bend News-Times* (IN), Oct 30, 1918.
29. "57 candidates here for congress ask

complete surrender." *New York Tribune*, Oct 31, 1918.
30. Ad. *Wood County Reporter* (Wisconsin Rapids WI), Oct 31, 1918.
31. Ad. *Harrisburg Telegraph* (PA), Nov 2, 1918.
32. Ad. *Wheeling Intelligencer* (WV), Nov 4, 1918.
33. "All Socialists defeated here for congress." *New York Tribune*, Nov 6, 1918.

Chapter 10

1. Ad. *New York Tribune*, May 1, 1917; Ad. *Sun* (NY), May 2, 1917.
2. "Security league to spend million in rousing nation." *New York Tribune*, May 13, 1917.
3. "Security league moves to offset pacifist activities." *New York Tribune*, May 28, 1917.
4. "Campaign launched to combat activities of pacifist bodies." *Honolulu Star-Bulletin*, Jun 18, 1917.
5. Albert Bushnell Hart. "Telling why we fight and why we're sure we're right." *Sun* (NY), Jun 24, 1917.
6. "Security league leaders to organize a nation-wide wake up America campaign." *Lake County Times* (Hammond IN), Jun 25, 1917.
7. S. Stanwood Menken. "A speakers' Plattsburg." *New York Tribune*, Jun 26, 1917; "Dr. Baker overflows to entire nation." *Grand Forks Herald* (ND), Jul 16, 1917.
8. "Patriotism overflows to entire nation." *Grand Forks Herald* (ND), Jul 16, 1917.
9. "To stir war enthusiasm." *Sun* (NY), Jul 16, 1917.
10. "One way to discourage spies." *Carson City Appeal* (NV), Jul 21, 1917.
11. "McElroy to stir patriots." *Sun* (NY), July 25, 1917.
12. "Educational campaign by National Security League." *Evening Herald* (Washington), Jul 26, 1917.
13. Robert M. McElroy. "Nation's war ideals basis of America's unity in peace." *Sun* (NY), Aug 5, 1917.
14. "Hexamer resents loyalty creed." *Evening Public Ledger* (Philadelphia), Aug 6, 1917; "Ex-Teutons resent loyalty request." *Sun* (NY), Aug 6, 1917.
15. "Should acknowledge it." *Pensacola Journal* (FL), Aug 10, 1917.

16. Shailer Mathews. "Why we fight Germany—in plain words." *Hope Pioneer* (ND), Aug 16, 1917.
17. William J. Black. "Great chautauqua movement has become mobilization agency for national policies." *New York Tribune*, Aug 19, 1917.
18. "Finds loyalty agitation was needed in country." *Evening Star* (Washington), Aug 20, 1917.
19. "Teuton publisher rejects Kaiserism; is loyal to U.S." *New York Tribune*, Aug 20, 1917.
20. "Vigilantes aim in tightening slackers' net." *Evening Public Ledger* (Philadelphia), Aug 23, 1917; Ad. *Washington Times*, Jan 17, 1918.
21. "W. M. Musgrave to speak here Friday night." *Grand Forks Herald* (ND), Aug 30, 1917.
22. "Townley can't stomach governor's peace council." *Washburn Leader* (ND), Sep 7, 1917.
23. "Ignorance endangering country, says National Security League." *Honolulu Star-Bulletin*, Sep 20, 1917.
24. Irvin S. Cobb. "Victory or defeat; which will it be?" *Bridgeport Evening Farmer* (CT), Sep 21, 1917.
25. "Tell the people the facts." *Hartford Republican* (KY), Sep 21, 1917.
26. "Plans annual convention." *Evening Star* (Washington), Sep 24, 1917; "Loyalty campaign gains." *New York Tribune*, Sep 18, 1917; "Speakers to tour for loyalty week." *New York Tribune*, Sep 17, 1917; "Other states plan loyalty week." *Sun* (NY), Sep 24, 1917.
27. "T. R. would send La Follette to the German lines." *Wheeling Intelligencer* (WV), Sep 27, 1917; "La Follette unfit to sit in Congress." *Bismarck Tribune* (ND), Sep 25, 1917.
28. Ad. *Sun* (NY), Oct 16, 1917.
29. "Security leaguers to talk war at training camps." *Harrisburg Telegraph* (PA), Nov 5, 1917.
30. "Women in National Security League." *Tulsa World* (OK), Nov 20, 1917.
31. "Call is made on professors for war work." *Washington Times*, Nov 5, 1917.
32. "Teachers to take loyalty pledge." *Sun* (NY), Nov 26, 1917.
33. "Drive to keep pacifists out of congress to be started." *Grand Forks Herald* (ND), Jan 1, 1918.

34. "Labor heads tell of loyalty in war." *Sun* (NY), Jan 8, 1918.
35. "Plan patriotic propaganda for school children." *New York Tribune*, Jan 21, 1918; "Teachers decide on loyalty campaign." *Sun* (NY), Jan 21, 1918.
36. "Importance of labor of shipyard workers." *Norwich Bulletin* (CT), Feb 8, 1918.
37. "Educators loyalty." *Pensacola Journal* (FL), Feb 13, 1918.
38. "Attack on Darrow brings a defense of his patriotism." *New York Tribune*, Mar 16, 1918.
39. "Darrow to preach Americanism." *Sun* (NY), Mar 16, 1918.
40. "N. Y. and Chicago teachers unite for patriotism." *New York Tribune*, Mar 19, 1918.
41. [No title] *Evening Public Ledger* (Philadelphia), Mar 18, 1918.
42. Melanchton Fennessey Libby. *Suggestions for the Organization of a State for Patriotic Education*. New York: National Security League, 1918.
43. "Where volunteers are needed for war work." *New York Tribune*, Mar 26, 1918.
44. Robert McNutt McElroy. "Teaching teachers." *Wheeling Intelligencer* (WV), Mar 27, 1918.
45. "Will instill loyalty in foreign born citizens." *New York Tribune*, Apr 1, 1918.
46. "War apathy laid to lack of teaching." *Sun* (NY), Apr 15, 1918.
47. "West is crowded with pro-Germans, Dr. McElroy says." *New York Tribune*, Apr 17, 1918.
48. "Flying squadron to start." *New York Tribune*, Apr 17, 1918.
49. "Col. Roosevelt to speak." *Evening Star* (Washington), Apr 28, 1918.
50. "German newspapers." *Washington Herald*, Apr 30, 1918.
51. "Study of German dropped by more schools in nation." *New York Tribune*, May 27, 1918.
52. "Nation-wide war on things German is started here." *New York Tribune*, Jun 3, 1918.
53. "Sing song for honoring flag." *Rock Island Argus* (IL), Jun 4, 1918.
54. "Teaching patriotism." *Pensacola Journal* (FL), Jun 15, 1918.
55. "The patriot." *Ocala Evening Star* (FL), Jun 25, 1918.
56. "Anti-German language is fruitful." *Evening Star* (Washington), Jul 19, 1918.
57. "A message from the Divine Sarah." *New York Tribune*, Jul 28, 1918.
58. "She helps inspire patriotism through teachers' Plattsburgs." *Evening Star* (Washington), Jul 28, 1918; "Security league sends out tons of pamphlets." *New York Tribune*, Aug 4, 1918.
59. "Germany not just as good." *Sun* (NY), Aug 17, 1918.
60. "Street speakers' squadron to fight propaganda widely." *New York Tribune*, Aug 18, 1918.
61. "Million people are reached at patriotic meetings." *Evening Capital and Maryland Gazette* (Annapolis), Aug 26, 1918.
62. "Teach patriotism in schools, says educators." *East Oregonian* (Pendleton), Sep 4, 1918; "She tells teachers how to make pupils patriotic." *Albuquerque Morning Journal* (NM), Sep 8, 1918.
63. Upton Sinclair. "A socialist view of German victory." *Albuquerque Morning Journal* (NM), Sep 18, 1918.
64. "Husband and brothers are fighting Hun; aids U.S. at home." *News Scimitar* (Memphis TN), Oct 26, 1918.

Chapter 11

1. Ad. *Wheeling Intelligencer* (WV), Apr 5, 1917.
2. Ad. *New York Tribune*, Apr 27, 1917; Ad. *New York Tribune*, Apr 28, 1917; Ad. *New York Tribune*, Apr 30, 1917.
3. "Walsh in doubt on universal training." *Butte Post* (MT), May 26, 1917; [No title] *Richmond Times-Dispatch* (VA), May 30, 1917.
4. Ad. *Evening Star* (Washington), Jul 23, 1917.
5. "Security league writes to papers." *West Virginian* (Fairmont), Jul 24, 1917.
6. "Vigilance bodies to track slackers." *Missoulian* (Missoula MT), Aug 3, 1917.
7. "Industrial draft urged for camps." *New York Tribune*, Aug 26, 1917.
8. "Universal military training is needed, says Gen. Young." *New York Tribune*, Aug 27, 1917.
9. "Allies spend ten million daily in America." *Harrisburg Telegraph* (PA), Aug 28, 1917.
10. "Training for all steadily winning favor in congress." *New York Tribune*, Sep 16, 1917.

11. "Many converts for universal military service." *Missouri Valley Times* (Iowa), Nov 22, 1917; *Why We Are at War*. New York: National Security League, n.d.
12. Ad. *Evening Star* (Washington), Dec 22, 1917.
13. "Training must be compulsively if America is to have peace." *Albuquerque Morning Journal* (NM), Dec 26, 1917.
14. "Women's war congress near." *Sun* (NY), Feb 11, 1918.
15. "Security league congress to hear Taft and Whitman." *New York Tribune*, Feb 18, 1918; "Two ex-war secretaries for congress in Chicago." *Albuquerque Morning Journal* (NM), Feb 19, 1918.
16. "Labor loyalty rally final session called." *Evening Star* (Washington), Feb 23, 1918.
17. "Win the war with patriotism." *Richmond Palladium* (IN), Feb 23, 1918.
18. "American business men are firmly behind war declared at National Security League." *Tulsa World* (OK), Feb 23, 1918.
19. "War to last three more years, is belief in Washington." *New York Tribune*, Feb 24, 1918.
20. "Plans training for youths of the nation." *New York Tribune*, Feb 17, 1918.
21. "Walter Camp seeks mayor's co-operation." *Richmond Times-Dispatch* (VA), Feb 25, 1918.
22. "Source books on the war." *Sun* (NY), Mar 31, 1918.
23. "For God's sake, hurry, appeal made to congress." *Washington Herald*, Apr 9, 1918.
24. "Arms production meeting all needs says McRoberts." *New York Tribune*, Apr 14, 1918.
25. "President's widow in war work." *Herald and News* (Newberry SC), Apr 19, 1918; "Editorial." *Alexandria Gazette* (VA), Apr 25, 1918.
26. Marguerite Mooers Marshall. "The daily dozen set-up 1." *Evening World* (NY), Apr 25, 1918.
27. "Seeking physical fitness high in air." *New York Tribune*, Jul 17, 1918.
28. "Ellen Key pacifist book under ban." *Sun* (NY), May 31, 1918.
29. "Prizes for telling how to spread war aims." *New York Tribune*, Jun 8, 1918; "Balloons to bear message of U.S. into Germany." *Washington Times*, Jun 29, 1918.
30. "To train new draftees." *New York Tribune*, Jul 29, 1918.
31. "Security league to train drafted men before call to cantonments." *Bismarck Tribune* (ND), Aug 3, 1918.
32. "Crowder approves nation-wide plan to train draftees." *New York Tribune*, Aug 19, 1918.
33. S. Stanwood Menken. "Following false gods." *Bottineau Courant* (ND), Aug 22, 1918.
34. "Writers condemn premature peace." *Evening Star* (Washington), Sep 23, 1918.

Chapter 12

1. "Thousands line streets to give Teddy Roosevelt warm welcome to Chicago." *Day Book* (Chicago), Apr 28, 1917.
2. "The so-called security league." *Nonpartisan Leader* (Fargo ND), Feb 11, 1918.
3. "The National Security League." *Nonpartisan Leader* (Fargo ND), Sep 2, 1918.
4. "Reaching for the schools." *Nonpartisan Leader* (Fargo ND), Oct 14, 1918.
5. "The workingman's right to vote." *South Bend News-Times* (IN), Nov 2, 1918.
6. "Declares war on security league." *Evening Star* (Washington), Sep 23, 1918; James A. Frear, wikipedia page, accessed Apr 10, 2019.
7. "League quiz asked house." *Washington Herald*, Sep 24, 1918.
8. "House will probe security league." *South Bend News-Times* (IN), Oct 8, 1918.
9. J. Hampton Moore. "What a congressman sees." *Evening Public Ledger* (Philadelphia), Oct 16, 1918.
10. "Other editors than ours." *South Bend News-Times* (IN), Oct 19, 1918.

Chapter 13

1. "Directs league's speaker bureau." *Richmond Palladium* (IN), Nov 12, 1918; "Ghost of the Navy League arrives." *South Bend News-Times* (IN), Nov 21, 1918; "Peace and the security league." *Nonpartisan Leader* (Fargo ND), Nov 25, 1918.
2. "League wants beaten legislators kept from seats." *New York Tribune*, Dec 21, 1918.
3. "Security league article o.k." *Nonpartisan Leader* (Fargo ND), Apr 14, 1919.
4. "League favors Reds, is belief of Poindexter." *New York Tribune*, May 8, 1919.

5. "Hanson in security league." *Sun* (NY), Dec 22, 1919; "C. D. Orth new president of security league." *New York Herald*, Jan 14, 1920.
6. "Garrison named honorary head of security league." *New York Tribune*, May 6, 1920.
7. "A. J. Hemphill, financier, dies at age 64." *New York Tribune*, Dec 30, 1920.
8. "S. Stanwood Menken." *Richmond Palladium* (IN), Dec 2, 1921; "Security league urges economic preparedness." *New York Tribune*, Dec 5, 1921.
9. "Board ousts Otis from security body." *Evening Star* (Washington), Jan 17, 1926.
10. "Col. Brown is elected security league head." *Evening Star* (Washington), Jun 21, 1928.
11. "Mrs. Thomas J. Preston dies; was Grover Cleveland's widow." *Evening Star* (Washington), Oct 30, 1947.
12. "Gen R. L. Bullard dies; led drive at Marne and fought Indians." *Evening Star* (Washington), Sep 12, 1947.

Chapter 14

1. "Red flag not barred here." *New York Tribune*, Nov 14, 1918.
2. "Stop the leak." *New York Tribune*, Nov 28, 1918.
3. "To combat red flagism." *El Paso Herald* (TX), Nov 29, 1918.
4. "Security league fights Bolshevism." *Sun* (NY), Dec 2, 1918.
5. "Security league to open double-barrel fight on reds here." *New York Tribune*, Dec 16, 1918.
6. "Socialists cannot hire hall, they say." *Sun* (NY), Jan 19, 1919.
7. "Hylan praised for move to wipe out Reds." *New York Times*, Apr 4, 1919.
8. "Security league is united in a great drive." *Public Ledger* (Maysville, KY), Apr 14, 1919; "High schools join in fight on Bolshevism." *New York Tribune*, Apr 16, 1919.
9. "The facts about Bolshevism in New York." *Sun* (NY), Apr 20, 1919.
10. "Million women pledged to fight Bolshevism." *New York Times*, May 4, 1919; "Composer's wife joins fight against Bolshevik." *Richmond Palladium* (IN), May 5, 1919.
11. "League favors Reds, is belief of Poindexter." *New York Tribune*, May 8, 1919.
12. "Anti-Bolshevism doctrine spread." *Wheeling Intelligencer* (WV), Jun 20, 1919.
13. "Security league tells anti-Bolshevik plans." *New York Tribune*, Jun 23, 1919.
14. [No title] *New York Tribune*, Aug 31, 1919; "Women of today." *Grand Forks Herald* (ND) Sep 13, 1919.
15. "Security league issues warning on spread of doctrine." *Public Ledger* (Maysville KY), Oct 20, 1919.
16. Mary Roberts Rinehart. "Radicalism is false idealism." *News Scimitar* (Memphis TN), Jan 16, 1920.
17. "Scores Debs nomination." *New York Tribune*, May 18, 1920.
18. "No more war is scored by league." *Seattle Star*, Jul 31, 1922.
19. "Jeers meet security league's attack on Countess Karolyi." *Evening Star* (Washington), Nov 12, 1924.
20. "Urges grim war on secret enemies." *Evening Star* (Washington), Apr 30, 1925.
21. "Washington observations." *Evening Star* (Washington), Sep 8, 1930; "Menken quits as head of security league." *Evening Star* (Washington), Nov 2, 1930.
22. "Anti-Soviet rally to hear notables." *Evening Star* (Washington), Apr 16, 1933.

Chapter 15

1. "Preaching Americanism." *New York Tribune*, Nov 18, 1918.
2. "Security league out to beat 3 Senators." *New York Tribune*, Nov 25, 1918; "Security league to urge reforms." *Sun* (NY), Nov 25, 1918.
3. "Women of America are warned against pleas from Germany." *New York Tribune*, Nov 25, 1918.
4. "Will aid Americanization." *Sun* (NY), Nov 29, 1918.
5. "50,000 teachers take citizenship course." *New York Tribune*, Dec 1, 1918.
6. "National plan of education is proposed." *New York Tribune*, Dec 15, 1918.
7. Ad. *Perth Amboy Evening News* (NJ), Jan 27, 1919.
8. Charles E. Lydecker. "Your boy, and the right military training for him." *New York Tribune*, Mar 2, 1919.
9. "Security body hits congress in new plans." *New York Tribune*, Mar 9, 1919.
10. "Governors and mayors united

against anarchy." *Albuquerque Morning Journal* (NM), May 6, 1919.
11. "Charges I.W.W. incites negroes." *New York Tribune*, Aug 4, 1919.
12. "Security league is combating Red menace." *Harrisburg Telegraph* (PA), Jul 29, 1919.
13. "Security league anti Red war has now spread." *Harrisburg Telegraph* (PA), Aug 15, 1919.
14. Ad. *Evening World* (NY), Sep 16, 1919; "Policemen's strike arraigned by Root." *Bisbee Review* (AZ), Sep 18, 1919; "Girl Red leader indifferent at her arraignment." *New York Tribune*, Sep 19, 1919.
15. "Security league fight against unrest." *New York Tribune*, Nov 24, 1919.
16. "Boy Scouts to see film." *Richmond Times-Dispatch* (VA), Dec 20, 1919.
17. "Favors military training." *Evening Star* (Washington), Feb 11, 1920.
18. "For higher grade of future citizens." Sun (NY), Feb 16, 1920.
19. "May 1 to be observed as American Day." Ogden Standard (UT), Feb 18, 1920; "American Day to offset schemes of Bolsheviks." *Bridgeport Times and Evening Farmer* (CT), Feb 24, 1920.
20. "The security league and the first of May." *Butte Bulletin* (MT), Mar 8, 1920.
21. Ad. *El Paso Herald* (TX), Apr 30, 1920.
22. "Mayor sees Rockefeller crowd in school plot." *New York Tribune*, Mar 19, 1920.
23. "C. D. Orth asks fusion to beat four Socialists." *New York Tribune*, May 31, 1920; "Fusion to defeat Socialists for congress urged." *New York Tribune*, Jul 26, 1920.
24. "Children of thirty-five states enter prize contest." *Public Ledger* (Maysville KY), Apr 14, 1921.
25. "Council formed for Americanism." *New York Tribune*, Mar 5, 1921; "Union to aid Americanism founded here." *New York Tribune*, May 19, 1921.
26. "How does public opinion stand?" *Evening World* (NY), Jun 3, 1922.
27. "Wants translations with poster." New York Herald, Jun 11, 1922.
28. "Plan passage of law requiring schools to teach provisions of the Constitution." *Bemidji Pioneer* (MN), Sep 28, 1922.
29. "Views on preparedness for congressmen." *Evening Star* (Washington), Aug 18, 1924.
30. "Patriotic bodies discuss alien." *Evening Star* (Washington), Mar 6, 1929; "Out-of-town stations." *Evening Star* (Washington), Aug 31, 1929.
31. National Security League, wikipedia page, accessed May 20, 2019.

Chapter 16

1. "Ghost of the Navy League arrives." *South Bend News-Times* (IN), Nov 21, 1918.
2. "Root and Parker and the so-called National Security League." *South Bend News-Times* (IN), Nov 22, 1918.
3. *Ibid.*
4. "A fable." *Butte Bulletin* (MT), Jul 1, 1919.
5. "Scathing attack made on security league." *Evening Star* (Washington), Dec 5, 1918.
6. "Congress asked to order inquiry of security league." *New York Tribune*, Dec 5, 1918.
7. "Sweeping investigation of National Security League demanded by Congressmen." *South Bend News-Times* (IN), Dec 8, 1918.
8. *Congressional Record: Sixty-Fifth Congress, Third Session*, vol. LVII, Pt. 1, p. 260; "Security league rapped in House." *Evening Star* (Washington), Dec 10, 1918; *Hearings Before a Special Committee of the House of Representatives*. Wash.: Government Printing Office, 1918.
9. "Security league is under inquiry." *Evening Star* (Washington), Dec 19, 1918.
10. "Security league aims explained." *Evening Star* (Washington), Dec 20, 1918; "League fought for best men for Congress." *New York Tribune*, Dec 20, 1918.
11. "Security million drops to $6,000." Sun (NY), Dec 20, 1918.
12. "League wants beaten legislators kept from seats." *New York Tribune*, Dec 21, 1918.
13. [No title] *Montana Nonpartisan* (Great Falls), Dec 28, 1918.
14. "The security league." *South Bend News-Times* (IN), Dec 27. 1918.
15. "Frear defends league probe." *Washington Herald*, Jan 3, 1919.
16. "Put security league on pan." *Labor World* (Duluth MN) Jan 4, 1919; "Congress pulls mask from security league." *Labor World* (Duluth MN) Jan 4, 1919.
17. "Sharp reprimand for security league

Notes—Chapter 16

head." *Richmond Times-Dispatch* (VA), Jan 7, 1919.
18. "Security league is put on the grill." *Nonpartisan Leader* (Fargo ND), Jan 13, 1919.
19. Hearings... *op. cit.*, pp. 17–140.
20. *Ibid.*, pp. 143–221.
21. "Should probe a little further." *Butte Bulletin* (MT), Jan 16, 1919.
22. "National Security League investigation." *South Bend News-Times* (IN), Jan 17, 1919; Hearings... *op. cit.*, pp. 774, 926, 930, 946, 988.
23. "Contempt threat for Orth." *Sun* (NY), Jan 18, 1919.
24. "Less than $6,000 spent in election." *Evening Star* (Washington), Jan 21, 1919.
25. "West retained as paid agent for District." *Washington Herald*, Jan 22, 1919; Hearings... *op. cit.*, pp. 1018–1084.
26. *Ibid.*
27. "Called Wilson great idealist." *Washington Herald*, Jan 24, 1919.
28. "Security league not partisan, says Orth." *New York Tribune*, Jan 21, 1919.
29. "Wealthy Chicagoans called to testify security league quiz." *Evening Capital News* (Boise ID), Jan 30, 1919; "Favors sliding scale in 'wrong' vote test." *Evening Star* (Washington), Feb 2, 1919.
30. "Couples league with railways." *Washington Herald*, Feb 5, 1919.
31. "Security league opposed Ford on account of lack of war loyalty." *Albuquerque Morning Herald* (NM), Feb 7, 1919; "Root supports security league acid test chart." *Arizona Republican* (Phoenix), Feb 7, 1919.
32. "Almost disloyal says Root of Ford." *Sun* (NY), Feb 7, 1919.
33. "Security league investigation by Congress silly." *Public Ledger* (Maysville KY), Feb 7, 1919.
34. "McCulloch asks accusers be tried." *Washington Times*, Feb 9, 1919.
35. "National Security League is criticized." *Evening Star* (Washington), Feb 10, 1919; "Plan security league fight." *Washington Herald*, Feb 11, 1919.
36. "Plan security league fight." *Washington Herald*, Feb 11, 1919.
37. "Parker apologizes for security league." *New York Tribune*, Feb 12, 1919.
38. "Truth of the investigation." *Butte Bulletin* (MT), Feb 13, 1919.
39. "Wall Streets' black hundred exposed." *Nonpartisan Leader* (Fargo ND), Feb 24, 1919.
40. *Ibid.*
41. "Security league is pronounced guilty." *Arizona Republican* (Phoenix), Mar 4, 1919.
42. "Menken league styled as tool." *Sun* (NY), Mar 4, 1919.
43. *Ibid.*
44. "Congressman tells of security league." *Nonpartisan Leader* (Fargo ND), Mar 10, 1919; "A loyalty league found guilty. *Nonpartisan Leader* (Fargo ND), Mar 24, 1919.
45. "Loyalty league guilty." *Nonpartisan Leader* (Fargo ND), Mar 17, 1919.
46. "Security league origin exposed." *Bottineau Courant* (ND), Apr 3, 1919.
47. "Prosecution of security league is recommended." *Seattle Star*, May 7, 1919.
48. Hearings... *op. cit.*, pp259–281.
49. *Ibid.*, pp. 377–518.
50. "Security spent $176 in recent election." *Washington Times*, Nov 17, 1922.

Bibliography

Ad. *Bisbee Review* (AZ), Oct 29, 1918.
Ad. *El Paso Herald* (TX), Apr 30, 1920.
Ad. *Evening Star* (Washington), Jul 23, 1917.
Ad. *Evening Star* (Washington), Dec 22, 1917.
Ad. *Evening World* (NY), Sep 11, 1915.
Ad. *Evening World* (NY), Sep 16, 1919.
Ad. *Harrisburg Telegraph* (PA), May 17, 1916.
Ad. *Harrisburg Telegraph* (PA), Nov 2, 1918.
Ad. *New York Tribune,* Jul 5, 1915.
Ad. *New York Tribune,* Jan 2, 1917.
Ad. *New York Tribune,* Apr 27, 1917.
Ad. *New York Tribune,* Apr 28, 1917.
Ad. *New York Tribune,* Apr 30, 1917.
Ad. *New York Tribune,* May 1, 1917.
Ad. *New York Tribune,* Oct 29, 1918.
Ad. *Perth Amboy Evening News* (NJ), Sept 12, 1918.
Ad. *Perth Amboy Evening News* (NJ), Oct 30, 1918.
Ad. *Perth Amboy Evening News* (NJ), Jan 27, 1919.
Ad. *Richmond Palladium* (IN), Oct 29, 1918.
Ad. *Shepherdstown Register* (WV), Oct 24, 1918.
Ad. *Sun* (NY), Jun 14, 1915.
Ad. *Sun* (NY), Mar 2, 1917.
Ad. *Sun* (NY), Mar 22, 1917.
Ad. *Sun* (NY), May 2, 1917.
Ad. *Sun* (NY), Oct 16, 1917.
Ad. *Topeka State Journal,* February 11, 1916.
Ad. *Washington Times,* Jan 24, 1917.
Ad. *Washington Times,* Mar 29, 1917.
Ad. *Washington Times,* Jan 17, 1918.
Ad. *Wheeling Intelligencer* (WV), Apr 5, 1917.
Ad. *Wheeling Intelligencer* (WV), Nov 4, 1918.
Ad. *Wood County Reporter* (Wisconsin Rapids WI), Oct 31, 1918.
"Against American militarism." *Twin Falls Herald* (ID), Mar 23, 1915.
"Aim revolution in America." *County Record* (Kingstree SC), Nov 6, 1919
"A. J. Hemphill, financier, dies at age 64." *New York Tribune*, Dec 30, 1920.
"All for defense." *Topeka State Journal* (KS), Sep 10, 1915.
"All Socialists defeated here for congress." *New York Tribune,* Nov 6, 1918.
"Allies spend ten million daily in America." *Harrisburg Telegraph* (PA), Aug 28, 1917.
"Almost disloyal says Root of Ford." *Sun* (NY), Feb 7, 1919.
"American business men are firmly behind war declared at National Security League." *Tulsa World* (OK), Feb 23, 1918.

"American Day to offset schemes of Bolsheviks." *Bridgeport Times and Evening Farmer* (CT), Feb 24, 1920.
"American mayors meet in St. Louis." *Evening Star* (Wash), Mar 3, 1916.
"Annual Report." *Our Country,* May 1916.
"Another insidious lobby." *Commoner* (Lincoln NE), Sep 1, 1915.
"Anti-Bolshevism doctrine spread." *Wheeling Intelligencer* (WV), Jun 20, 1919.
"Anti-German language is fruitful." *Evening Star* (Washington), Jul 19, 1918.
"Anti-military pastor assailed." *New York Tribune,* Jan 30, 1917.
"Anti-Soviet rally to hear notables." *Evening Star* (Washington), Apr 16, 1933.
"Are we prepared." *Evening Public Ledger* (Philadelphia), October 30, 1915.
"Armament agitation." *Grand Forks Herald* (ND), Jun 21, 1915.
"Armored car on way west." *Harrisburg Telegraph* (PA), May 27, 1916.
"Arms production meeting all needs says McRoberts." *New York Tribune,* Apr 14, 1918.
"Ask to be investigated." *Barre Times* (VT), January 20, 1916.
"Attack on Darrow brings a defense of his patriotism." *New York Tribune,* Mar 16, 1918.
"Balloons to bear message of U.S. into Germany." *Washington Times,* Jun 29, 1918.
"Band together to urge nation's preparedness." *Evening Star* (Washington), Jan 16, 1917.
"Bares inferiority of American navy." *Evening Star* (Washington).
"Baseball players' frat is in favor of national defense." *Albuquerque Morning Journal* (NM), Mar 19, 1916.
"Big campaign to elect loyal war congress." *Alexandria Gazette* (VA), Jun 22, 1918.
Black, William J. "Great chautauqua movement has become mobilization agency for national policies." *New York Tribune,* Aug 19, 1917.
"Board ousts Otis from security body." *Evening Star* (Washington), Jan 17, 1926.
Bonaparte, Charles J. "Increase size of our army and navy, PDQ, says Charles J. Bonaparte." *Sun* (NY), Dec 27, 1914.
"Boy Scouts to see film." *Richmond Times-Dispatch* (VA), Dec 20, 1919.
Bryan, William J. "Investigate." *Commoner* (Lincoln NE), Nov 1, 1915.
"Bryan accused of falsifying." *Harrisburg Telegraph* (PA), Nov 5, 1915.
Bryant, Louise. "A day with lady militarists." *New York Tribune,* Mar 11, 1917.
"Business men in defense league." *New York Tribune,* Dec 2, 1914.
"C. D. Orth asks fusion to beat four Socialists." *New York Tribune,* May 31, 1920.
"C. D. Orth new president of security league." *New York Herald,* Jan 14, 1920.
"Call is made on professors for war work." *Washington Times,* Nov 5, 1917.
"Called Wilson great idealist." *Washington Herald,* Jan 24, 1919.
"Campaign launched to combat activities of pacifist bodies." *Honolulu Star-Bulletin,* Jun 18, 1917.
"Capital press and munitions makers get a panning at C. F. of L. meeting." *Day Book* (Chicago), Nov 22, 1915.
"Champ Clark and O'Gorman declare in favor of preparedness." *Washington Herald,* Oct 11, 1915.
"Charges I.W.W. incites negroes." *New York Tribune,* Aug 4, 1919.
"Charles E Lydecker, lawyer, dies at 68." *New York Times,* May 7, 1920.
"Chicago's mayor ignored." *Evening Star* (Washington), August 29, 1917.
"Children of thirty-five states enter prize contest." *Public Ledger* (Maysville KY), Apr 14, 1921.
"Citizen soldiers." *Topeka State Journal* (KS), Jul 14, 1915.
"Civilian leaders under army officers." *Evening Star* (Washington), August 9, 1915.
"Claim Japan is menace to U.S." *El Paso Herald* (TX), Jan 22, 1916.
"Claude Kitchin's statement on the nation's preparedness—he gives facts." *Commoner* (Lincoln NE), Dec 1 1915.
Cobb, Irvin S. "Victory or defeat; which will it be?" *Bridgeport Evening Farmer* (CT), Sep 21, 1917.
Collins, Paul V. "President may roar like lion for preparedness." *Perth Amboy Evening News* (NJ), Jan 26, 1916.
Collman, Charles A. "Why the money trust wants war." *New Ulm Post* (MN), Nov 5, 1915.
"Col. Brown is elected security league head." *Evening Star* (Washington), Jun 21, 1928.

Bibliography

"Col. Roosevelt to speak." *Evening Star* (Washington), Apr 28, 1918.
"Columbus ships deported I.W.W. back." *Arizona Star* (Tucson), Jul 13, 1917.
"Company formed to buy Belgium." *Washington Times,* Jul 28, 1915.
"Composer's wife joins fight against Bolshevik." *Richmond Palladium* (IN), May 5, 1919.
"Conference is held on national defense." *Richmond Times-Dispatch* (VA), Sep 17, 1915.
"Congress asked to order inquiry of security league." *New York Tribune,* Dec 5, 1918.
"Congress can shake off grip of war trust." *Day Book* (Chicago), Oct 20, 1915.
"Congress pulls mask from security league." *Labor World* (Duluth MN), Jan 4, 1919.
"Congress will decide great army and navy problem." *Bridgeport Evening Farmer* (CT), Dec 3, 1914.
"Congressman tells of security league." *Nonpartisan Leader* (Fargo ND), Mar 10, 1919;
"Congressmen for national defense." *Perth Amboy Evening News* (NJ), Oct 18, 1915.
"Congressmen strongly favor adequate defense." *Grand Forks Herald* (ND), Oct 20, 1915.
"Constructive patriotism for America." *Grand Forks Herald* (ND), Dec 4, 1916
"Contempt threat for Orth." *Sun* (NY), Jan 18, 1919.
"The cost of defense." *East Oregonian* (Pendleton), Aug 16, 1915.
"Council formed for Americanism." *New York Tribune,* Mar 5, 1921.
"Country is aroused over Creel's unprepared speech." *New York Tribune,* Apr 21, 1918.
"Country not prepared for war." *Evening Public Ledger* (Philadelphia), March 12, 1915.
"Couples league with railways." *Washington Herald,* Feb 5, 1919.
"Crowder approves nation-wide plan to train draftees." *New York Tribune,* Aug 19, 1918.
"Daniels attacks many detractors." *Tulsa World* (OK), May 16, 1915.
"Darrow picked for security league." *Free Trader-Journal* (Ottawa IL), Sept 11, 1917.
"Darrow to preach Americanism." *Sun* (NY), Mar 16, 1918.
"Declare nation in sad state." *Evening Herald* (Albuquerque NM), May 10, 1915.
"Declares war on security league." *Evening Star* (Washington), Sep 23, 1918.
"Defense inquiry aims of security league defined." *Sun* (NY), Dec 9, 1914.
"Defense league is enlisting aid." *Washington Herald,* Apr 8, 1915.
"Defense, marchers' slogan." *Evening Star* (Washington), Apr 2, 1916.
"Defense petitions out." *Evening Public Ledger* (Philadelphia), Feb 17, 1917.
"Defense plan at Mill City." *Bemidji Pioneer* (MN), Aug 14, 1915.
"Dent strikes at security league." *Pensacola Journal* (FL), Sep 7, 1918.
"Directs league's speaker bureau." *Richmond Palladium* (IN), Nov 12, 1918.
"Dr. Baker overflows to entire nation." *Grand Forks Herald* (ND), Jul 16, 1917.
"Dr. Bell for preparedness." *Evening Star* (Washington), Apr 24, 1916.
"Down with the extremists." *West Virginian* (Fairmont), Jan 21, 1916.
"The draft and the war." *South Bend News-Times* (IN), Sep 16, 1918.
"The drama, the stage and the actors." *Labor World* (Duluth MN), Nov 25, 1916.
"Drive to keep pacifists out of Congress to be started." *Grand Forks Herald* (ND), Jan 1, 1918.
"Duck the Natural Security League." *Labor Advocate* (Cincinnati), Apr 8, 1916.
"The duty of preparedness." *Sun* (NY), Jun 15, 1915.
"Editorial." *Alexandria Gazette* (VA), Apr 25, 1918.
"Educational campaign by National Security League." *Evening Herald* (Washington), Jul 26, 1917.
"Educators loyalty." *Pensacola Journal* (FL), Feb 13, 1918.
"Elect loyal men to congress, plea of Elihu Root." *New York Tribune,* May 9, 1918.
"The election case of Truman H. Newberry of Michigan (1922)." www.senate.gov/artandhistory/history/common/contested_elections. Accessed June 20, 2019.
"Election of loyal congressmen urged." *New York Tribune,* Jul 8, 1918.
"Elihu Root hold out for a monster federal army." *Harrisburg Telegraph* (PA), January 7, 1916.
"Ellen Key pacifist book under ban." *Sun* (NY), May 31, 1918.
"Employers urged to help militia." *Sun* (NY), Jul 7, 1915.
"Ex-Teutons resent loyalty request." *Sun* (NY), Aug 6, 1917.
"A fable." *Butte Bulletin* (MT), Jul 1, 1919.
"The facts about Bolshevism in New York." *Sun* (NY), Apr 20, 1919.
"Famous men say United States must get ready." *Guthrie Leader* (OK), May 24, 1915.

"Favored by most editors." *Evening Star* (Washington), Mar 22, 1917.
"Favors military training." *Evening Star* (Washington), Feb 11, 1920.
"Favors sliding scale in 'wrong' vote test." *Evening Star* (Washington), Feb 2, 1919.
"Few sales on local market." *Washington Herald,* Aug 8, 1916.
"57 candidates here for congress ask complete surrender." *New York Tribune,* Oct 31, 1918.
"50,000 teachers take citizenship course." *New York Tribune,* Dec 1, 1918.
"Fight on war profits at cost of U.S. buyers." *Sun* (NY), Aug 22, 1914.
"Finds loyalty agitation was needed in country." *Evening Star* (Washington), Aug 20, 1917.
"A first army of defense." *Richmond Palladium* (IND), May 18, 1915.
"500 leave city to learn war's ways at camp." *New York Tribune,* Aug 10, 1915.
"Five hundred dollar prize for good story." *Logan Republican* (UT), Oct 5, 1915.
"Florida to get branch of Nat'l Security League." *Lakeland Evening Telegram* (FL), Oct 1, 1915.
"Flying squadron to start." *New York Tribune,* Apr 17, 1918.
"Fools and their war talk." *Tribune* (Cape Girardeau MO), Dec 17, 1915.
"For God's sake, hurry, appeal made to congress." *Washington Herald,* Apr 9, 1918.
"For higher grade of future citizens." *Sun* (NY), Feb 16, 1920.
Ford, Henry "Humanity—and sanity." *Rock Island Argus* (IL), Apr 13, 1916.
"Former Secretary of Navy will talk of preparedness." *Bridgeport Evening Farmer* (CT), Jun 10, 1915.
"47 of 347 members of Congress called 100 per cent loyal." *New York Tribune,* Aug 5, 1918.
"Frear defends league probe." *Washington Herald,* Jan 3, 1919.
"Fusion call issued by security league to beat Socialists." *New York Tribune,* Jul 15, 1918.
"Fusion to defeat Socialists for congress urged." *New York Tribune,* Jul 26, 1920.
"Gardner makes inquiry into pacifist and propagandist." *Evening Public Ledger* (Philadelphia), Dec 6, 1915.
"Gardner says conscription is only safe plan." *Honolulu Star-Bulletin,* Jan 11, 1916.
"Gardner thinks city forts can't stop foe." *Sun* (NY), Jan 11 1916.
"Garrison named honorary head of security league." *New York Tribune,* May 6, 1920.
"Gen R. L. Bullard dies; led drive at Marne and fought Indians." *Evening Star* (Washington), Sep 12, 1947.
"George von L. Meyer." wikipedia page, accessed May 10, 1919.
"George von L. Meyer, once Secretary of the Navy is sure it is now going to pot." *Evening Herald* (Albuquerque NM), Jun 15, 1915.
"German newspapers." *Washington Herald,* Apr 30, 1918.
"Germany not just as good." *Sun* (NY), Aug 17, 1918.
"Get ready now for war, urged." *El Paso Herald* (TX), May 10, 1915.
"Ghost of the Navy League arrives." *South Bend News-Times* (IN), Nov 21, 1918.
"Girl Red leader indifferent at her arraignment." *New York Tribune,* Sep 19, 1919.
"Give him a chance." *Richmond Palladium* (IN), Mar 30, 1917.
"Governors and mayors united against anarchy." *Albuquerque Morning Journal* (NM), May 6, 1919.
"The gray ghost of socialism." *New Ulm Post* (MN), Jul 30, 1917.
"Great defense move launched." *Washington Herald,* Nov 28, 1915.
"Gunboat hat joins in national propaganda for preparedness." *Evening Public Ledger* (Philadelphia), February 11, 1916.
"Hang him in effigy." *Topeka State Journal* (KS), Sep 5, 1917.
"Hanson in security league." *Sun* (NY), Dec 22, 1919.
Hart, Albert Bushnell. "Telling why we fight and why we're sure we're right." *Sun* (NY), Jun 24, 1917.
"Hate war but fight says Jane Addams." *Sun* (NY), Jul 10, 1915.
"He helped make the National Security League." *Tombstone Epitaph* (AZ), Sep 22, 1918.
Hearings Before a Special Committee of the House of Representatives. Wash.: Government Printing Office, 1918.
"Henry L. Stimson heads advocates of bigger American Army." *Evening Times-Republican* (Marshalltown IA), Jan 22, 1915.

Bibliography

"Here's how Morgan makes war pay." *Tacoma Times* (WA), Sep 20, 1915.
"Hexamer resents loyalty creed." *Evening Public Ledger* (Philadelphia), Aug 6, 1917.
"High schools join in fight on Bolshevism." *New York Tribune,* Apr 16, 1919.
"House will probe security league." *South Bend News-Times* (IN), Oct 8, 1918.
"How does public opinion stand?" *Evening World* (NY), Jun 3, 1922.
"How United States field artillery compares with that of other nations." *Grand Forks Herald* (ND), Dec 14, 1914.
"Hudson Maxim's interest in preparedness." *Commoner* (Lincoln NE), January 1, 1916.
Huidekoper, Frederic L. "The Argentine system of military training." *Wheeling Intelligencer* (WV), Jan 29, 1917.
Huidekoper, Frederic L. "Making Americans." *Wheeling Intelligencer* (WV), Mar 6, 1917.
"Husband and brothers are fighting Hun; aids U.S. at home." *News Scimitar* (Memphis TN), Oct 26, 1918.
"Hylan praised for move to wipe out Reds." *New York Times,* Apr 4, 1919.
"Ignorance endangering country, says National Security League." *Honolulu Star-Bulletin,* Sep 20, 1917.
"Importance of labor of shipyard workers." *Norwich Bulletin* (CT), Feb 8, 1918.
"Industrial draft urged for camps." *New York Tribune,* Aug 26, 1917.
"Industrial preparedness." *Bisbee Review* (AZ), Apr 19, 1916.
"Inquiry planned to sift strikes." *Washington Herald,* Jan 6, 1914.
"The interest back of preparedness." *Commoner* (Lincoln NE), Dec 1, 1915.
"James A. Frear." wikipedia page, accessed Apr 10, 2019.
"Jeers meet security league's attack on Countess Karolyi." *Evening Star* (Washington), Nov 12, 1924.
"Jersey urged to prepare." *New York Tribune,* Mar 11, 1917.
"John B. Stanchfield." Wikipedia page, accessed March 12, 2019.
"John Wanamaker quits chairmanship of security league." *Evening Public Ledger* (Philadelphia), Jul 28, 1915.
Johns, E. B. "The Herald's army and navy department." *Washington Herald,* Dec 23, 1915.
"Join in fight to build army." *Washington Herald,* Feb 26, 1915.
"Labor heads tell of loyalty in war." *Sun* (NY), Jan 8, 1918.
"Labor loyalty rally final session called." *Evening Star* (Washington), Feb 23, 1918.
"La Follette unfit to sit in Congress." *Bismarck Tribune* (ND), Sep 25, 1917.
"Late president's widow at her desk working for patriotism." *Albuquerque Morning Journal* (NM), Feb 4, 1918.
"League bares war record of Hearst guests." *New York Times,* Jul 6, 1918.
"League favors Reds, is belief of Poindexter." *New York Tribune,* May 8, 1919.
"League fought for best men for Congress." *New York Tribune,* Dec 20, 1918.
"League of women for war service." *Evening Star* (Washington), Jan 27, 1917.
"League quiz asked house." *Washington Herald,* Sep 24, 1918.
"League wants beaten legislators kept from seats." *New York Tribune,* Dec 21, 1918.
"Leonard Wood." wikipedia page, accessed May 9, 2019.
"Less than $6,000 spent in election." *Evening Star* (Washington), Jan 21, 1919.
Levish, Thomas "Influences." *Day Book* (Chicago), Jun 7, 1916.
Libby, Melanchton Fennessey. *Suggestions for the Organization of a State for Patriotic Education.*
"Like a bright red flag before a herd of bulls." *Gate City* (Keokuk IA), Nov 28, 1915.
"Loyalists only in congress." *New York Tribune,* October 21, 1918.
"A loyalty league found guilty." *Nonpartisan Leader* (Fargo ND), Mar 24, 1919.
"Loyalty league guilty." *Nonpartisan Leader* (Fargo ND), Mar 17, 1919.
"Lusitania was carrying first world war explosives from New York when sunk in May 1915, British files reveal." Centenarynews.com May 2014, accessed June 20, 2019.
Lydecker, Charles E. "Your boy, and the right military training for him." *New York Tribune,* Mar 2, 1919
"Major Putnam explains the purpose of the National Security League." *Sun* (NY), Dec 5, 1914.

"Make nation look silly." *Little Falls Herald* (MN), October 15, 1915.
"Making war profitable." *Washington Socialist* (Everett WA), Aug 27, 1914.
"Many converts for universal military service." *Missouri Valley Times* (Iowa), Nov 22, 1917.
"Marching with the legions of Preparedness." *New York Tribune*, May 21, 1916.
Marshall, Marguerite Mooers. "The daily dozen set-up 1." *Evening World* (NY), Apr 25, 1918.
Mathews, Shailer. "Why we fight Germany—in plain words." *Hope Pioneer* (ND), Aug 16, 1917.
Maxim, Hudson. "Why the government should not make its war supplies." *Richmond Times-Dispatch* (VA), Feb 13, 1916.
"May 1 to be observed as American Day." *Ogden Standard* (UT), Feb 18, 1920.
"Mayor leads 800 in defense demand." *Sun* (NY), Dec 17, 1915.
"Mayor Mitchel heads delegation." *Evening Star* (Washington), Jan 16, 1916.
"Mayor sees Rockefeller crowd in school plot." *New York Tribune*, Mar 19, 1920.
"Mayor shows nation's weariness in defense." *Sun* (NY), Apr 19, 1916.
"Mayor's defense plan acclaimed." *New York Tribune*, Nov 18, 1915.
"Mayors of 75 cities in league for defense." *Sun* (NY), Jan 23, 1916.
"McCulloch asks accusers be tried." *Washington Times*, Feb 9, 1919.
McElroy, Robert M. "Nation's war ideals basis of America's unity in peace." *Sun* (NY), Aug 5, 1917.
McElroy, Robert McNutt. "Teaching teachers." *Wheeling Intelligencer* (WV), Mar 27, 1918.
"McElroy to stir patriots." *Sun* (NY), July 25, 1917.
Menken, S. Stanwood. "End haphazard control of the nation's defenses." *Sun* (NY), Dec 27, 1914.
Menken, S. Stanwood. "Following false gods." *Bottineau Courant* (ND), Aug 22, 1918.
Menken, S. Stanwood. "Patriotism to nation what soul is to man—without it come decay and death." *Mexico Missouri Message*, Mar 15, 1917.
Menken, S. Stanwood. "A speakers' Plattsburg." *New York Tribune*, Jun 26, 1917.
"Menken denies Bryan's charges." *New York Times*, Nov 16, 1915.
"Menken league styled as tool." *Sun* (NY), Mar 4, 1919.
"Menken names board." *New York Tribune*, Dec 7, 1914.
"Menken quits as head of security league." *Evening Star* (Washington), Nov 2, 1930.
"A message from the Divine Sarah." *New York Tribune*, Jul 28, 1918.
"Military census urged for capital." *Evening Star* (Washington), April 3, 1917.
"Military officers making arrests." *Fergus County Democrat* (Lewistown MT), Sep 3, 1914.
"Military training in public schools." *Commoner* (Lincoln NE), Jul 1, 1916.
"Military training straw vote." *Ardmoreite* (Ardmore OK), Aug 28, 1916.
"Million defenders sought by league." *Sun* (NY), May 11, 1915.
"Million people are reached at patriotic meetings." *Evening Capital and Maryland Gazette* (Annapolis), Aug 26, 1918.
"Million women pledged to fight Bolshevism." *New York Times*, May 4, 1919.
"Mr. Gompers' dinner." *Bridgeport Evening Farmer* (CT), Jan 30, 1917.
"Modern war engines shown at exhibition." *Evening Star* (Washington), Jun 12, 1915.
Moore, J. Hampton. "What a congressman see." *Evening Public Ledger* (Philadelphia), Oct 16, 1918.
"Morgan firm's war contracts now $500,000,000." *New York Tribune*, July 5, 1915.
"Most vigorous arraignment of militaristic tendencies." *Labor Journal* (Everett WA), Mar 23, 1917.
"Movement for adequate defense meeting nation-wide response." *Sun* (NY), May 23, 1915.
"Mrs. Thomas J. Preston dies; was Grover Cleveland's widow." *Evening Star* (Washington), Oct 30, 1947.
"Must be either for or against the government." *Arizona Republican* (Phoenix), Sep 4, 1917.
"Must crush Bolshevism, says Gompers." *NY Tribune*, Feb 23, 1918.
"N. Y. and Chicago teachers unite for patriotism." *New York Tribune*, Mar 19, 1918.
"Nation aroused to sense of need of preparedness." *Sunday Telegram* (Clarksburg WV), May 28, 1916. "Throngs in Kansas City wildly cheer Roosevelt." *Sun* (NY), May 31, 1916.

Bibliography 251

"Nation-wide campaign for adequate defense." *Richmond Times-Dispatch* (VA), August 22, 1915.
"Nation-wide war on things German is started here." *New York Tribune*, Jun 3, 1918.
"National Defense Act of 1916." Wikipedia, accessed Jun 21, 2019.
"National plan of education is proposed." *New York Tribune*, Dec 15, 1918.
"National security congress will discuss America's vital needs." *Pensacola Journal* (FL), Jan 13, 1916.
"The National Security League." *New York Tribune*, Nov 25, 1917.
"The National Security League." *Nonpartisan Leader* (Fargo ND), Sep 2, 1918.
"The National Security League." *Sun* (NY), Dec 3, 1914.
"National Security League." Wikipedia page, accessed May 20, 2019.
"The National Security League and its purpose." *Sun* (NY), Jun 18, 1916.
"National Security League fever has reached Florida." *Lakeland Evening Telegram* (FL), Jul 29, 1915.
"National Security League investigation." *South Bend News-Times* (IN), Jan 17, 1919.
"National Security League is criticized." *Evening Star* (Washington), Feb 10, 1919.
"National Security League organized." *Missoulian* (Missoula MT), Dec 2, 1914.
"National Security League selects new president." *Albuquerque Morning Journal* (NM), Jul 17, 1918
"National Security League voices cry for preparedness." *Evening Star* (Washington), Jan 20, 1916.
"Nation's demand heard by Congress." *New York Tribune*, Dec 8, 1914.
"New York open to foe, expert says." *Washington Times*, March 19, 1915.
"News in brief." *New York Tribune*, Jan 1, 1918.
"No more war is scored by league." *Seattle Star*, Jul 31, 1922.
No title. *Capital Journal* (Salem OR), Mar 17, 1915.
No title. *Capital Journal* (Salem OR), Jan 21, 1918.
No title. *Capital Journal* (Salem OR), Jan 29, 1918.
No title. *Commoner* (Lincoln NE), July 1, 1915.
No title. *Commoner* (Lincoln NE), Nov 1, 1915.
No title. *Evening Public Ledger* (Philadelphia), Mar 18, 1918.
No title. *Hattiesburg News* (MS), Dec 22, 1915.
No title. *Montana Nonpartisan* (Great Falls), Dec 28, 1918.
No title. *New York Tribune*, Aug 31, 1919.
No title. *Richmond Times-Dispatch* (VA), May 30, 1917.
"Now for the preparedness parade!" *Richmond Times-Dispatch* (VA), May 21, 1916.
"Offer prize for the best essay on security." *Perth Amboy Evening News* (NJ), Dec 16, 1915.
"Old party leaders shy at fusion offer." *New York Tribune*, Jul 10, 1918.
"149 speakers to give preparedness talks." *Evening Public Ledger* (Philadelphia), Mar 15, 1916.
"1,500 business men cheer pleas for U.S. defenses." *Sun* (NY), Dec 16, 1914.
"One way to discourage spies." *Carson City Appeal* (NV), Jul 21, 1917.
"Opens Mex fight." *Topeka State Journal* (KS), Jan 6, 1916.
"Organize branch of security league." *Gate City* (Keokuk IA), May 30, 1915.
"Organize league tomorrow night." *Gate City* (Keokuk, IA), Aug 18, 1915.
"Other editors than ours." *South Bend News-Times* (IN), Oct 19, 1918.
"Other states plan loyalty week." *Sun* (NY), Sep 24, 1917.
"Our country." *Washington Times*, Jan 20, 1916.
"Out-of-town stations." *Evening Star* (Washington), Aug 31, 1929.
"Over-preparedness made war, he says." *Ordway New Era* (CO), April 23, 1915.
"Parker apologizes for security league." *New York Tribune*, Feb 12, 1919.
"The patriot." *Ocala Evening Star* (FL), Jun 25, 1918.
"Patriotic bodies discuss alien." *Evening Star* (Washington), Mar 6, 1929.
"Patriotic congress to meet in Washington." *Richmond Times-Dispatch* (VA), Nov 27, 1916.
"Patriotism at so much per." *Labor Advocate* (Cincinnati), Apr 1, 1916.
"Patriotism overflows to entire nation." *Grand Forks Herald* (ND), Jul 16, 1917.
"Peace." *Day Book* (Chicago), May 31, 1916.

"Peace and the security league." *Nonpartisan Leader* (Fargo ND), Nov 25, 1918.
"Peace conference here June 14–15." *Evening World* (NY), June 3, 1915.
"Peace convention now labor's plan." *Sun* (NY), Jun 10, 1915.
"Peace folk arm against armament." *New York Tribune*, Feb 16, 1915.
"Peace; prepare." *Topeka State Journal* (KS), Jun 14, 1915.
"Pershing in security league." *Perth Amboy Evening News* (NJ), May 18, 1917.
"Plan for a union of all increased armament bodies." *Evening Star* (Washington), Jan 22 1916.
"Plan passage of law requiring schools to teach provisions of the Constitution." *Bemidji Pioneer* (MN), Sep 28, 1922.
"Plan patriotic propaganda for school children." *New York Tribune*, Jan 21, 1918.
"Plan security league fight." *Washington Herald*, Feb 11, 1919.
"Plans annual convention." *Evening Star* (Washington), Sep 24, 1917.
"Plans training for youths of the nation." *New York Tribune*, Feb 17, 1918.
"Pledge personal service." *Richmond Times-Dispatch* (VA), Oct 29, 1915.
"Policemen's strike arraigned by Root." *Bisbee Review* (AZ), Sep 18, 1919.
"Preaching Americanism." *New York Tribune*, Nov 18, 1918.
"Predicts Security League will win." *New York Tribune*, Dec 27, 1914.
"Preparations for peace." *Capital Journal* (Salem OR), Jun 24, 1915.
"Preparedness educator named." *Bryan Eagle and Pilot* (TX), Jan 9, 1917.
"Preparedness sessions in Charleston end." *Evening Star* (Washington), Apr 29, 1916.
"President's widow in war work." *Herald and News* (Newberry SC), Apr 19, 1918.
"Press reports untrue." *Evening Star* (Washington), Jun 15, 1915.
"Prizes for telling how to spread war aims." *New York Tribune*, Jun 8, 1918.
"Prosecution of security league is recommended." *Seattle Star*, May 7, 1919.
"Purchase of Belgium urged by Wanamaker." *Evening Star* (Washington), Jul 23, 1915.
"Put security league on pan." *Labor World* (Duluth MN), Jan 4, 1919.
"Queen of Reds on Soviet Ark, predicts ruin." *Washington Herald*, Dec 22, 1919.
"Questionnaire on war views sent to all candidates." *Evening Capital and Maryland Gazette* (Annapolis), Aug 12, 1918.
"Ralston on record favoring Wilson policies on war." *South Bend News-Times* (IN), May 27, 1915.
"Reaching for the schools." *Nonpartisan Leader* (Fargo ND), Oct 14, 1918.
"Red flag not barred here." *New York Tribune*, Nov 14, 1918.
"Red Russians plan anarchy." *Watchman and Southron* (Sumter SC), Jul 2, 1919.
"Rep. Barnhart exposes lies of security league." *South Bend News-Times* (IN), Oct 30, 1918.
"Republicans lead in war support." *Abilene Reflector* (KS), Aug 29, 1918.
"Reserve of 20,000,000 men planned for U.S." *Evening Star* (Washington), Jan 21, 1917.
"Revolution?" *Nonpartisan Leader* (Fargo ND), Jan 13, 1919.
"A revolution approaching." *Northwest Worker* (Everett WA), Apr 5, 1917.
Rinehart, Mary Roberts. "Radicalism is false idealism." *News Scimitar* (Memphis TN), Jan 16, 1920.
"Ripley—labor would have all." *Evening Times-Republican* (Marshalltown IA), Sep 13, 1916.
"Robert Bacon." wikipedia page, accessed Mar 24, 2019.
"Robert Bacon, Senate candidate." *Sun* (NY), Aug 18, 1916.
"Roosevelt tells league pacifists are undesirable." *Evening World* (NY), Jun 14, 1915.
"Roosevelt urges a loyal Congress." *Sun* (NY), August 20, 1918.
"Root and Parker and the so-called National Security League." *South Bend News-Times* (IN), Nov 22, 1918.
"Root defines treason to America in the war." *Richmond Times-Dispatch* (VA), Sep 15, 1917.
"Root heads security league." *New York Tribune*, Sep 16, 1917.
"Root supports security league acid test chart." *Arizona Republican* (Phoenix), Feb 7, 1919.
"Rumor U.S. is to quit Haiti and San Domingo." *Evening Star* (Washington), Jan 25, 1917.
"S. Stanwood Menken." *Richmond Palladium* (IN), Dec 2, 1921.
"S. Stanwood Menken, who believes in being prepared." *New York Tribune*, Feb 24, 1918.
"Safety first, League's cry." *Washington Herald*, March 7, 1915.
"Says vast army can invade U.S." *Washington Herald*, Jul 26, 1915.

Bibliography 253

"Scathing attack made on security league." *Evening Star* (Washington), Dec 5, 1918.
"Scores Debs nomination." *New York Tribune,* May 18, 1920.
"Security." *Democratic Banner* (Mt. Vernon OH), Mar 3, 1916.
"Security body hits congress in new plans." *New York Tribune,* Mar 9, 1919.
"Security congress to meet January 20." *Evening Star* (Washington), Jan 2, 1916.
"The security league." *South Bend News-Times* (IN), Dec 27. 1918.
"Security league aims explained." *Evening Star* (Washington), Dec 20, 1918. "The security league and the first of May." *Butte Bulletin* (MT), Mar 8, 1920.
"Security league anti Red war has now spread." *Harrisburg Telegraph* (PA), Aug 15, 1919.
"Security league article o.k." *Nonpartisan Leader* (Fargo ND), Apr 14, 1919.
"Security league calls a congress." *Sun* (NY), Nov 12, 1917.
"Security league calls U.S. defense lacking." *Evening Star* (Washington), Jul 26, 1915.
"Security league congress to hear Taft and Whitman." *New York Tribune,* Feb 18, 1918.
"Security league dodges socialism." *Northwest Worker* (Everett WA), Apr 27, 1916.
"Security league fight against unrest." *New York Tribune,* Nov 24, 1919.
"Security league fights Bolshevism." *Sun* (NY), Dec 2, 1918.
"Security league in congress fight." *Sun* (NY), May 6, 1918.
"Security league investigation by Congress silly." *Public Ledger* (Maysville KY), Feb 7, 1919.
"Security league is combating Red menace." *Harrisburg Telegraph* (PA), Jul 29, 1919.
"Security league is pronounced guilty." *Arizona Republican* (Phoenix), Mar 4, 1919.
"Security league is put on the grill." *Nonpartisan Leader* (Fargo ND), Jan 13, 1919.
"Security league is under inquiry." *Evening Star* (Washington), Dec 19, 1918.
"Security league is united in a great drive." *Public Ledger* (Maysville, KY), Apr 14, 1919.
"Security league issues warning on spread of doctrine." *Public Ledger* (Maysville KY), Oct 20, 1919.
"Security league leaders to organize a nation-wide wake up America campaign." *Lake County Times* (Hammond IN), Jun 25, 1917.
"Security league moves to offset pacifist activities." *New York Tribune,* May 28, 1917.
"Security league not partisan, says Orth." *New York Tribune,* Jan 21, 1919.
"Security league opposed Ford on account of lack of war loyalty." *Albuquerque Morning Herald* (NM), Feb 7, 1919.
"Security league origin exposed." *Bottineau Courant* (ND), Apr 3, 1919.
"Security league out to beat 3 Senators." *New York Tribune,* Nov 25, 1918.
"Security league praises solons." *Missoulian* (Missoula MT), Jan 20, 1918.
"Security league puts 17 senators on its honor roll." *New York Tribune,* Oct 30, 1918.
"Security league rapped in House." *Evening Star* (Washington), Dec 10, 1918.
"Security league says nation cries out for better defenses." *Bridgeton Pioneer* (NJ), Aug 26, 1915.
"Security league sends out tons of pamphlets." *New York Tribune,* Aug 4, 1918.
"Security league sessions wind up with banquet." *Evening Star* (Washington), Jan 23, 1916.
"Security league should put the punch in its platform." *Tacoma Times* (WA), May 24, 1915.
"Security league tells anti–Bolshevik plans." *New York Tribune,* Jun 23, 1919.
"Security League to form branch here." *Washington Herald,* Feb 15, 1915.
"Security league to open double-barrel fight on reds here." *New York Tribune,* Dec 16, 1918.
"Security league to oust Thompson." *East Oregonian* (Pendleton), Aug 22, 1917.
"Security league to spend million in rousing nation." *New York Tribune,* May 13, 1917.
"Security league to train drafted men before call to cantonments." *Bismarck Tribune* (ND), Aug 3, 1918.
"Security league to urge reforms." *Sun* (NY), Nov 25, 1918.
"Security league urges economic preparedness." *New York Tribune,* Dec 5, 1921.
"Security league want 500 members in city Pensacola." *Pensacola Journal* (FL), Feb 24, 1916.
"Security league wants 'war navy.'" *Sun* (NY), May 4, 1915.
"Security league wants dynamite." *New York Tribune,* Jul 29, 1915.
"Security league wants members." *Gate City* (Keokuk IA), Jul 22, 1916.
"Security league writes to papers." *West Virginian* (Fairmont), Jul 24, 1917.
"Security leaguers to talk war at training camps." *Harrisburg Telegraph* (PA), Nov 5, 1917.

"Security league's new chairman tells what it will do here." *Evening Public Ledger* (Philadelphia), Aug 3, 1915.
"Security million drops to $6,000." *Sun* (NY), Dec 20, 1918.
"Security spent $176 in recent election." *Washington Times*, Nov 17, 1922.
"Seek public views on bills." *Evening Star* (Washington), Mar 9, 1917.
"Seeking physical fitness high in air." *New York Tribune*, Jul 17, 1918.
"Senator warns of peril to U.S." *Evening Star* (Washington), Jan 28, 1917.
"Sharp reprimand for security league head." *Richmond Times-Dispatch* (VA), Jan 7, 1919.
"She helps inspire patriotism through teachers' Plattsburgs." *Evening Star* (Washington), Jul 28, 1918.
"She tells teachers how to make pupils patriotic." *Albuquerque Morning Journal* (NM), Sep 8, 1918.
"Ships and men ready, Daniels and Dewey say." *New York Tribune*, May 16, 1915.
"Should acknowledge it." *Pensacola Journal* (FL), Aug 10, 1917.
"Should probe a little further." *Butte Bulletin* (MT), Jan 16, 1919.
Sinclair, Upton. "A socialist view of German victory." *Albuquerque Morning Journal* (NM), Sep 18, 1918.
"Sing song for honoring flag." *Rock Island Argus* (IL), Jun 4, 1918.
"The so-called security league." *Nonpartisan Leader* (Fargo ND), Feb 11, 1918.
"Socialism in Huntington." *Socialist and Labor Star* (Huntington WV), Oct 16, 1914.
"Socialists cannot hire hall, they say." *Sun* (NY), Jan 19, 1919.
"Socialists predict 300,000 votes as a result of fusion." *New York Tribune*, Aug 1, 1918.
"Society day at the Automobile Show." *Sun* (NY), January 5, 1916.
"Society in Washington." *Washington Herald*, Feb 3, 1918;
"Society News." *Chicago Eagle*, Feb 9, 1918.
"Songs and saws." *Richmond Times-Dispatch* (VA), Dec 12, 1914.
"Source books on the war." *Sun* (NY), Mar 31, 1918.
South Bend News-Times (IN), Dec 8, 1918.
"Speakers to tour for loyalty week." *New York Tribune*, Sep 17, 1917.
"Spiritual drill in nation urged." *New York Tribune*, July 3, 1915.
"Squadron of orators to urge U.S. defense." *Evening Public Ledger* (Philadelphia), Mar 2, 1916.
"Standing by the president." *New York Tribune*, May 21, 1915.
"Steps taken to remove Mayor Thompson of Chicago." *Norwich Bulletin* (CT), Aug 16, 1917.
"Stop the leak." *New York Tribune*, Nov 28, 1918.
"Street speakers' squadron to fight propaganda widely." *New York Tribune*, Aug 18, 1918.
"Study of German dropped by more schools in nation." *New York Tribune*, May 27, 1918.
"Sweeping investigation of National Security League demanded by Congressmen."
"T. R. would force all into military service." *Sun* (NY), Jan 21, 1916.
"T. R. would send La Follette to the German lines." *Wheeling Intelligencer* (WV), Sep 27, 1917.
"Target practice is urged." *Princeton Union* (MN), Dec 24, 1914.
"Teach patriotism in schools, says educators." *East Oregonian* (Pendleton), Sep 4, 1918.
"Teachers decide on loyalty campaign." *Sun* (NY), Jan 21, 1918.
"Teachers to take loyalty pledge." *Sun* (NY), Nov 26, 1917.
"Teaching patriotism." *Pensacola Journal* (FL), Jun 15, 1918.
"Tell the people the facts." *Hartford Republican* (KY), Sep 21, 1917.
"10 governors for league." *South Bend News-Times* (IN), Oct 7, 1915.
"Teuton publisher rejects Kaiserism; is loyal to U. S." *New York Tribune*, Aug 20, 1917.
"Thousands line streets to give Teddy Roosevelt warm welcome to Chicago." *Day Book* (Chicago), Apr 28, 1917.
"Timeline of United States military operations." Wikipedia, accessed June 21, 2019.
"Times and persons." *Evening World* (NY), Sep 6, 1917.
"To argue for national defense." *Evening Star* (Washington), Feb 15, 1915.
"To combat red flagism." *El Paso Herald* (TX), Nov 29, 1918.
"To form security league branch." *Evening Star* (Washington), Apr 24, 1916.
"To investigate defenses." *Sun* (NY), Jan 15, 1915.
"To show the need of defense is aim." *Evening Star* (Washington), Jan 12, 1916.

Bibliography 255

"To spread preparedness." *Sun* (NY), Sep 17, 1915.
"To stir war enthusiasm." *Sun* (NY), Jul 16, 1917.
"To train new draftees." *New York Tribune,* Jul 29, 1918.
"Townley can't stomach governor's peace council." *Washburn Leader* (ND), Sep 7, 1917.
"Training for all steadily winning favor in congress." *New York Tribune,* Sep 16, 1917.
"Training must be compulsively if America is to have peace." *Albuquerque Morning Journal* (NM), Dec 26, 1917.
"Trio bind man, get $150,000 gems." *Evening Star* (Washington), Jun 17, 1931.
"Truth of the investigation." *Butte Bulletin* (MT), Feb 13, 1919.
"Try to extend military service." *Labor World* (Duluth MN), Jan 6, 1917.
"Twelve governors cooperating in move for preparedness." *Sun* (NY), Oct 24, 1915.
"Two ex-war secretaries for congress in Chicago." *Albuquerque Morning Journal* (NM), Feb 19, 1918.
"U.S. assembles powerful armada." *Grand Forks Herald* (ND), Dec 14, 1914.
"U.S. preparedness." *Evening Star* (Washington), Jan 25, 1917.
"Union to aid Americanism founded here." *New York Tribune,* May 19, 1921.
"Unions attacked." *Labor Journal* (Everett WA), Apr 3, 1914.
"United States Army not able to conduct war of magnitude." *Albuquerque Morning Journal* (NM), Jun 15, 1915.
"Universal military training is needed, says Gen. Young." *New York Tribune,* Aug 27, 1917.
"Urges development of National Guard." *Evening Star* (Washington), Jul 14, 1915.
"Urges grim war on secret enemies." *Evening Star* (Washington), Apr 30, 1925.
"Urges navy bigger than Wilson plans." *Washington Times,* Nov 28, 1915.
"Veterans at eighty urge U.S. defense." *Washington Times,* Feb 18, 1916.
"Views on preparedness for congressmen." *Evening Star* (Washington), Aug 18, 1924.
"Vigilance bodies to track slackers." *Missoulian* (Missoula MT), Aug 3, 1917.
"Vigilantes aim in tightening slackers' net." *Evening Public Ledger* (Philadelphia), Aug 23, 1917.
"W. M. Musgrave to speak here Friday night." *Grand Forks Herald* (ND), Aug 30, 1917.
"Wall Streets' black hundred exposed." *Nonpartisan Leader* (Fargo ND), Feb 24, 1919.
"Walsh in doubt on universal training." *Butte Post* (MT), May 26, 1917.
"Walter Camp seeks mayor's co-operation." *Richmond Times-Dispatch* (VA), Feb 25, 1918.
"Wanamaker wants U.S. to buy Belgium." *Sun* (NY), Jul 23, 1915.
"Wants committee appointed on national defense." *Lakeland Evening Telegram* (FL), Oct 14, 1915.
"Wants translations with poster." *New York Herald,* Jun 11, 1922.
"War apathy laid to lack of teaching." *Sun* (NY), Apr 15, 1918.
"War men to talk peace." *New York Tribune,* Jun 12, 1915.
"War orders will make J. P. Morgan the richest man in the world." *Mitchell Capital* (ND), Sep 16, 1915.
"War to last three more years, is belief in Washington." *New York Tribune,* Feb 24, 1918.
"Washington men in list of nation's defenders." *Evening Star* (Washington), Jul 30, 1917.
"Washington observations." *Evening Star* (Washington), Sep 8, 1930.
"Washington, or any other American city near coast, could be destroyed by enemy airmen, Peary says." *Albuquerque Morning Journal* (NM), Jan 28, 1917.
"Watchful waiting's end sure Nov. 2, says Choate." *Sun* (NY), Feb 17, 1916.
"We are weak as a military power." *Ogden Standard* (UT), May 13, 1915.
"Wealthy Chicagoans called to testify security league quiz." *Evening Capital News* (Boise ID), Jan 30, 1919.
West, Henry "Criminal neglect of national defenses." *Richmond Times-Dispatch* (VA), Oct 24, 1915.
"West is crowded with pro–Germans, Dr. McElroy says." *New York Tribune,* Apr 17, 1918.
"West retained as paid agent for District." *Washington Herald,* Jan 22, 1919.
"What happened to Capper?" *Sun* (NY), Feb 7, 1916.
"Where volunteers are needed for war work." *New York Tribune,* Mar 26, 1918.
"Whitman pledges preparedness aid." *Sun* (NY), Nov 4, 1915.

"Why should we not defend ourselves?" *New York Tribune,* Dec 3, 1914.
Why We Are at War. New York: National Security League, n.d.
"Wide interest in defense." *Evening Star* (Washington), Mar 13, 1917.
"Will aid Americanization." *Sun* (NY), Nov 29, 1918.
"Will direct speakers." *Tulsa World* (OK), Nov 3, 1918.
"Will instill loyalty in foreign born citizens." *New York Tribune,* Apr 1, 1918.
"Will investigate National Security League." *Newark Post* (DE), Oct 9, 1918.
"Wilson estimates national defense cost $400,000,000." *Little Falls Herald* (MN), Oct 15, 1915.
"Wilson urged to move for defense." *Evening Times-Republican* (Marshalltown IA), Jun 16 1915.
"Win the war with patriotism." *Richmond Palladium* (IN), Feb 23, 1918.
"Woman heckles ex-Senator Young." *New York Tribune,* Dec 15, 1915.
"Womanhood, the Glory of the Nation, displays feminine patriotism." *Evening World* (NY), Mar 29 1917.
"Women in National Security League." *Tulsa World* (OK), Nov 20, 1917.
"Women of America are warned against pleas from Germany." *New York Tribune,* Nov 25, 1918.
"Women of today." *Grand Forks Herald* (ND), Sep 13, 1919.
"Women prominent in civic and social service work." *Grand Forks Herald* (ND), Jan 24, 1917.
"Women urged to serve country." *Washington Herald,* May 13, 1916.
"Women will raise funds to help train 5,000 aviators for national defense." *Sun* (NY), Feb 11, 1916.
"Women's war congress near." *Sun* (NY), Feb 11, 1918.
"Working for real preparedness." *Richmond Times-Dispatch* (VA), Oct 14, 1915.
"The workingman's right to vote." *South Bend News-Times* (IN), Nov 2, 1918.
"Would help in case of war or disaster." *Evening Star* (Washington), Jan 21, 1916.
"Would recruit and train 5000 men as U.S. officers." *El Paso Herald* (TX), Dec 2, 1914.
"Writers condemn premature peace." *Evening Star* (Washington), Sep 23, 1918.

Index

Abbott, Lawrence F. 14
activities, NSL 114
Adams, E.D. 144
Addams, Jane 91, 93
advertisements (NSL) 155
aims and objectives of NSL 34, 178
air power, military 58
Alexander, Mrs. William 30-31
Allen, Henry 199
Allies' purchases in America 157
America to "buy" Belgium campaign 64-65
American Constitution 196
American Day, to replace May Day 199-200
American Defense Society 183
American Express 69
American Federation of Labor 21-22
American League to Limit Armaments 69, 91
American Union Against Militarism 59
Americanism 143; uniqueness of 134
Americanization 146, 178, 188; of aliens 203; campaign 196-200
Americanization Advisory Service (NSL) 197
anarchistic literature distribution 198
annual meetings 179-180
anti-war demonstrations 43
anti-Bolshevik campaign, scope of 188
Argentina 85
arguments, ludicrous 7
Armour, J. Ogden 170
assault on NSL speaker 151
Atherton, Gertrude 169
athletes 71
auditorium rentals, blocked 185
Automobile Show, NYC 77

Bache, Jules S. 74
Bacon, Robert 42, 48, 50, 52, 57, 130
Bancroft, Edgar 224
Barnhart, Henry A. 124, 127
Barry, Herbert 14, 136
Baruch, Bernard 225, 227
baseball players 79
The Battle Cry of Peace (film) 74, 99, 103
Belgium 7
Bell, Alexander Graham 53

Benson, Allan 99
Berger, Victor 192
Bernhardt, Sarah 149-151
Bestor, Arthur E. 132
bipartisanship 48
Black, Mrs. William 188-189
Black, William 135-136
Blackton, J. Stuart 89-90
Bliss, Anna B 96
Boardman, Mabel T. 54
Bolsheviks 22-23, 161, 183-191; definition of 187
Bolshevism defined, by Menken 227-228
Bonaparte, Charles, J. 13, 98
book, suppressed 166-167
Bowden, J.E.T. 36
Bowers, George M. 125
Bradford, Mary C. C. 145, 152-153
Brady, J.C. 96
Brady, Nicholas F. 96, 222
branch
branches: 7, 28-30, 48, 119; number of 33-34, 81-82; organizing 26-27; university 74
Brewster, William B. 29-30, 74-75
Briggs, Olive M. 166-167
Britain 72
Britten, Fred A. 37, 217-218
Brough, Charles H. 161
Brown, Franklin Q. 14
Browne, Edward E. 207
Browne, George E. 128
Bryan, William Jennings 75, 93-94, 96, 104-105
Bryant, Louise 87
Bullard, Robert 180-182, 190
bullying 59, 117, 123
Burton, Theodore E. 147
business interests 171
Business Men's Club, Richmond, VA 30
businessman's march, for preparedness 79-80
Butler, Nicholas Murray 91
Byllesby, H.M. 179

Cadwaller, J, Augustus 95-96
Cambridge Business Men's School 82

Camp, Walter 162–166, 169
campaign against premature peace 169
campaign against Reds 184–186
campaign against slackers 136–137
campaign against social and industrial unrest 198–200
campaign for patriotism in schools 141–144
campaign to arouse war enthusiasm 132–134
campaign to consecrate and sanctify American citizenship 201–202
Campbell, Calvin C. 143
capitalism, dangers to 161
capitalist class: and World War I 16–20
capitalist trusts 17–18
Capper, Arthur 101
Caraway, Thaddeus 207
Carnegie, Andrew 22, 75
Carnegie Corporation 209
Carnegie Foundation 212
Carr, George Wentworth 79
cartoons and cartoonists 149–150
Cashman, Joseph T. 178
Catchings, Waddell 161
Caulfield, Henry S. 100
celebrities: as figureheads 149–151, 153–154, 158–159, 189–190; recruited by NSL 138
Central Federated Union 43
Chamberlain, George 35, 58, 117
chautauquas 134, 135–136
Chemical National Bank 174–175
Chicago 109–111; public schools 143–144; road trip for special committee 217
Chicago Federation of Labor 98–99
Child, Richard Washburn 169
children to adult propaganda pipeline 144
Childs, Eversly 227
Choate, Joseph A. 30, 33, 41, 111
Chomsky, Noam 25
Church, William C. 11, 63, 101
Citizens' Preparedness Parade 80
citizenship requirements 58
civilian employees, wartime 156–157
Clark, Champ 36–37
class: aspects 45, 71–72, 102; conflict 102; nature of 30; in NSL 92, 104; violence 22
Clothier, W.J. 72
Cobb, Irvin S. 138
Cochran, George C. 71
Colby, Bainbridge 49, 50
Collman, Charles 96–98
Colorado 144–145
Commercial Men's National Patriotic League 132
commercial tie-ins 84
commercialism 101
committee against un-American propaganda 184–185
Committee of One Thousand, NYC 38–39
Committee on Extension 36
committee on organized education (NSL) 192–196

Committee on Patriotism Through Education 108–111, 134
Committee on Physical Reserve (NSL) 163
Committee on Preliminary Training and Instruction of Men Registered for Draft (NSL) 168–169
committees of citizens 38
common language, for America 147–149
The Commoner 94
Communists 183–191
composition, of NSL 6
Conference of American Patriotic Societies 34
conferences 43–59
conflicts of interest 212–213, 214
Congress of Constructive Patriotism 53–59
Congress of Constructive Patriotism, women 54–55
Congress of National Service 159–162
Congressional Campaign Committee (NSL) 121–125
Congressional districts targeted 125
Congressional elections, 1918 118–128
Congressional reform 192
conscription 117; human vs conscription, of capital 156–157; industrial 156–157
Constitution instruction, schools, compulsory 202
contracts: no-bid 78; war 93
conventions 43–59; annual 47, 111–113
Converse, Edmund C. 97
Coolidge, Calvin 189
corporations: protection of 55–56; ties 179
Corrupt Practices Act 222
corruption, political 94
Coudert, Frederic R. 50, 60–61
Cowell, A. Lawrence 49
Creel, George 118
criminal neglect 76
critics of 91–103, 170–185, 204–228
Curley, James M. 28, 45
curriculum for public schools 140
Curtis, Charles G. 49
Cutts, William 103–104

Daniels, Josephus 45, 63
Darrow, Clarence 108, 111, 143–144
Davies, J. Clarence 167
Davis, Richard Harding 198
death of NSL, de facto 191, 203, 228
Debs, Eugene V 190
decline of NSL 180–181
Deering, Charles 225
Defenders of America parades 199–200
defense conference of mayors 52–53
De Koven, Mrs.Reginald 187
Denny, Early C. 145
Dent, S. Hubert 124
Dickinson, Jacob M. 46, 111
directors, boards intertwined 180
directors, first 26
disloyalty 110–111; higher education 142–143

dissent, attempts to suppress 183-191
Dix, William Frederick 27
Dodge, Kern 137
donations 68, 96, 209, 216, 212, 220-221, 222, 225; corporations 96; in kind 96, 145, 152, 213-214; questionable 227
Donovan, Bill 79
draftees: brainwashing 168-169; physical rejections 161; pre-training by 168
Dupont, T. Coleman 225
Durango, CO 145
duties: of citizens 148, 160; of draftees 168-169
Dwight, William B. 199-200

editorials 8, 62-63; against NSL 11, 52, 91-93, 118, 171-173, 200; attacks 204-206; dissections 100-101, 102; favorable 46-48, 74, 160-161; investigation 210-211; lack of war spirit 138-139; ratings 124
editors, mailings from 156
education, patriotic 144-145, 171-172
education campaigns 130-153
education program, explained 131
education system, attacked 130-131
educational camps, summer 151
effigies 110
elections: feared 116; targeting 116-129
Elvebach, J.N. 132
enemies 98
English language, spoken 58
Enright, Richard 184, 185
essay contests 74, 76-77, 101, 159; winners 167-168
exaggerations, egregious 58

Farnam, Henry W. 108
fashion, female, preparedness related 77
fear, use of 60-64
fear mongering 58, 76, 96-97, 188-189
figureheads 35
figures, newsworthy 13, 26, 114
film, propaganda 198
finances of NSL 208-210, 213
Fish, Hamilton, Jr. 72
flag, red 183-184
Flag Day, 1918 148-149
Flood, Emmet 98-99
Ford, Henry 23, 75, 103, 216-217
foreign languages: speakers of 146; suppression of 147-149
formation of NSL 6-24
Fosdick, Harry E. 139
Frayne, Hugh 142
Frazier, Lynn J. 137
Frear, James A. 173-174, 206-207, 210, 220
Frick, Henry 96, 222
fusion candidates 121-124, 128-129, 200-201

G. P. Putnam's Sons 15
Gardner, August Peabody 6, 8-10, 15, 40-41, 67, 106
Garfield, Mrs. James 114

Garrison, Lindley M. 66, 180
Garvan, Francis P. 23
Gary, Elbert H. 22, 97
General Committee, makeup 11
General Electric 69, 98, 179
George, Mrs. A. J. 80
George E. Stifel Company 155
Gerard, James W. 113
German-American National Alliance 134-135
German-American societies and citizens 134
German language 147-149
Germany 72; pro-German sentiment 146
Giddings, Franklin H. 144
Gilder, Rodman 27
Gildersleeve, Virginia C. 159
Goldfogle, Henry 129
Gompers, Samuel 21-22, 30, 102-103, 111
good citizenship courses, for teachers 194
Gordon, Alexander 54
Graham, George S. 37
Grayson twins 78
Greene, Frances V. 63
Greenhut, A. 32-33
Gronna, Asle 192
Guggenheim, Daniel 221
Guggenheim, Murray 221
"gunboat" hat 77
Gunter, Julius C. 145

Hall, Walter P. 144
Hamill, D.B. 29
Hamilton, Cosmo 169
Hancock, B.S. 32
Hanson, Ole 179, 189
Harrison, Pat 207
Hart, Albert Bushnell 54-55, 130, 131
Harvey, E.L. 187, 217
Hay, James 8
Hayden, Carl 157
Hayden, Charles 220-221
headquarters, moved 113
Hearst, William Randolph 119-120, 178-179
Hedges, Job E. 139, 147
Heinze, F. Augustus 50
Hemphill, Alexander J 180
Hexamar, Charles S. 134-135
Hill, David Jayne 48, 50, 188
Hillquit, Morris 22, 116, 121, 129
Holmes, John Haynes 58-59
Holt, Frank 93
Honolulu 40
Hoover, William D. 90
Hornaday, William T. 13, 67
Hornblower, George 108
Hoyt, Colgate 92
Hubbard, Thomas Hamlin 10
Huidekoper, Frederick L. 85
Humphrey, A.E. 27
Humphrey, A.R. 66
Hunt, Henry T. 102
Hylan, John 183, 186, 200

260 Index

immigrants 58
imperialism 96
indifference, by public 137–138
Industrial Workers of the World (IWW, Wobblies) 21, 186, 189, 196–197
influence of NSL, 1919 194
Insull, Samuel 170
internal control 104
International Nickel Company 98
internationalism 187, 188
invasion, of U.S.: as easy 60–61; as fear 41; by Germany 87; ludicrous 58, 60–61; of west coast 50–51
investigation of NSL: calls for 96, 105–106, 170, 173–175, 206–207; hearings 208–228; impact of 204; investigators 61–65; majority report 223; minority report 223; scope of 207; summary 221; verdict 224–225
irrelevancy of NSL 190–191
Irwin, Wallace 169
Iselin, John R. 27

J.P. Morgan and Company 93, 97, 157
J.P. Morgan contracts 18–19
Johnson, Ben 207
Johnson, Morton L. 99
Jones, Mary (Mother) 20–21

Kahn, Julius 117
Keller, Frances A. 54
Keokuk Iowa 29
Key, Ellen 166–167
Kiel, Henry 41–42, 53, 99–100
King, Edward John 219–220, 223–224
Kirkpatrick, George K. 103–104
Kitchin Claude 214
Koop, George 99

labor: agitators 196–197; representation 108; strife 20–21
labor, organized 102–103, 141–142; sympathetic to NSL 143–144
Lackawanna Steel Corporation 97
La Follette, Robert 116, 139, 192
Lane, Franklin K. 113, 132
Lane, John 40
Lansing, Isaac J. 152
Lawrence, MA 149
The League of Nations, attacked 187–188
Lee, Algernon 185–186
Leighton, Etta V. 153, 159, 186, 192, 197
letter campaigns 36; to clergy 68–69
Levish, Thomas 104
Libby, Melanchton Fennessey 144–145
Libby, M.F. 144
Liberty Loan bond drive 147, 174
Liesering, Adolph 151
literature, from NSL 36
Littleton, Martin W. 184
lobbying 66; judges 198; paid 216–217; states 42; Washington 94–95
Lodge, Henry Cabot 49

London, Meyer 93–94, 121, 128–129
Loveland, John Winthrop 7
Lowden, Frank O. 110, 199
Lowell Massachusetts Normal School 149
loyalty 123; campaigns 130–153; checks 140–141; oaths 136, 155; of organized labor 141–142
loyalty test, reality 173
Loyalty Week, NY 139
Lusitania (ship) 20, 64, 68
Lydecker, Charles E. 7 14, 15, 46, 168–169, 178, 183, 187–188, 194–195; reprimanded 211; testimony 208–211
Lynch, Frederick 69, 92

Mackay, Clarence H. 96
Mann, James 206
Manning, Mrs. Richard 159
Mason, B.S. 156
Mason, William E. 217
Mathews, Shailer 135
Maxim, Hudson 43, 45, 78, 99–100
Maxim Munitions Corporation 99–100
May Day, denigrated 199–200
mayors 38, 52–53
McAdoo, William 68
McAndrew, William 141
McCormack, R, R, (Bertie) 170
McCullouch, Roscoe C. 207, 219–220
McElroy, Robert M. 108, 134, 142, 145–146, 196–197; booed during speech 147
McRoberts, Samuel 164
media coverage 8, 37, 45, 63; critical 76; of election targeting 119–120; favorable 47; preparedness 78–83
media outlets, loyalty demanded 134–136
Meeker, Arthur 170
meeting, first 6–8
Mellen, Chase 54
membership: categories 30, 113; dues 33; numbers 30, 34, 54, 179, 198; statistics 119
Menken, S. Stanwood 6–9, 10, 14–15, 35, 56–57, 78, 89, 96, 104–105, 130, 132, 162, 178–179, 180–181, 190–191; and outbreak of World War I 14–15; testimony 225–228; wealth of 15
Merchants Association, NYC 12–13, 35–36
Merrick, H.H. 109, 170
Metcalf, Menton B. 108
methods of NSL 35
Mexico 47, 103
Meyer, George L. von 28–29, 43, 46
militarism and public schools 13
military: abroad 16–17; assertions refuted 47; displays, cross-country 65; expenditures 68, 75; "facts" from NSL 66–67; as helpless 16–17; impotence, of U.S. 57; increase 10, 46; instruction 46; position, reality 103; reserve force 40–41; size 7–8, 12–13; statistics 47, 70, 72; strength 11, 202; training 71–73, 83, 104–105; training camps 79–83; weakness, exaggerated 11–12

Index

Militia Committee, of NSL 69–70
militias 26
Mills, Ogden L. 97
Minneapolis 29
Mitchel, John Purroy 22, 33, 39–40
Moffet, Cleveland 63, 139
money 23, 93, 156–157
money trust 96–98
Moore, J. Hampton 175
Moore, L.B. 196–197
Moore, Mrs. Philip N. 55
Moran, Thomas F. 108
Moree, Edward A. 83–84
Morgan, Anne 54
Morgan, J.P. 22, 97, 227
Morris, Robert 96
motion picture promotion 74, 89–90
munitions display 44
munitions manufacture 78
munitions manufacturers 100
Murphy, Charles F. 121
Musgrave, Wayne M. 137

National Committee of Mayors 41–42
National Defense Act 17
national defense campaign, February 1915 35–40
National Guard 13, 40–41, 61–62, 70, 82; campaign to join 69; and employers 69; federalized 16–17, 40, 195
National Nonpartisan League 116
National Security Congress 48–53
National Special Aid Society 31–32
National Surety Company 97
naturalization 198
Navy Committee (NSL) 67
Nearing, Scott 127
Neill, Charles 160
New Jersey 42
New York City Board of Education 140–141
New York City delegation 120
New York State Committee on National Defense 38–39
New York State Industrial Commission 166
New York Telephone 69
Newberry, Truman H. 23–24
Nonpartisan Leader (Fargo ND) 170
Norris, George 192

obedience 35, 105
objectives and aims 113; as defined by Lydecker 212
officers, list of 114–115
O'Gorman, James A. 36–37
Olander, Victor A. 99, 160
organizations, umbrella 34, 51–52
origins of 225
Orth, Charles D. 119–120, 123, 192; testimony 214–216
Otis, William Bradley 150–151, 180

Pacific Island possessions 76
pacifists 117, 160; countered 131
packers, Chicago 170
Palmer, Frederick 78
pamphlets 114, 144
Parker, Alton B. 27–28, 45–46, 171, 205
Parker, Grace 55–56, 87, 130
Parkhurst, Charles H. 169
patriotism 17, 130; militant, speakers' numbers 152; as required subject 144–145; teachings, in public school 152–153
peace, premature, campaign against 169
Peace and Preparedness Conference 43–47
peace conferences 43, 137
Peary, Robert E. 58
Pelton, J.L. 179
Pensacola, FL 31–32
People's Council of America 137
Pepper, George Wharton 71
Perkins, George W. 225
Pershing, John J. 108–109
Peters, Joan 84
petitions 42, 114
Phelan, James 50
Philadelphia 29
physical exercises 165–166
physical fitness: for capitalist labor 162–166; military recruits 99
physical training program 161–167
Pinchot, Amos 105
Plattsburgh camps 84
Plattsburgh, NY 71
Plymouth Business Men's School 82
Poindexter, Miles 187
police strike, Boston 189
political activities, admission of engagement 216
politicians 23, 35–42, 116–129; attack NSL 124–127; attempt at removal 109–111; bullied 40–41; canvassed 202–203; lobbied by 36–40; named 36–37; opposed 68; praised 117; ratings of 121–123; 171, 175; state and local 38–40; targeted 217–221; vindicated 207, 222–223
politics, corrupted 23–25
Polland, Mary B. 180
polo players 72
Pope, George 20
poster campaign 67–68
posters, foreign language 202
Prall, Anning S. 200
preparedness: media coverage 79–82; as national demand 10
preparedness conference, admission prices 44
press releases 92; printed as news 60–62, 73–74, 158–159, 165
Preston, Mrs. Thomas J. 111, 114, 115, 151, 161, 178, 181
Price, Raymond 34
Proctor, William Cooper 102
profits: excess 156–157, 222; war 16–20

Index

proletarian: as defined by Lydecker 211
propaganda, patriotic 185; for schools 142
propaganda pieces, placed 131–132
property: capitalists fears for 102
prosecution of NSL 225, 228
public aroused 83
public opinion 74; awakening 66; molded 95; shift in 50
publicizing of NSL 28
purpose of NSL 11; extrapolated 30
Putnam, George Haven 7, 10, 14, 15

questionnaires: to NYS candidates 127–128; to politicians 123

race riots, 1919 196–197
radicals 183–191
Ralston, Samuel 68
Rankin, Jeannette 218
ratings 124; *see also* politicians
Reavis, C. Frank 207
Reds: attacks on through schools 186–187; preoccupation with 183–191
Reed, James A. 47
registration 35
reinvention, of NSL 131, 178
Remington, Franklin 108
reporters, as gullible 60–63
responsibility, individual 140
rights of property 189
Rinehart, Mary Roberts 189–190
Ripley, E.P. 21
Robinson, Herman 142
Rock, Frank 170
Rockefeller, John D. 209
Rockefeller, Percy 98
Rockefeller Foundation 200
Roll of Honor 194
Roosevelt, Franklin D. 132
Roosevelt, George Emlen 10
Roosevelt, Mrs. Theodore 114
Roosevelt, Theodore 45, 49, 50–51, 57–58, 83, 89–90, 139, 147, 170
Root, Elihu 35, 111, 205, 214; testimony 218–219
Rucker, W.C. 83
Russell, Charles Edward 160
Russia 72; invasion of 23; recognition of 190–191
Russian Revolution 16–17

St. Louis 53
salaries: executive 212; NSL 208
sanitary education 168
Satterlee, H.L. 68
Saunders, Edward 207
Schofield, W.H. 144
school boys and military training 194–195
school teachers 144
schools, quality of 200
Schrader, Frederick F. 136
Schroeder, Raymond C 219–220

Schwab, Charles M. 22
Scully, Thomas 124, 127, 194
sermons, topics urged by 69
Sherwood, Isaac 220
ship building 156
shipyard workers 142
Siegel, Isaac 129
Sinclair, Upton 153–154
singing, patriotic 148–149
slackers, war 136–137, 156
slogans 57, 58
Smiley, Emory E. 145
Smith, Alfred E. 199
Smith. Henry Louis 167–168
soapbox orators, open air 192
social control 14, 46, 85, 102, 104
socialism/communism threat 20–23
Socialist Party 116, 190, 192
socialists 121, 183–191
Soldiers of Fortune 198
Somers, Arthur C. 143
songs, patriotic 148–149
speakers: anti–Bolshevik 184, 188; tours 66, 133; training camp 132; venues 79; war bond drive 147
speakers' bureau 115, 134, 152, 178; Philadelphia 78–79
Special Committee, operating budget 211
Spencer, J. Beaumont 36, 63
Spooner, Willet M. 113, 116
sports, "manly" urged 70
Stanchfield, John B. 50
Steele, Charles 98
Steiner, Mollie 197–198
Stellwagon, Edward J. 90
Sterling, John A. 37
Stettinus, Edward R. 19–20, 157
Stimson, Henry L. 26, 35–36, 70
Stodden, William T. 199–200
Strauss, Oscar S. 120–121
street speakers' squadrons 151
submarine 130
subordination, of self to state 80
Sunny, B.E. 170

Taft, Helen 160
Taft, Mrs. William Howard 114
Taft, William Howard 198
Tarkington, Booth 158–159
Taylor, Lloyd 202
teachers, exchanges 144
Terhune, Albert Payson 169
Thomas, Mrs. M. Carey 159
Thompson, Robert M. 103
Thompson, William Hale 109–111
Towner, Horace 207
Tracy, Benjamin F. 63
traitors 111
Trammell, Park 36
troops, abroad 57
Tyler, T. DeWitt 227

Index

unions, radical vs. safe 21–22
U.S. Army resources, use of 65
U.S. Chamber of Commerce 84
U.S. Committee on Public Information 118
U.S. Congressional investigation of 206–220
U.S. House Judiciary Committee 173
U.S. House Special Committee struck 207
U.S. Navy 45–46
United States Rubber 69
U.S. Senators 125–126, 192
U.S. Steel Corporation 42
U.S. system, danger of overthrow 188–189
Universal Military Training (UMT) 34, 42, 53, 54, 84–87, 117–118, 155–156, 194–195, 198–200, 213; and Americanization 85–87; canvass 157–158, 159; class aspects 53; favored by editors 89; for social control 85; media coverage, critical 84–85; naming legislative supporters 155–156; petitions 155–156; publicity push 89–90; votes and referendum 84
university professors, as agents 144
unpreparedness 75–76

Vanderbilt, Cornelius 10, 41, 97
Vanderbilt, W.H. 225
Vanderbilt, Mrs. William 55
van Rensselaer, Mrs. Coffin 159
Van Tyne, C.H. 144
vigilant committees 136–137, 156
Villa, Pancho 47, 103
Vogel, August H. 116
volunteer service, condemned 53
volunteer war workers 145
voting records, of politicians 118–128

Wadsworth, James, Jr. 132
Wainwright, J. Mayhew 14
Walcott, Frederick C. 139
Waldo, Rhinelander 72
Walker, Bernard 26
Walker, J. Bernard 130
Walsh, David I. 28
Walsh, Joseph 207
Wananaker, John 64–65
war: financing of 157; contracts 164–165; curriculum, for schools 141; hysteria 101; production, U.S. factories 164; profiteering 174, 222; propaganda 135; as protection racket for money 60–61; stocks 98; trusts 18–19
War, Peace and the Future 166–167
Warner, Hazel 154
wartime decrease, criticism of 170
watch fob 84
Watts, Ridley 174–175, 216
wealth: of members and backers 14–15; prejudice against17–138
Wendell, Mrs. Barrett 55
West, Henry L. 30, 38, 75–76; testimony 215–216
west coast 73, 76
Westinghouse Electric 98
Wetmore, Maude 49, 54, 111
Wetter, Emil C. 224
Whitman, Charles 39–41, 139
Wickersham, George 132
Wiedersheim, Theodore E. 29
Williams, Talcott 139
Wilson, Woodrow 8, 57, 94
Wingate, George 13
Winthrop, Beekman 26
Wisconsin Loyalty League 116
Womanhood, the Glory of the Nation (film) 89–90
women 45, 113–114; admitted as members 140; anti-Red campaigns 187; Congress of National Service 159–160; directors (NSL) 180; idle rich 161; league of, proposed 57; loyalty campaigns 139–140; militarists 87; membership 111; and the NSL 30–32; section of the movement 52, 54; warned 192; wives of former U.S. presidents 113
women's committee 113
Women's Peace Society 190
Wood, Henry Wise 58–59
Wood, Leonard 12, 35–36, 63–64
workers enrolled 142
Wright, Luke E. 113
Wright, William 151
writers, celebrity, NSL propaganda 138
World War II entry 108

Young, Lafayette 58, 76
Young, S.B.M. 157

Zimmerman, Eugene 149–150

www.ingramcontent.com/pod-product-compliance
Ingram Content Group UK Ltd.
Pitfield, Milton Keynes, MK11 3LW, UK
UKHW041933140426
5217IPUK00014B/457